Walking in Shakespeare's Shoes

Walking in Shakespeare's Shoes

Connecting His World and Ours Using Primary Sources

Sheridan Lynn Steelman

National Council of Teachers of English
340 N. Neil St., Suite #104, Champaign, Illinois 61820
www.ncte.org

Staff Editors: Kurt Austin and Cynthia Gomez
Manuscript Editor: The Charlesworth Group
Interior Design: Jenny Jensen Greenleaf
Cover Design: Pat Mayer
Cover Images: iStock.com/SDI Productions (student photo) and iStock.com/bigemrg (books)

ISBN: 978-0-8141-4452-7 (paperback); 978-0-8141-4454-1 (ebook)

It is the policy of NCTE in its journals and other publications to provide a forum for the open discussion of ideas concerning the content and the teaching of English and the language arts. Publicity accorded to any particular point of view does not imply endorsement by the Executive Committee, the Board of Directors, or the membership at large, except in announcements of policy, where such endorsement is clearly specified.

NCTE provides equal employment opportunity to all staff members and applicants for employment without regard to race, color, religion, sex, national origin, age, physical, mental or perceived handicap/disability, sexual orientation including gender identity or expression, ancestry, genetic information, marital status, military status, unfavorable discharge from military service, pregnancy, citizenship status, personal appearance, matriculation or political affiliation, or any other protected status under applicable federal, state, and local laws.

Every effort has been made to provide current URLs and email addresses, but, because of the rapidly changing nature of the web, some sites and addresses may no longer be accessible.

Library of Congress Control Number: 202294

If you don't enter that world, hold your breath with the characters and become involved in their destiny, you won't be able to empathize, and empathy is at the heart of the novel. This is how you read a novel: you inhale the experience. So start breathing.

—Azar Nafisi, *Reading Lolita in Tehran*

We know what we are, but know not what we may be.

—William Shakespeare, *Hamlet*

Contents

Preface

The book you are about to read is the culmination of a teaching pilgrimage. What I have learned is I am a teacher first, scholar second. By this, I mean that I am in constant doubt that I know enough about the Bard's work; his meaning often eludes me, yet I often teach through my doubts until I come to a place of understanding. Learning to teach Shakespeare's plays and sonnets has been one of the greatest challenges and joys of my long tenure as a teacher. For the past fifty years, I have experimented, learned, succeeded, relapsed, and laughed, picking myself up over and over again to try again. Sometimes I get it *right*, but mostly I get it *enough* to know that I can always improve. If you feel unsure, uncomfortable, unled, or unsettled about how to go about traveling with your students through the early modern puzzle we call *William Shakespeare*, this book is for you.

My second home, the school district where I work, has changed dramatically over the years. When I began teaching, I worked with middle- to lower-income families, mostly white. Today I am happy to say that the school district is growing in diversity. The number of students of color continues to rise. Our LGBTQIA2S+ population is a source of pride as my new learning swells with respect for gender identity. The changing demographics are significant in that I understand that I must be vigilant about my own growth and willingness to adapt. My classroom will always be filled with the noise, laughter, shouts, and movement often known as the American teenager but, as our world changes, so too do our classroom library, our discussions, and our focus. Today's vibrancy is often offset with the silent scrutiny of books from my classroom library and the soft whisper of turning pages. When we write, I hear the tap of Chromebook keys, rather than the scratch of pencil lead, pausing briefly as they close their eyes or look out the window for inspiration.

I invite you to enter this sacred space, the place I have intentionally created to be inviting and instructional. When you turn the pages here, you will open my classroom door, but you must imagine the aroma of freshly brewed mocha coffee, the green of potted plants, and the view of teenagers all over the room, some swiveling in green Node chairs, some voraciously—and some nonchalantly—browsing my shelves, chatting. You will notice both keen and subtle differences: pink hair, shaved heads, dirty clogs, worn hoodies, caps, wraps, fuzzy pajamas, ripped jeans. Some confirm their identities with bare skin in winter, and some doubt with coverings in spring. They are, in essence, a conglomeration of open-hearted, open-minded young adults, ready for life to begin.

If it's a Monday, we all settle and prepare for a mindfulness session. If it's a Friday, empty doughnut boxes line the walls. On any day, we are engaged with language as if our lives depended on it. They say it's inviting and cozy; I say it's the place to be. I have stools all over the room, so I can change my teaching space, but I often sit at a student desk so we can talk. Sometimes we discuss a topic of urgency, but sometimes it's all about the basketball game or what they are wearing to Homecoming. We are all in this place of learning together.

I urge you to consider a new approach to teaching Shakespeare as if you are preparing for the first day of school. We are hungry to begin. Our minds are ready for the newness of learning and the start of another year. Begin with the Introduction, so you find your footing. You'll know which pedagogical path you've been traveling and if and where you might pause for a drink of clean water. Then find the chapter that quenches your thirst because you have been there before. Then try another, and another.

The *document approach* is one you can dabble in while you are teaching your own Shakespeare unit. If you have taught *Romeo and Juliet* for one year or twenty, you will find ideas for incorporating some primary documents into any part of your tried-and-true activities. You may be the novice who dreads having to coerce students into reading act 1 or the veteran who has an eclectic approach, using combinations of close reading and performance. The document approach to teaching Shakespeare can be used fully or partially in any classroom. Yesterday, my students watched their remix multimedia projects after experiencing Shakespeare Book Clubs. One student remarked, "Learning what was happening back then made me realize that things haven't changed that much." It's true. My students' responses electrify my own, and I am alive. Join me in the journey.

With respect for all you do,
Sheri

Acknowledgments

I would like to thank Northview Public Schools for their continued faith and support as I traveled my own path of continued learning. They have encouraged my interest in Shakespeare and in literature, in general, and allowed me to work with middle school teachers to introduce a new approach to teaching *A Midsummer Night's Dream* alongside amazing English language arts teachers. A special thank you to the two superintendents who facilitated my work within the district, Dr. Michael Paskewicz and Dr. Scott Korpak, as well as assistant superintendent and curriculum director Liz Cotter for listening, supporting, pushing, and reminding me of how to balance and juggle with grace. Their words have kept me going.

Many teachers worked directly with me to incorporate new methods, strategies, content, and language with one goal in mind: student learning and achievement. Several middle and high school educators made this happen: Kathy Vogel, Andy Galmish, Benson Mitchell, Linda Parker, Mary V., Kevin Weber, and Emily Alt. Thank you for trying out a new approach and for going off the beaten path with me.

My principal, Mark Thomas, has been inspiring in his devotion to continued learning as well as a mentor and friend throughout the years I worked on my doctorate and this book. His continued faith in me is very much appreciated. He taught me how to lead by stepping to the back of the pack.

The Northview High School English Department has been instrumental in helping me improve my teaching on a daily basis. I thank them for their professionalism, their uplifting support, and soothing humor as we have traveled our English paths together, including but not limited to the many challenges we faced during the pandemic. I am grateful to all of you: Audra Whetstone, Sara Pitt, BJ Schroder, Betsy Verwys, Emily Alt, Shelli Tabor, Megan Porter, Mary VanderWilt, Nancy Hoffman, Ali McNulty, Alex Hower, Anna Reynolds, Karen Michewicz, Kevin Weber, and Matt Howe. My heart will always live on the second floor.

Two teachers who worked with me on Shakespeare Book Clubs deserve my grateful acknowledgement. Alison McNulty and Mindi Cottriel walked with me during the most challenging time in education, the 2020–2021 pandemic. We experimented with virtual, hybrid, and face-to-face block learning, overcoming great odds to achieve wonderful outcomes. I am indebted to them for their willingness to learn about Shakespeare's problem plays, to explode their comfort zones, to reflect on their teaching, and to share ideas.

My dissertation chairperson and champion, Dr. Allen Webb, has been a friend, advisor, and writing coach before, during, and after I tackled the idea of a new approach to teaching Shakespeare. He encouraged me to write this book. I will always be grateful for his friendship and advice.

Dr. Jo Miller deserves my utmost thanks for her belief in me as a Shakespeare scholar. Her faith in my writing, both poetry and prose, has been a source of confidence as I have overcome challenges in my path to new learning. Her kindness and quiet strength have fed me when I most needed it.

I would also like to thank Megan Henning, who became my *teacher reader* throughout the initial phases of my research and writing. Her sensitivity to teacher concerns and love of language pushed my thinking constructively and with great insight. Many of the Document Discussions in this book were based on her feedback.

Two writers and English teacher practitioners push my thinking in such important ways: I am indebted to Penny Kittle and Kelly Gallagher, who model choice reading, workshop methods, conferring, and writing with fidelity. My teaching changed dramatically after reading *Book Love* (2013) and *Readicide* (2009). Student choice has been at the heart of their work, and reading has been in their souls. I credit them for guiding me and steering the paths of so many teachers who want to continue learning, growing, and loving language.

Kurt Austin, my NCTE editor, deserves the highest praise for helping me create a book in its best form. He has been honest, compassionate, and forthright in his efforts to help me write with fidelity. His steadfast encouragement is his claim to fame and my resolve to revise, revise, revise. Thank you, Kurt, for believing in this book.

My family's support and encouragement need top-shelf recognition. Thank you, Bob, for the many sacrifices and your undying support and love. You have bravely and consistently picked up the pieces when I laid them down. To my children—Kelly, Kristin, Kerri, Kassandra, Kevin, and Katherine—thank you for saying "yes" when I asked if I should. You will always be the wind under my wings.

Introduction

I looked over the sea of thirty faces in my second hour English class and knew I was in trouble. Body language told me these juniors were not eager to begin reading *Hamlet*. Aiden had his eyes closed. Charlanda rolled hers. Hunter put his head against the wall in the back, trying to use it as a flat pillow. Elissa frowned.

Sound familiar? I am a veteran teacher, but the story is the same, regardless of experience. Most middle and high school English teachers know the challenges of teaching Shakespeare. We seek to have our students engage with the richness of Shakespeare's language, envision his stagecraft, and generate fresh ideas about the plays and human experience. Despite the fact that Shakespeare is the most often taught author in American high schools and the only author specifically named by the Common Core State Standards adopted by forty-one states, today's teachers know their students will encounter difficulties with early modern language. My own students tell me: "I just don't get this old stuff."

Perhaps, today's students are reading with less tenacity than in former years. In the twenty-first century, social media and increased screen time can be distractions and deterrents to reading. When English teachers do successfully engage their students in reading, they are more likely using young adult literature. Reading contemporary literature as a whole class, in book clubs, or independently is easier compared to older, denser, poetic texts. Shakespeare, especially, is harder work.

This book proposes an approach to teaching Shakespeare in secondary English classes, one that effectively develops student interest and ability to read Shakespeare in rich and complex ways. I call this method of teaching the *document approach*. In every chapter, working with the plays that you are most likely already teaching, I show students in my own and other teachers' classrooms engaging more deeply with the plays, examining meaningful questions about their relevance to the present, and developing important knowledge and questions often overlooked in other approaches. I won't say that the document approach makes the teaching of Shakespeare *easy*, but I have found that a cultural approach engages students, raises academic and intellectual expectations, and provides me the satisfaction and joy of great teaching.

You might wonder about which primary documents I use for the plays, where I find examples that are age appropriate and relevant, and how I have time to add more material to an already tight teaching schedule. The answer is in thematic connections, the ties that bind Shakespeare's world to our own. Once students see the relevance of the plays through characters who react to their sixteenth-century world the same way my students react to their own twenty-first-century popular culture, the distance melts. Compassion grows. The goal of the document approach is to foreground historical and cultural materials, issues, and questions from the early modern period, helping students better understand Shakespeare in his own time and, by making significant thematic connections, better understand Shakespeare's relevance in today's world.

I have chosen cultural themes that surface during each of the four plays that are most often taught in middle and high school—*Romeo and Juliet*, *Hamlet*, *Macbeth*, and *A Midsummer Night's Dream*—to capture attitudes, thinking, and trends that define Shakespeare's early modern period (see also Appendix A). Some themes, such as witches and religion or ghosts and the supernatural, are popular discussion points and elicit rapid-fire questions and comments from my students. It turns out that marriage and sexuality intrigues as much as violence and death in relation to *Romeo and Juliet*. Excerpts from sixteenth-century books on manners and customs also provide context for Macbeth's behavior at the feast in act 3, and a portrait of eight of the conspirators responsible for the Gunpowder Plot raises questions about Shakespeare's writing during the same year. Students love discussing the "hot-button" issues that provide context for his plays, especially those that surface from their own questions. You will also read about how Shakespeare Book Clubs, using the Bard's problem plays, transform a whole-class play approach to a student-centered, inquiry-based workshop. Shakespeare's narratives and insights spring to life as students engage: he, a creative cartographer, and we, the hungry travelers. Connection is the only road to understanding.

Every teacher envisions those "Aha" moments when students willingly dig into scenes, excited about discovering meaning. It happened to me when I used the *Rainbow Portrait*[1] (see Figure I.1) during a class discussion on spies and spying in *Hamlet*. The beautiful depiction of Queen Elizabeth I's

Every teacher envisions those "Aha" moments when students willingly dig into scenes, excited about discovering meaning.

gown, covered with embroidered eyes and ears, made sense in light of Hamlet's betrayal when he asks if Rosencrantz and Guildenstern were "sent for," Ophelia's dismay when she falls prey to her father's demands, and Hamlet's agency when he becomes spymaster and manipulator, rather than spied upon and manipulated. My students wondered if the Queen's dress was a warning to her subjects, or if Shakespeare's scenes illuminated a problem that was more than fictional intrigue.

FIGURE I.1. The *Rainbow Portrait*. Circa 1600–1602.

Providing sketches, paintings, poetry, treatises, letters, sermons, laws, catalogues, plays, frontispieces, proclamations, plant lore, tables, speeches, and news reports allows students to compare sixteenth-century thinking with the attitudes of today's writers, artists, politicians, and medical experts. What they learn is that visual and digital expressions of thought during the early modern period were as complex and varied as they are today. Laws about carrying weapons and challenging authority in 1595 when Tybalt baits and kills Mercutio continue to be relevant today, especially in light of school shootings and national uprisings. Our own laws on purchasing, owning, and carrying assault weapons continue to be scrutinized.

In addition to students' increased ability and desire to read Shakespeare's language, my students' focus on "what happened in act 1" has shifted to inquiry-based and student-led discussions on cultural/historical issues during the early modern period and how these connect to their own place and time in the world. They now use a broader lens. Instead of merely focusing on Capulet's anger at his daughter when she refuses to marry Paris, they now debate family relationships, normative gender roles, and power hierarchies during the early modern period. Students today "get it" when they read about family tensions and understand a Lord's power over his household. Today, feelings of entrapment and control are the same if a teenager has no agency. Reading sixteenth-century primary documents, such as a sermon, where the roles of a child, wife, and husband are carefully outlined is now the impetus for impromptu class discussions. Students are thirsty for "how it was back then," and their small- and large-group discussions often evolve dynamically when they tackle the big ideas in the plays within the framework of the documents. It has been a refreshing change to listen to students talk about how Juliet manipulates her situation despite the powerful constraints she faces.

According to Paula Marantz Cohen, Shakespeare does more than write stories about marginalization that is both external and internal. Shakespeare teaches us about empathy. "We are destined to lose power and become marginal figures, if we live long enough," Cohen writes (*What Shakespeare* 13–14). Students today, especially during the isolating forces of a pandemic, understand. Using primary sources, particularly those that illuminate the dynamic and devastating fabric of Shakespeare's world, allows students to feel more deeply to "probe the wellsprings of his characters' actions" (Cohen, *What Shakespeare* 14). In other words, Shakespeare transforms.

The document approach provides invaluable historical and cultural information, but the most important feature is how students make connections to their own world. Shakespeare's characters—the villains, the heroes, the alienated—provide mirrors to the soul, reflecting base truths about human nature. As students situate the plays within the context of early modern thinking, they understand how a tour de force exposes and challenges the status quo. The social pressures William Shakespeare faced in sixteenth-century London are often illuminated by other writers and artists of his time, and students often hinge their desire to plow through difficult language on finding relevance. Personal connection is key.

Undoubtedly, the rude mechanicals in a fairyland are hilarious in *A Midsummer Night's Dream*, but the relevance issue in past years of teaching this play has been a struggle. Once students began to read competing ideas about the supernatural, such as Robert Burton's (aka Democritus Junior) *The Anatomy of Melancholy* in which he depicts fairies as good-natured yet mischievous, as opposed to Reginald Scot's descriptions of them as dangerous and foreboding, they found their footing. Not all writers depicted fairies in the same way. Early modern parents, conflicted about supernatural beings, may have warned their children about fairies abducting them in the middle of the night. As today's students read diverse documents on similar themes, they realize, similar to today's popular culture, thinking varies. We often have lively discussions about today's movies, books, video games, fashion, and memes—and how they connect to Shakespeare's plays. One of my favorite days while I was teaching *Midsummer* to middle school students was when we talked about Puck's antics and made a list of all the tricksters in today's movies and TV shows. It was wild.

Other approaches to teaching Shakespeare—close reading, reader response, and performance—influence our teaching and learning practices. I am sure you will recognize these approaches and be able to see how they influence pedagogy. For this reason, I will review these approaches. They all have their value and strengths, and taken together in careful measure, combined with a document approach, have a great deal to offer to students.

Close Reading

When I first began teaching, a colleague taught *Julius Caesar*, carefully working through the play with her students, line by line, as they decoded the meaning of Shakespeare's words. As a proponent of the close reading approach, they explicated passages, emphasizing the play's poetic devices, such as rhyme, meter, figurative language, and irony. Students were encouraged to find meaning through explicit analyses of scenes, dialogue, and soliloquies without connecting ideas beyond the text. This pedagogical approach—*new critical* or close reading—includes a focus on "text alone," rather than considerations of student background knowledge or early modern cultural beliefs. A new critical approach often emphasizes the formal structure of Shakespeare's plays and sonnets, which may include verse form, rhyme scheme, stanza divisions, and the five-act structure. Many anthologies, individual editions, and professional books for teachers emphasize close reading and help students understand and appreciate Shakespeare's language, establishing the pedagogical priorities found in many classrooms.

Editors of contemporary high school literature anthologies often adopt a close reading, new critical approach. In the *Insights* anthology published by McGraw Hill, for example, the *Romeo and Juliet* text has *glossed* margins, defining words, such as "star-crossed," "in choler," and "bite my thumb" (Carlsen et al. 324, 325). Comprehension checks at the end of each scene include short summaries with questions, such as "What character traits do you see revealed in this scene in both Romeo and Juliet?" Reading for Details, Reading for Meaning, and Reading for Appreciation elements are spaced between acts and include questions based on text alone. Students rely on literal and inferential interpretations but miss the historical or cultural influences during the time the play was written. In essence, students stay within the four corners of the text to determine meaning.

Separate editions of the plays also include this emphasis on close reading of language. The exemplary Folger Shakespeare series, for example, uses *glossed* text where words and phrases are defined in accessible, contemporary language. Students who read these editions in school are able to see the full text on one page and the glossary of difficult or early modern language on the facing page. In the Folger edition of *Macbeth*, for example, "screw your courage to the sticking place" (1.7.70) is defined as an archery term in the provided glossary, giving students immediate access to the meaning without having to interrupt the flow of reading. In most cases, glossed editions, such as the Folger ones, provide substantial definitions or contemporary substitutions of words and phrases within the context of the scene.

Some professional books for teachers, such as Mary Ellen Dakin's *Reading Shakespeare with Young Adults*, also emphasize the new critical approach. Dakin provides resource material for building units of study to help students comprehend Shakespeare's language through categorized lists and vocabulary definitions to help students comprehend text. Defining archaic or early modern English, Dakin claims, challenges the frequently held stereotype that Shakespeare's wording is "too hard." One list, vocabulary specific to stage directions, provides students with terms commonly seen in comedies, tragedies, or histories. Other lists include high-frequency words, problematic pronouns, and definitions tied to specific plays. The anthologies, separate editions, and professional books for teachers that emphasize close reading help students gain a better understanding of Shakespeare's notoriously difficult language.

While understanding the lines is important, emphasizing only close reading—the exclusive study of language and form—reinforces the belief in one "correct" interpretation of Shakespeare's work. Students often believe that "true" understanding can only happen when glossed editions or simplified versions, such as *No Fear Shakespeare*, *WordPlay Shakespeare*, or *SparkNotes*, provide meaning.

Performance

Jake has taught eleventh-grade English primarily using a close reading approach but, over time, increasingly felt *Hamlet* was not coming alive for his students. Instead of reading the entire play as a shared text, he integrated performance strategies, directing students to choose, study, and prepare specific scenes to perform. They set about editing scripts, rehearsing lines, blocking movement, creating costumes, and designing scenery. The process was chaotic but beautiful. As a student emerged in a ragged sheet, boldly stating, "Remember me!" Jake remarked, "I haven't seen so much activity and excitement in my classroom before!"

Language is key to Shakespeare's dramatic scripts, but movement, body language, intonation, costuming, props, lighting—natural in his day—all engage the audience and are also important to meaning. Humor and anger, as well as all of the other intense emotions, are inherent not only in words, but also in hand gestures, facial expressions, and physical movement.

Some professional books for teachers, such as Rex Gibson's *Teaching Shakespeare*, include performance ideas, thus adding another layer to his close reading approach. Gibson introduces theatrical experiences, suggesting that teachers and students take on the roles of characters, which significantly increases opportunities to experience Shakespeare's language.

Edward Rocklin's *Performance Approaches to Teaching Shakespeare*, published by the National Council of Teachers of English, also provides ideas to help high school and college students experience the play in dramatic form. Taking on roles of director, player, or audience, students are challenged to divide the script into practical scenes and arcs, which Rocklin asserts will provide a deeper engagement when they understand "what words do" (xx). A more recent performance approach to Shakespeare is described in *Bring on the Bard: Active Approaches for Shakespeare's Diverse Student Readers* (Long and Christel) and offers a Folio technique that includes cue scripts much like Shakespeare might have used when players rehearsed and performed several different plays in a week.

Whether incorporating viewing, acting, or analyzing, performance approaches appeal to middle and high school teachers and students because of the energy that physical engagement affords. Viewing professional performances, either live or on film, allows students to experience Shakespeare by listening to early modern language supported by nonverbal cues. One actor at the Chicago Shakespeare Theater compared the experience of watching a play on stage to walking into a dark room: at first, nothing is clear. Eventually, however, the eyes adjust, shapes become more visible, and the path is easier to navigate. Shakespeare's language, despite the initial strangeness, becomes much clearer when we engage in the sound and cadence supported by expressive movement. Viewing a live performance is also a social experience, one that creates energy among students. During pre-performance talks, student audience members are often encouraged to laugh, clap, scream, and cry during performances because it creates energy for the actors on stage.

In addition to live performances, viewing film versions of the play appeals to both teachers and students because of the versatility of streamed film. Students can watch the entire play from beginning to end, which might include strategic places to "stop and jot." Teachers can also show clips of several versions of specific scenes or soliloquies, such as Hamlet's "To Be or Not to Be" speech or the witches on the heath in act 1 of *Macbeth*. Mary Ellen Dakin's *Reading Shakespeare: Film First* is an exploration of Shakespeare's plays through film analysis. Dakin describes her text as an opportunity for students to enter two worlds, visual composition and play construction. Students are introduced to the "trinity of telling," including text, theater, and cinema (10). What is unique about *Film First* is its attention to commercial images. The focus on how Shakespeare's plays are displayed and publicized incorporates another dimension: graphic design.

Viewing film versions of plays does not provide the same intense sensory experience as performing in class, but it can be used for students to compare different interpretations of the same play. The witches in *Macbeth*, for example, can be portrayed as men, women, monsters, nurses, garbage collectors, or hags, depending on the period in which the production is set or the director's choice. Students benefit from analyzing film, practicing media literacy skills as well as viewing diverse interpretations. Shakespeare's genius is often imagined in popular culture using unique set designs, outlandish special effects, and gender changes. In a recent Chicago Shakespeare Theater production of *Romeo and Juliet*, a female played Mercutio. Her stage presence and combat skill created a positive and passionate stir among the audience. She was a hit.

If teachers do not have experience in dramatic performance and do not have strong theater departments in their schools, they may find this approach somewhat daunting. Others may not have the option to take their students to performances or to invite local performers to the classroom. Teacher training courses traditionally use a new critical approach where teachers study Shakespeare through reading and discussion and may not experience a performance approach until they begin teaching and go to workshops or seek ideas from colleagues. Anxiety about using a performance approach can affect students too. Not all students are willing or able to engage physically, preferring seated activities. In this case, teachers may turn to less dramatic yet more responsive strategies.

Reader Response Approach

Alyssa began her teaching career with ninth-grade English classes and confided that she often felt insecure about how she taught Shakespeare. "I love this play," she said, "but I'm not sure my students really understand the nuances—and beauty—of the language, even after I taught it! And I know they don't see the relevance. All they think about is that Romeo and Juliet got married after a day and a half. They just don't relate." Alyssa's commitment to her students and to Shakespeare propelled her each year to try something new. Her students often read the play, followed by their own performances of other Shakespeare plays. Small groups chose tragedies or comedies and using summaries as well as the text, performed fifteen-minute "Short Shakes,"[2] complete with costumes and props. Still, Alyssa felt her students had not personalized the play in ways that invited Shakespeare into their own lives. How could her students inhale the relevance of four-hundred-year-old writing?

The answer came to her by accident. Our high school was under construction, and the builders had constructed temporary walls that Alyssa deemed perfect.

She invited her students to express their feelings about *Romeo and Juliet*, as well as other plays, by painting giant murals. Watching students with buckets of paint and smocks cover entire walls with Shakespeare quotes and symbols gave our newest English teacher a feeling of accomplishment. "These students have loved the creativity of expressing Shakespeare's language in their own way. It's awesome!" Alyssa's approach, known as *reader response*, provided her students with opportunities to internalize Shakespeare's words and construct meaning through art. Some students collaborated on initial sketches and then brought their ideas to life through color, texture, and form. This ninth-grade class may not remember Shakespeare's exact language, but they will remember their personal responses to *Romeo and Juliet*.

The reader response approach, described by Louise Rosenblatt in *Literature as Exploration*, argues that the meaning of text depends on reciprocal, personal transactions with the reader. Rather than focusing on one correct interpretation inherent in a text through a study of language and form, Rosenblatt emphasizes that, for each reader, meaning depends on the prior knowledge and experience they bring to the text. Teachers may wonder how students can gain prior knowledge and experience with the issues posed in Shakespeare's work. Rosenblatt suggests that teachers can counteract that concern by helping students "submit vicariously to a cultural pattern and code different from his own" (252). What this means is that students can build empathy as they approach literature personally, resulting in deep connections to the successes and failures that Shakespeare's characters encounter.

Similar to Alyssa, teachers who use the reader response approach find ways for students to understand Shakespeare based on personal interpretations that can be expressed through Socratic Seminars (see Appendix B), creative writing, sketch notes, one-pagers, memes, or social-media platforms. Rosenblatt's reader response approach takes into consideration the meaning derived when readers "live through what is being created during the reading" (33). Rosenblatt concedes that the same text, depending on time and circumstance, "will have a very different value and meaning" (35). Thus, living through the poetry of *Romeo and Juliet* may not necessarily provide opportunities to acquire information; rather, the acquisition of experiences teaches them the joy of new love, the pain of family discord, the heartache of death. And these understandings may vary not only based on prior knowledge, but also at different life junctures. According to Rosenblatt, the most valuable part of the reading experience is the ability to register others' responses with understanding and empathy.

Although the reader response approach recognizes and respects different interpretations and is a rich and valuable way to teach literature, it may be a difficult approach to Shakespeare if reluctant readers do not initially engage with text that seems beyond comprehension or interest. Deborah Appleman believes literature teachers have a responsibility to "move students beyond their own personal responses" (25) and that using reader response as the sole lens through which students interact with imaginative literature may narrow their limited range of understanding.

Close reading, performance, and reader response complement one another, and can be combined, but something important is missing: the historical and cultural context of the plays and sonnets. Without context, it is much harder to see how Shakespeare is relevant to our own day.

Document Approach

Several years ago, my class was reading *Macbeth*, and I showed them an excerpt from Shakespeare's early modern source, Raphael Holinshed's 1577 *Chronicles of England, Scotlande, and Irelande* (Figure I.2). At first, the students were dumbfounded and a little "put off" by the spelling, but then Jamie asked, "Can I try reading it?" With just a little stumbling, she figured out that the letter *u* took the place of a *v* and the single letter *j* was replaced by an *i*.

Students laughed when "neither shall he leaue anie iffue" stumped her, but then Aiden asked, "What is *iffue*?"

"Those elongated *f*s are really the letter *s*, so the word is *issue*, and that word means children. So, what is this strange woman saying?" I asked.

"You mean the witch?" asked Jamie.

"In the Holinshed's excerpt, Banquho [spelling as per the source] refers to them as women. Let's go back and see how they are referred to in Shakespeare's text," I ventured. We went back to the play.

"The character names are called FIRST, SECOND, AND THIRD WITCHES," said John from the back.

"Yeah, but, when they sing, they call themselves 'Weird Sisters,'" said another student.

Then Banquho; "What manner of women (saith he) are you, that séeme so little fauorable vnto me, whereas to my fellow here, besides high offices, ye assigne also the kingdome, appointing foorth nothing for me at all?" "Yes (saith the first of them) we promise greater benefits vnto thée, than vnto him, for he shall reigne in déed, but with an vnluckie end: neither shall he leaue anie issue behind him to succeed in his place, where contrarily thou in deed shalt not reigne at all, but of thée those shall be borne which shall gouerne the Scotish kingdome by long order of continuall descent."

FIGURE I.2. Excerpt from Raphael Holinshed's 1577 *Chronicles of England, Scotlande, and Irelande.*

"Later, Macbeth calls them 'imperfect strangers,'" added Jamie.

"But Banquo says 'fantastical,'" said Aiden. "It says in the side note, 'figments of the imagination.'"

"Who wrote that?" asked Jenna. "And what about this Holinshed guy?"

Jamie spoke up. "He says, 'the prophefie of three women suppofing to be weird fifters or feiries."[3]

"Fairies?" asked Aiden.

"That's what it says. And look at the picture—they look like three women all dressed up with long skirts on and funny hats!"

"Well, that one hat looks kind of pointy, like a witch hat." Aiden looked up from the text for some verification.

"But they almost seem like royalty. If that's what the original story was, why would Shakespeare change it up? He says they look like hags and have beards!" Everyone laughed.

"That's a good question," I said. "Why do you think Shakespeare changed the source story?"

"Maybe he wanted Macbeth and Banquo to be scared," said Cierra.

"Maybe he wanted us to be scared," answered Colin.

"Beards aren't scary," said Nick. "It's weird!" More laughter. I had never seen such engagement in our discussions and wondered about what other documents might interest them. I knew King James VI had written *Daemonologie* within ten years of Holinshed's *Chronicles*. Other early modern writers would undoubtedly provide a rich context for *Macbeth* and cast a wider net on his culture's ideas about supernatural beings. If my students understood how different perspectives created a backdrop, situating Shakespeare's writing, they could then reflect and respond to his characters and their complex motivations.

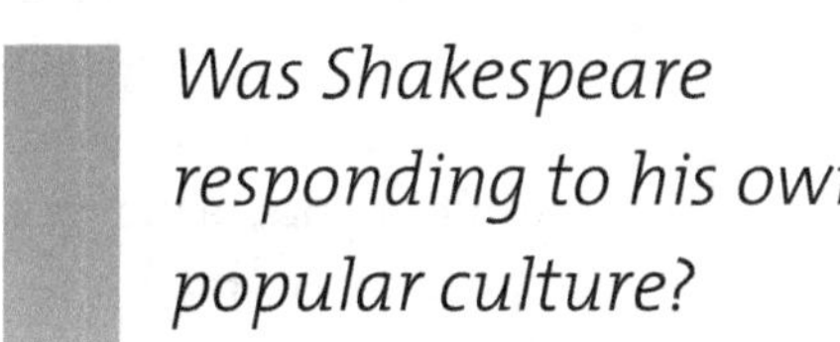

My review of the established approaches to teaching Shakespeare illuminates the need for a document approach. A close reading approach is important to understanding Shakespeare's language at a basic level but does not investigate historical and cultural questions and issues. The reader response approach does elicit personal responses but is culturally limited by the knowledge and background of the students. Performance approaches engage students in the plays as living, interpreted scripts but do not deepen knowledge of the time period nor raise questions about Shakespeare's relevance to the present.

Throughout this book, I will show how students are able to engage more deeply with Shakespeare's work, his words, and his world by combining the study of his works with key historical documents. Drawing on today's lively and diverse classrooms, I will reveal student engagement punctuated with deep thinking and great joy, where Shakespeare is the proffered example of an author whose work is drawn from a source play. In the Common Core English Language Arts eleventh- and twelfth-grade reading standard 11-12.1, students must "cite strong and thorough textual evidence" as they look at what the text says and infers, especially "where the text leaves matters uncertain." In standard 11-12.4, students must determine figurative and connotative meanings of words as they are used in a Shakespeare text and "analyze the impact of specific word choices on meaning and tone, including words with multiple meanings or language that is particularly fresh, engaging, or beautiful." In other words, as pinnacle standards for students who are on the cusp of post-secondary education, students must, in an analysis of craft through close reading, analyze the impact of Shakespeare's language. More important, and how the historical/cultural approach allows students to meet these standards, is how incorporating primary documents provides opportunities for critical thinking about language and issues involving the past and the present, thus synthesizing these two standards.

College Board national assessments, the SAT, AP Language and Composition, and AP Literature and Composition national exams include essay topics that require students to analyze how writers express complex ideas. In the 2021 AP Language and Composition national exam, for example, the synthesis essay asks students to "synthesize the material from at least three of the sources" to develop a position.[4] Students taking this exam will have scoured multiple primary documents, analyzing author's craft from a variety of genres to form an opinion and write a well-developed essay on a relevant issue. The SAT, now required in many states, also asks students to read a passage and analyze how the authors strategically add power to their writing.[5] Reading and studying early modern primary documents as part of the study of Shakespeare affords students multiple opportunities to examine how diverse artists and art forms speak to specific cultural issues. Writing about how Shakespeare and others develop relevant themes, based on varied viewpoints and genres, directly aligns with the skills needed to successfully meet and exceed academic standards. The document approach provides meaningful and real-life practice for priority standards and high-stakes tests. It's good teaching.

This book uses the document approach by addressing Shakespeare's plays and sonnets one chapter at a time. Teachers will be drawn first to the chapter about the plays they teach, which makes the organization accessible and useful. I urge you to read chapters about plays you do not teach, including his sonnets and the problem plays, to consider how to incorporate a workshop model through project-based book clubs. The chapters are filled with ideas that can be springboards to new classroom activities and writing prompts. Several appendices include strategies for teaching Shakespeare and the documents, assessment rubrics, contemporary literature based on Shakespeare's plays, and teacher online resources for further exploration. I invite you to learn a new approach to teaching Shakespeare and know you will enjoy the journey.

1

A Maiden Voyage with *Romeo and Juliet*

"We were told to read *A Midsummer Night's Dream* last year. I tried reading it on my own, but it was impossible."

"Yeah, we read that too at my old school," said Stephanie, "and it was all homework. I just went to *SparkNotes*. I had no idea what the play was about."

"I hate Shakespeare," said Tyler. "Well, really, I just don't get it. It's just too old."

All twenty-eight students were nodding. Colin, however, sitting in the back, was quiet. Just minutes before, he danced into the room on his toes with a smile on his face and gave me his best Romeo line: "What light through yonder window breaks? It is the east, and Juliet is the sun." This kid was beaming. "I love that part," he said.

Why do high school students have such diverse experiences studying the Bard? And why do many teachers loathe the thought of teaching Shakespeare for several weeks, knowing it will end with frustration, confusion, and defeat?

According to Turchi and Thompson, a secondary English teacher's primary goal is to "equip students with the tools to understand, decode, and analyze complex texts" as a way to satisfy the Common Core but often use methods that require students to simply summarize online plot summaries (par. 5). What often results, they claim, is a regurgitation rather than a discovery of universal themes. It *is* true, we sometimes fall into the trap of trying to cover an entire Shakespeare play without knowing exactly how to get through pages of early modern language. As one colleague said to me before we began our journey into *Romeo and Juliet*, "I dread this unit. I just don't know what to do with it. And I know my students dread it too." Turchi and Thompson give teachers "an opportunity to reboot," confirming we need to provide opportunities for students to *explore* complex texts in ways that are both challenging and empowering.

Most new middle and high school teachers expect to teach Shakespeare and consider it a staple in the curriculum. Unfortunately, how teachers approach his plays and sonnets varies widely, but most admit feelings of guilt if they do not read the play from cover to cover. Believing that "less is more," Turchi and Thompson suggest selecting key scenes and exploring ambiguities, which leads students to ask questions and to make sense of language, certainly, but to think deeply about big ideas, absolutely. The theme of violence, for example, can be explored in act 3, scene 1, when Tybalt challenges Romeo to "turn and draw," but the same theme can also be explored in Vincentio Saviolo's 1595 fencing manual (see Figure 1.1), the document Shakespeare may have consulted when he wrote the fight scene that ended in the stabbing and subsequent avenging of Mercutio's death.

I speake not as though those two fightes were not good for him which knowes how to vse them, because sometimes they are very necessary, according as a man findes his enemy prepared with his weapon: but then they must be doone with time and measure, when you haue got your enemye at an aduantage, with great dexteritie and readines. But as for me I will shewe you the wardes which I my selfe vse, the which if you well marke and obserue, you cannot but vnderstand the art, and withall keepe your bodye safe from hurte and danger.

L. At this present I take wonderfull delight in your companye, and nothing pleaseth me so much as this discourse of yours, to heare you giue me the reasons of those things which so much concerne the life and honour of a man: wherefore performe that which you haue promised, wherein you shall not onelye pleasure mee, but many other gentlemen and Noble-men will thinke themselues to haue receiued a fauour at your handes.

Rapier, and at this weapon will firste enter you, to the ende you maye frame your hand, your foote, and your body, all which partes must goe together, and vnlesse you can stirre and moue all these together, you shall neuer be able to performe any great matter, but with great danger.

FIGURE 1.1. Vincent Saviolo's *His Practise* (sig. D3 of "The Firft Booke"; 15).

Saviolo moved to London in the early 1590s and was teaching fencing in the Blackfriars playhouse, placing him in close proximity to Shakespeare when the latter was writing *Romeo and Juliet*. The manual, which first admonishes fighting—"Wherefore by way of advise, I wish all men to avoid evill companie" (68)—does give men permission not only to draw, if challenged, but also to strike the accuser if the challenged is unable to defend himself. And isn't that just what happened when Mercutio takes it upon himself to answer Tybalt's written challenge to Romeo? Both Shakespeare and Saviolo offer similar yet competing texts, providing students the opportunity for deep analysis. Despite what national standards, SAT preparation, and curriculum maps indicate, teachers already understand and desire a richly diverse classroom where students learn to approach a variety of text types actively and without trepidation.

> The fencing material in *Romeo and Juliet* typifies the eclectic nature of Shakespeare's borrowings and was probably culled from his own London experience as well as from various literary sources. (Holmer 163)

Beginning a New Approach

Having taught English for more than forty years, I can confirm that my classes always studied a Shakespeare play or sonnet. Only the very best students admitted *loving* the plays—perhaps ten percent of my students—and the rest simply endured. Some enjoyed performing bits and pieces or reading in groups, but the majority preferred movie versions where the meaning was often carried in the action. Still, despite the visual effects, some lines remained a mystery. The same questions or comments surfaced year after year:

- Why are the Montagues and Capulets so angry with each other?
- Why does the Prince threaten anyone who disturbs the peace with death?
- Why did Romeo and Juliet decide to get married when they just met?
- Why does the friar call Romeo's tears "womanish" when he is banished?
- Why are Romeo and Juliet so quick to commit suicide, and why are they buried side by side?

None of these questions are answered by the text, and yet students believe the actions to be incredible and incredulous by today's pop culture. Eventually, the play becomes just another old text lacking relevance.

Before approaching the text, we researched Shakespeare's world, delving into student-selected interests, such as clothing, food, living conditions, romance, and schooling. The Usborne *World of Shakespeare* (Claybourne and Treays) offers an accompanying, interactive website that expands on the content found within its colorful pages (Figure 1.2).

Students perused the pages, followed by taking virtual tours of the Globe Theatre, reading about the Elizabethan cure for lice and drunkenness, watching clips on medicine in London, or walking through photo galleries of play performances. They made lists of topics and questions to explore. Ryan, for example, wondered why women weren't allowed on stage and asked, "If people tried to shut down plays, but the Queen liked them, wouldn't they be disobeying her by shutting them down?" Kiara speculated why Shakespeare's wife didn't go to London with him. Nick asked how Shakespeare was different from other

FIGURE 1.2. Students use this book's accompanying interactive website for early modern cultural information.

authors of that time period. Brenna thought it might be hard to make murders look real on stage and wondered how people were stabbed. Eden considered why Shakespeare would leave his family, and Nick was confused about the Globe not having a roof. Elle asked what determined social rank and wondered if Shakespeare ever wore purple. Ainsley noticed that many of Shakespeare's plays were about love and violence and wondered why.

I wrote their questions on the board for us to revisit throughout the unit. How would we find the answers, I queried? Would Shakespeare's play reveal all? Or would we have to look at other documents? That was the beginning. Students first learned that Shakespeare would not be our sole text; other early modern documents would also be our source of learning.

My goal was for students to understand Shakespeare as a pop culture artist who might have been tapping into his own society for ideas to be explored, manipulated, and exploited in his own work, similar to Kendrick Lamar, Rupi Kaur, Lin-Manuel Miranda, Jill Soloway, and Chimamanda Ngozi Adichie, who have been recently touted as "culture defining" in the twenty-first century. Rather than study *Romeo and Juliet* as a single piece of literature from a specific time period, we explored the questions we had about Shakespeare's world by categorizing them into broad themes that might have been addressed by other sixteenth-century artists. In this way, any author's oeuvre, including Shakespeare's, could be considered a primary document and therefore "fair game" to be included in the quest to both challenge and empower.

Students soon learned that not all authors shared the same ideas; some disagreed but, by comparing several documents, they could compare competing early modern ideology. For example, act 1, scene 5, when Romeo and Juliet meet for the first time, and act 2, scene 2, when they exchange vows during the balcony scene, caused more than raised eyebrows. "But they just met!" said Nick. Other documents from the same time period, however, included records depicting the average age of marriage in 1595 in several areas north of London (Laslett Table 1.2; Young 470), a sermon on the legality of underage children who get married without parental consent, a *banne* or required marriage announcement from the pulpit, and Arthur Brooke's poem "The Tragicall Historye of Romeus and Juliet." Scrutinizing these documents tells more than a single story. According to Chimamanda Adichie, if we "show . . . people as one thing, as only one thing, over and over again . . . that is what they become" (09:14). A single story, she claims, is dangerous and often leads to viewing people through one lens, leading to misunderstanding and mistrust. Was sixteenth-century England a place where children married young? Were children impulsive and oblivious to their parents' wishes? Did parents disown their children for such infractions? During the first two weeks of reading *Romeo and Juliet*, as well as other primary documents, students found that ideas about marriage and sexuality may not have changed much in the past four hundred years. Jake's question from our first few days together drove the entire unit:

> "Why did Shakespeare write this play?"

Document Discussions

Reading several documents can lead to rich discussions in which students debate what the documents reveal: their variability, their complexity, and their relevance.

Working with Primary Documents

The first question I had to answer was how many documents I should incorporate and which broad themes would initiate student inquiry. Because the play opens with the fighting among servants of the Capulet and Montague households, I chose *gender* and *clothing*, knowing that students would be interested in how sixteenth-century gender identity may have contributed to the feud. Both documents and videos that incorporate period clothing, such as the 2013 film production (Carlei), starring Hailee Steinfeld (as Juliet) and Douglas Booth (as Romeo), help students picture early modern dress and cultural mores. I decided to include eight documents in booklet form to read and discuss after each act. Students each had at least one part in the play, so, when we read aloud, they practiced reading and followed character development. They also made *foldables* (see Appendix B) with five tabs, one for each act, and spaces for dramatic terminology, such as *aside*, *soliloquy*, and *stichomythia* (Figure 1.3).

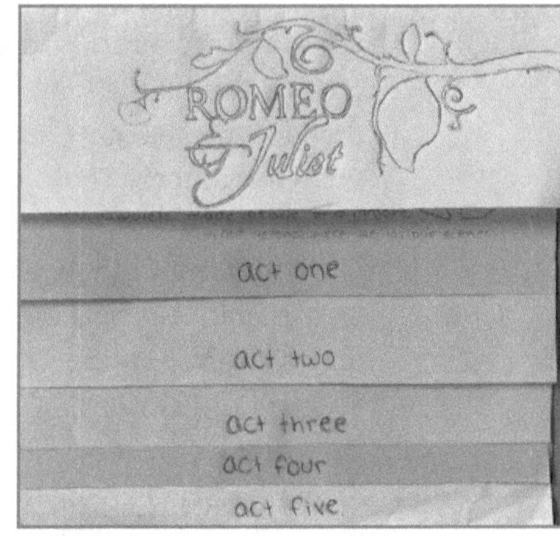

FIGURE 1.3. A student example of a *Romeo and Juliet* foldable.

Using foldables for class notes, scene titles, character sketches, and document reflections provided an interactive system for recording students' learning.

Beginning the play was the most difficult part, but I wanted their first experiences with language to be engaging. An idea from the Chicago Shakespeare Theater's education department, which used to host a teacher workshop annually, suggests students leave their seats and physically experience the language. I gave each pair of students a line from the prologue. Each group memorized this line and created motions to carry the message. They had fun figuring out their assigned ten syllables. I had to explain that "loins" were not *lions*, a common mistake. We formed a large circle with the groups in sequential order. Moving from group to group around the circle, students performed the prologue several times, laughing as they *played* with the language. Next, students chose the two most important words from their assigned line and adapted their motions. Finally, each group chose the most important word from their line and narrated the play in fourteen words and motions. We went around the circle quickly, filling the hall with laughter. Perfect.

To help students remember which characters were Montagues and which were Capulets, I made a class set of envelopes containing the names of all the characters that they could arrange as a family tree on their desks while I narrated the story. As I added characters, I wrote the names on the board while students created their own graphic organizers. Once students had all the characters' names in a meaningful assembly, they put them back in the envelopes and met with another student, trying to replicate their family tree. Before reading the play, students created these family trees several times, helping them to visualize relationships and to pronounce names.

The first scene of the play was slow going. I expected students would mispronounce words, fumbling through the first eighty lines, and that did happen. With practice and patience, though, we moved through the first scene. Most importantly, we talked about what it meant to be "at war" with other students, families, or countries in our world. We laughed about gestures, such as "I do bite my thumb, sir" and compared it to today's "flipping someone off." Students then listened as our class Prince Escalus read his lines. He read slowly, warning the two families. Their job was, first, to listen as Prince Escalus read aloud and, second, to reread his words with a partner. In their foldables, they explained what he meant by "If you ever disturb our streets again / Your lives shall pay the forfeit of our peace" (96–97). When they read Queen Elizabeth I's 1594 "Proclamation Prohibiting Unlawful Assembly" (qtd. in Callaghan 232–33; see also Hughes and Larkin), from one year before *Romeo and Juliet* was written, in which the Queen bestowed "a provost martial with sufficient authority to apprehend all such as shall not be readily reformed and corrected by the ordinary officers of justice; and them without delay to execute upon the gallows by order of martial law," students understood why Escalus was so harsh in his justice. The Queen's proclamation made clear the precedent for Shakespeare's scene. Early modern audiences would have understood the Prince's power—he could and would carry out her proclamation to "apprehend" and "execute" or defy his matriarch. Another proclamation they read was from 1562, one that defined who could carry a rapier and the parameters for the size of the blade; any person who was found to carry a weapon "passing the length of twelve inches," specifically with intent to harm, would be imprisoned. Where, I asked, does Shakespeare mention the law during the fight between Sampson, Gregory, and Abraham? Eden, who played Sampson's part, said, "When he says, 'Is the law of our side if I say ay?'" They were getting the idea. Shakespeare was not writing in isolation. He was writing to an audience who knew about fighting in the streets, who knew about wielding a rapier, what size was allowed, and what would occur if an enemy said, "I am for you."

Document Discussions

Using contemporary primary documents about gun control will help students understand the importance of looking to the past to understand the present. How do our weapons laws speak to who we are today?

This period is a landmark because for the first time in England women began to write in their own defense and for the first time anywhere significant numbers of women began to publish defenses. (Henderson and McManus 4)

At the end of act 1, students received eight documents about gender or clothing to read as a Jigsaw or Each Teach activity (see Appendix C). They first read one document together in groups of three to four while I circled the room and answered questions about wording. In Samuel Rowlands's poem "The Humors that Haunt a Wife" (*Humors Looking Glasse*), the speaker condemns the woman who tries to be too modern, a selection that could be compared to Jane Anger's 1589 pamphlet "Protection for Women," the possible rebuttal to Charles Pyrrye's "Disprayse of Women." The pamphlets, much like a contemporary, rousing debate we might read in editorials, listen to on podcasts, or watch on televised debates, were written responses to controversies over normative gender roles. The rise of printing made pamphlets disseminate quickly, more attacks than defenses on "the woman question."

Students were also intrigued by John Gerard's plants from his 1597 *Herball*; specifically, black hellebore, which is "good for mad and furious men" or those plagued with love melancholia. After much discussion on all the documents' main points, students formed three groups of eight students where all documents were represented. Students in each group spent several minutes teaching their documents to the rest of the group, explaining the meaning, the theme, and the purpose (Figure 1.4).

Excerpts from *The Praise and Dispraise of Women* by C. Pyrrye

Here Beginneth the Disprayse of Women	***Here Beginneth the Prayse of Women***
This Monster is the woman kinde, *whose ougelye shape and port:* *I meane to paint, writ thou my minde,* *not forcing her report.* *This woman kinde I know right well,* *is comelie to the eye:* *Of perfect shape she beares the bell,* *I can it not denie.*	*I thinke thou doost not call to minde,* *in sicknes or in health:* *How we are holpe by woman kinde,* *whose care is for our wealth.* *First (as thou knowst) she takes great paine,* *by trauelinge in bed:* *And greuous groninges doth sustaine,* *before she see our head*

FIGURE 1.4. Students compared controversial early modern pamphlets written about women, such as these excerpts from Pyrre's *The Praise and Dispraise of Women*.

As a final activity, our large-group discussion centered on what students learned about Shakespeare's world: What attitudes were unearthed from the documents? How might Shakespeare have exposed some of these attitudes in his play? (See also Appendix D.)

"They sure had attitudes about girls back then!" said one student.

"How do you know? I asked.

"Well, look at what it says about being a virgin!" said another. "It says she is 'the beauty of nature' and 'her parents' joy.'"

"And what is a 'wanton' woman?" asked a student from the back.

"I think it's someone who hooks up," said another. They all laughed.

"Well, this document calls her a witch and a devil!"

"Same as now, then," said someone else. They all laughed again.

"Devin, do you have a question?" I asked the student on the side of the room who normally seemed rather quiet but now had his hand up.

"Well, I was just wondering why Shakespeare makes Juliet seem so different. When she meets Romeo, she is not shy at all, like in the document on virgins. But she isn't a devil either. Romeo treats her like she's perfect, but she's definitely interested."

Document Discussions

Early modern historical and cultural attitudes are embedded within the primary documents and provide a framework for student learning.

"If the audience knew about the pamphlet wars and had the impression that women were a problem, as you read in the documents, why do you think he portrays Juliet this way?" I asked.

"Maybe he was trying to make people mad."

"Maybe he was making people wonder if they were wrong."

"Maybe he was trying to get them to think."

"Maybe he was trying to get them to come to his plays."

"I think all of you could be right," I ventured.

Working through the Tough Stuff

If I'm giving you the impression that students read the documents easily without struggle, confusion, or questions after the first "go," I should admit that this was not the case. Some students, especially those who were trying to make sense of John Lyly's *The Anatomy of Wit*, could not comprehend his point. I joined their small group to help them break it down. William Whately's sermon on women's roles from 1619 was no easier because of the spelling and sentence structure. Students did pick up on certain lines that jumped off the page, though, such as "mine husband is my superiour, my better" (36).

"Seriously?" asked Shayna. "They really thought that?"

"I know, right?" I answered. "What ideas and thoughts will you share with your Jigsaw group that explains this document?" I asked.

Brooke admitted she didn't get half the language: "Why does it say that women must give men leave to 'chew the cud'? What does that mean? And what is 'good carriage'? How can her 'good carriage be withered'?"

We worked through as many language issues as possible the first time we tackled the documents, but working in small groups helped to build confidence and skill. During their collaborative work, I met with each group and asked students the following:

- What will you share in your Jigsaw group?
- How does this document help your reading of Shakespeare's play?

Students who needed more support benefited from having a list of ideas to share before joining others who read different pieces.

Jigsaw Strategy

1. Teacher provides overview of each document and its genre (letter, pamphlet, poem).
2. Teacher assigns numbered documents to eight small groups.
3. Students individually read assigned document for general meaning, underlining key ideas: *first reading*.
4. Students join small groups with same document. One student reads aloud slowly, stopping halfway to recap meaning: *second reading*.
5. Students choose three important points to share with larger group.
6. Teacher visits each group to listen to conversations and to help clarify meaning.
7. A second student in small group rereads document aloud: *third reading*.
8. Students form groups of eight with each document represented.
9. Each student shares their document's content while others jot notes.
10. Students reflect on thread running through all documents.

Ready to share, students formed groups of eight, with all documents represented. Discussions began slowly, tentatively. Most students walked through their documents, reporting "what it said." Some, however, made text-to-text connections. Alana noticed, for example, that the compliments in John Gough's poem "Encomiums on the Beauty of His Mistress" mimicked Romeo's compliments of Juliet's beauty: "She doth teach those torches to burn bright" (86).

"Isn't that plagiarism?" Rena asked.

"Not really," I answered. "Copyright laws in 1595 did not exist, and writers often borrowed from other writers. What does this similarity tell you?"

"Shakespeare probably read a lot," they said. My thought was—and I told them—that they were thinking through so much more than what was happening in the play.

Immediately following discussions, writing about cultural issues that surfaced in *Romeo and Juliet* became our norm. Their reflections solidified their understandings about the connective tissue between Shakespeare and other writers of his day. The more genres they explored, such as letters, poems, treatises, pamphlets, and sketches, the more they realized that other writers were also grappling with troubling issues within their society. The writing helped them sort out their own thinking about how the documents related to Shakespeare's tragedy.

Student-Written Reflections

- Women had "barely any rights."
- Juliet's father says he will allow her to select any husband she wants but forbids her to see Romeo.
- Women needed to accept they were inferior to men.
- Men were controlling, but women received a lot of compliments.
- Men thought they were more knowledgeable than women.
- Rosaline prefers to stay chaste, but Romeo acts like he's not used to having girls saying no to him.
- Men treated women like animals.

"'Love-Melancholy' makes it sound like love is a disease," wrote Eden, whose writing made it seem as though she was trying to work out her own thoughts about gender equality and finally came to the conclusion that it was not only young, forbidden love, but also diseased love from the viewpoint of many others. Eden's ideas surprised me, not because of what she said, but because the vast majority had opinions about what they were discovering about early modern writers. For several students, this was their first experience with primary documents, and yet I had never witnessed so much discussion during a Shakespeare unit of study and particularly during the first few weeks. I was both stunned and excited.

Working with Shakespeare's Text

If students know about *Romeo and Juliet*, many know about the balcony scene. When Juliet asks, "Romeo, Romeo, wherefore art thou, Romeo?" most commonly believe she is asking him where he is, rather than why he is called Romeo. This scene, however, can be considered somewhat "steamy." Are they planning to have sex? Is he getting her to agree? And, of course, when Romeo asks Juliet, "Oh wilt thou leave me so unsatisfied?" (2.2.125), most of us expect hormonal snickers. If any act hits the mark squarely when it comes to student interest, it revolves around the theme of love and sexuality. Act 2, specifically, has the potential to be pivotal. Is Shakespeare friend or foe? Young love and heartbreak are emotions they understand.

Lessons in ninth-grade English classrooms must activate, engage, inspire. I decided to play the audio of act 2, scene 1, when Mercutio and Benvolio, in their post-party stupors, call out for Romeo and make fun of his Petrarchan love for Rosaline. I knew professional readers would provide the intonation and cadence necessary to carry the meaning. For the next section, I put two stools in front of the room for our student players, Romeo and Juliet, to read the balcony scene as they profess their love for each other. Before they began, I asked students to think about how Juliet might react to Romeo's proclamation of love. Was he only interested in sex? Did this new love seem real?

They read. We listened. We discussed. They wrote.

I am hoping this is the point that you notice I use combinations of performance, close reading, and reader response while I teach. The document approach is not necessarily a solo act. Many of us do use a variety of activities, an eclectic pedagogical recipe that, when combined in strategic ways, offers students variety. For example, I use close reading as a rereading technique. On this particular day, I assigned several lines from the balcony scene to each partner group. I directed them to *reread* the lines and to explicate or unfold the meaning. What were Romeo and Juliet saying to each other?

How to Unfold Meaning

1. Teacher assigns one to two lines to partner groups.
2. Each student reads lines aloud to partner, then in unison.
3. Partner groups read aloud to class in chronological order.
4. Partner groups decide on how to say lines in today's language.
5. Partner groups read new lines sequentially to create contemporary poem.

After approximately fifteen minutes, students reported their findings to the class. I asked them to share their most powerful line as well as a contemporary way to express the words. First, in sequential order, each group recited their Shakespearean line, creating a poem. Next, each group read their contemporary line, creating the modern version. I found that rereading excerpts often resulted in clearer understanding, but I also realized that numerous exposures to shorter pieces of text was how students learned about how early modern language worked.

Students balked at Shakespeare's language far less than in other years. They were more confident in their ability to decipher what he was saying and less concerned if they did not know every single word. They were beginning to see how the Montague and Capulet feud was affecting Romeo and Juliet. Students now understood why the timing of their marriage was so important. The fear of parents finding out about what they were doing was also known by twenty-first-century fourteen year olds.

Numerous exposures to shorter pieces of text was how students learned about how early modern language worked.

Each day, we actively engaged with the play, including the day a colleague dressed up as Romeo and I as Friar Laurence. We placed ourselves in the middle of the room, *fishbowl* style (see Appendix B), and read act 2, scene 3, when Romeo confides his love for Juliet to Friar Laurence (Figure 1.5).

FIGURE 1.5. Teachers can use a fishbowl strategy to demonstrate small-group discussion techniques.

We mustered up as much emotion as possible, then discussed the scene together. We talked about what the friar is doing with plants when Romeo arrives. Was that a normal activity for a friar during this time? How did the friar feel about the knowledge that Romeo was no longer in love with Rosaline and now loved Juliet? Was the friar Romeo's friend? Would he tell Romeo's parents what he was doing? Our discussion would provide a model for students to read the next scene—when Peter and the nurse speak to Romeo about his intent to marry Juliet—in small groups. I was learning that students needed time to talk about what they were reading and to ask each other questions about uncertainties. During act 2, we engaged in a vast array of activities: small-group readings, large-group discussions, audios, reflections, fishbowl discussions, poetry writing, close reading explications, movie clips, and performance. The key? Variety.

Students moved through activities like fish through water, gliding and turning through currents of language that sometimes confused and overwhelmed them. Yes, they struggled, but it was the type of struggle where they did not feel submerged. No one said, "I can't" or "I won't."

Group Activities

I was excited to share the documents on marriage and sexuality, but I knew varying, active reading strategies were needed (Figure 1.6). In this activity, I had arranged the room so that we had four large groups of six or eight. Roaming Team Leader (see Appendix E) is an activity in which small groups choose a leader to move to a different group to share thinking.

Each group reads, annotates, and discusses one document together before sending the "roaming team leader" off to another group. The roaming leader or new group member shares the group thinking about their document and then listens while the new group members reciprocate. After roaming team leaders have shared with each group, students have learned about all the documents. The repetition of shared information found in this activity provides struggling readers opportunities to take leadership positions as they showcase their documents while building confidence and skill. I occasionally and intentionally choose roaming team leaders in each group to provide students the practice they need to improve verbal skills.

Act 2 documents on marriage and sexuality included William Whately's sermon "On Rushing into Marriage" in which he warns, "He that leapes over a broad ditch with a short staffe, shall fall into the midst" (45–46), words akin to Friar Laurence's "Wisely and slow. They stumble that run fast" (line 101). Students also read about the plant sowbreade, considered by John Gerard as a "good amorous medicine" (000) (Figure 1.7).

Activities for Reading Shakespeare
3 – 2 – 1
Big Chunk / Little Chunk
Blocking Scenes
Cognitive Mind Maps
Digital to Visual
Divide and Conquer
Document Walk
Explicate or Unfold
Family Tree
Fishbowl Discussion
Foldables
Inquiry Dive
Five Types of Writing
Jump-In Reading
Page-to-Stage
Play it Again, Sam!
Quick Writes
Read-Around
Re-Enactments
Samoan Circles
Silent Annotations
Socratic Seminar
Think-Aloud
Turn and Talk
Verbal Fluency
Whip-Around
Who Said What?

FIGURE 1.6. Appendix B provides further descriptions of classroom activities for teaching any Shakespeare play.

The lawful age of marriage, assumed to be fourteen for men and earlier for women, who are "soon ripe than men" (Swinburne 48), contrasts with the chart from 1550 that lists the average age of marriages, specifically for females, in Devon, England, as twenty-six (Laslett Table 1.2; Young 470). Students read, annotated, and discussed the document types and messages before moving to the next partner group to share findings.

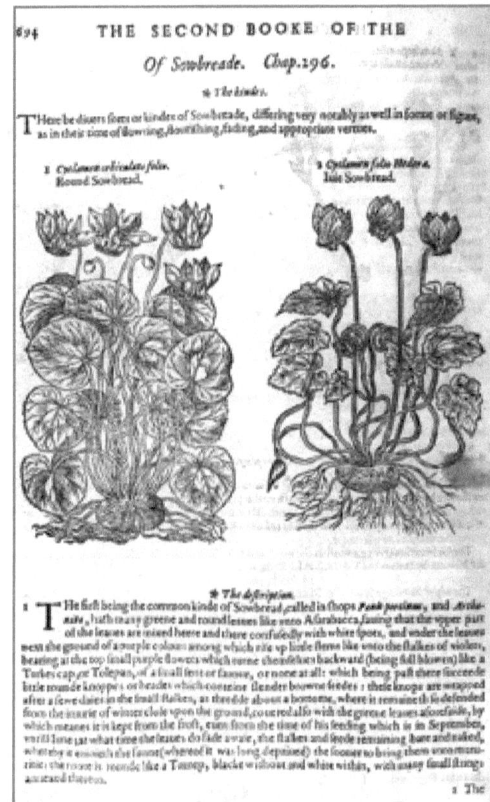

694 THE SECOND BOOKE OF THE

Of Sowbreade. *Chap.*196.

The kindes.

Round Sowbread.

Iuie Sowbread.

The description.

2 The

FIGURE 1.7. "Of Sowbreade," *The Herball or Generall Historie of Plantes* (Gerard 694)

Reading primary documents for act 2 posed far less difficulty (Figure 1.8). Even so, I knew I would need more arrows in my quiver to help students comprehend early modern documents (Figure 1.9). Reading strategies that included active rereading, discussion, and movement were paramount.

Students had now read two acts in *Romeo and Juliet* and expected variant spelling and syntax, such as in William Miller's 1676 letter of advice about marriage when he states that a "Huswife dedicates her time and pains: her Children are her Garden, her Park, nay her Court" (15–16). After the "roaming" discussions, I asked students to choose a document they considered the most shocking or interesting and write about their reactions. Elle thought it was "absurd that society thought they could control such personal and private habits." Marissa agreed with Elle and added that these ideas were "overstepping the boundaries a bit." Eden discussed the sowbreade document and wondered if people really believed it worked. Another student conjectured that "this plant could've increased testosterone in males and strengthened women's sex drive." Breana paired up two

FIGURE 1.8. Small groups reading and annotating act 2 primary documents to discuss early modern plant lore.

Activities for Reading Documents
Diminishing Maps and Notes
Document Walk
Four Reads
Gradual Release
GRAPES
Genre, Rhetorical schemes, Audience, Purpose Effect, Speaker
Jigsaw
Listen and Bubble
OPTIC
Overview, Parts, Title, Interrelationships, Conclusion
PAPER
Purpose, Argument, Presuppositions, Evaluate, Relate
Q & A
Questioning
Say Something
Shared Reading
Shift and Share
SOAPSTone
Subject, Occasion, Audience, Purpose, Speaker, Tone
Student Writing
T-Square Notes
Text Comparison
Text-to-Text
Text-to-World

FIGURE 1.9. Appendix C describes classroom activities for working with primary documents.

articles and noted, "It's interesting to hear their rules, like you're only supposed to have sex for kids, not for pleasure, yet Romeo tries to have sex with Rosaline, and he wants to have sex with Juliet before they get married." After asking students about what questions they still had, Kyla wanted to know about the father's role, and Cody was curious about whether they used sowbreade as a prank. After reading John Donne's letter of apology to Sir George More for eloping with his daughter Anne, Spencer was curious about whether Donne was punished. Their questions revealed deep thinking about the early modern society, a thirst for knowledge that entrenched them in Shakespeare's popular culture.

Conquering the Midpoint Slump

We were at the pivotal act 3, where structurally the play moves toward tragedy or comedy. In a mini-lesson, we considered how both comedies, such as *A Midsummer Night's Dream*, and tragedies, such as *Romeo and Juliet*, began with a block to love by an authority figure. Although Hermia's father Egeus demands she marry Demetrius, she desires Lysander, much in the same way that Juliet's father demands she marry Paris and forbids any liaison with the Montagues. Structurally, both comedies and tragedies move from the *block to love* to an escape. Hermia and Lysander escape to the green world whereas Romeo and Juliet secretly marry by escaping to Friar Laurence's cell. From this point, however, in *Romeo and Juliet*, act 3, we see the *pivot* or turn in action that leads to tragedy. In this case, it is Mercutio's death that is the inciting event, placing all characters on the path to destruction: the death of Tybalt and the exile of Romeo lead to unintended, tragic consequences. This is an action-packed part of the play, yet many students often lose steam.

To maintain engagement, we watched how the act 3 violence begins in the 2013 film version (Carlei). Next, I asked our student players, Romeo, Tybalt, and Mercutio, to demonstrate what they noted in the film using plastic *Star Wars* sabers. They reenacted (see Reenactments, Appendix B) the duel in silent slow motion, so students could see in real time how Romeo blocks Mercutio, allowing Tybalt's sword to hit its mark using a *passado* or quick thrust under Romeo's arm. Finally, we divided the class into acting groups, so students could block some short scenes:

- Benvolio, Mercutio (lines 1–9)
- Benvolio, Mercutio (10–33, up to where Tybalt enters)
- Benvolio, Mercutio, Tybalt (34–44)
- Mercutio, Benvolio, Tybalt (45–54, up to where Romeo enters)
- Tybalt, Mercutio, Romeo (55–71)
- Mercutio, Tybalt, Romeo (swords: 72–88, up to where Tybalt stabs Mercutio)
- Mercutio, Benvolio, Romeo (swords: 89–107, to where Mercutio exits)
- Benvolio, Romeo (108–19, to where Tybalt enters)
- Benvolio, Romeo, Tybalt (swords: 120–35, to where Romeo exits)
- First citizen, Benvolio, Romeo, Tybalt, Capulet's wife (136–49)
- Prince, Benvolio, Capulet's wife, Montague, Prince (150–96).

Students had fun getting out of their seats to practice scene work, but the highlight of the week was working with an expert in stage combat (Figure 1.10). Moving our class to a larger space, a local stage combat professional first

FIGURE 1.10. Ninth-grade students learning stage combat from a theater director.

FIGURE 1.11. Di Grassi's depiction of the *true art of defence* (fig. 19).

reviewed the parts of the rapier and demonstrated some of the moves that were used in act 3, scene 1, such as *passado, alla staccata, punto reverso,* and the *hai*. Students used foam swords to fight each other, incorporating a demi-lunge, thrusting—both straight and around the side—and circling. Our expert taught us about Giacomo di Grassi,[6] an Italian swordsman whose 1570 document, which was translated into English in 1594, Shakespeare may have used as a source for the scene (Figure 1.11).

Back in the classroom, we analyzed another publication, Vincentio Saviolo's *His Practise*, which, according to Joan Holmer in "'Draw, If You Be Men': Saviolo's Significance for *Romeo and Juliet*," conveys how Saviolo stresses "much more the importance of the occasion for the gentleman's quarrel" (176). Holmer emphasizes the sequence of events in a challenge, which is explained in the document: an oral confrontation must occur, followed by a concise, polite letter of challenge. In gentlemanly fashion, the appointed time and location, a field, are specifically named. When the two documents—Saviolo's *His Practise* and Shakespeare's *Romeo and Juliet* (2.4.6–35, 3.1.26–106)—are placed side by side, students are then able to compare texts. "How do both documents develop the theme of violence and death?" I asked.

Document Discussions

Using a side-by-side comparison of Saviolo and Shakespeare helps students understand the cultural influences on the act 3 violence. Shakespeare manipulates the sixteenth-century protocols of a gentleman's challenge, duel, and technique.

Collin said, "Well, it doesn't seem like Shakespeare followed this guy's rules. Romeo did receive a letter, but there wasn't any confrontation before that."

"Yeah," said Devin. "When Romeo was at the Capulet house, Tybalt wanted to fight, but the old guy Capulet held him back."

Collin quipped, "Go to! Go to!" We all laughed, but Devin made his point.

"Another thing you should know," I said, "is that Saviolo moved to London in 1594 and rented a room in the Blackfriars playhouse from owner Philip Henslowe to teach fencing lessons the year before Shakespeare wrote *Romeo and Juliet* and two years before it was first performed at the Globe. If Shakespeare had done any rehearsing at the Blackfriars or had heard about London's newcomer, he may have met Saviolo and perhaps watched some of the fencing lessons."

An interesting comparison we noted is how Saviolo compares the art of the rapier to music: "I thinke it necessarye that euery one should learne this arte of rapier, for as a man hath voice and can sing by nature, he shall neuer doo it with time and measure of musicke" (qtd. in Holmer 172).

"What music terminology do you notice in this section of the play?" I asked. Three of the band students shouted,

"Minstrels!"

"Fiddlesticks!"

"Discords!"

"What about yesterday, when you learned about di Grassi, the Italian fencing teacher who may have also written a book on dueling? Do we know which document Shakespeare may have relied upon for his terminology?"

"He probably used both," said Brenna. "How would anyone know?"

"You're right. We don't. But we do know that many documents from that time period used similar wording, including Shakespeare's."

"How do we know Shakespeare didn't know fencing? Maybe he already knew these words," said Nate.

"Does anyone have an answer to that?" I asked. The silence was palpable. "Good. More questions than answers. That's exactly what learning is all about."

"Writing Floats on a Sea of Talk"

When writing either precedes or follows a discussion, magic happens. My students expected *short-writes*, bursts of three- to five-minute opportunities to write into their thinking. We had read and discussed Shakespeare's and Saviolo's documents, and now I wondered how student thinking about sixteenth-century violence would deepen. Brenna and Jake both wrote about the obvious fight scenes in the play, but Brenna pointed out that "Mercutio thinks he [Romeo] is soft and cannot fight." She noted that Saviolo mentions if it is appropriate for a third party [Mercutio] to step in. "It's talked about," she wrote, "when he says, 'when one doth call another for an offence done unto him by a third person,' and the passage talks about how a third challenger needs a reason." Jake discussed this same idea by pointing out, "Mercutio duels Tybalt even though Romeo was the one who was challenged by Tybalt. Shakespeare must have been aware of Saviolo's fencing manual." Reading the students' writing about how sixteenth-century writers speak to cultural issues, such as violence and death, energizes me. In past years, student writing focused primarily on scene summaries or character descriptions, exactly as required. Using primary documents to help situate Shakespeare's writing moves students beyond the storyline. They are more equipped to discuss how Shakespeare's writing reflects the cultural views of his time. Similar to today's artists, he was very much aware of competing views and created believable yet controversial characters and situations.

Discussing the controversial issues that permeate today's society is a necessary yet natural transition. Young adult and pop culture books, such as bullying in *The 57 Bus* (Slater), identity in *Educated* (Westover), or senseless crime in *Concrete Rose* (A. Thomas), become logical extensions of early modern thinking about challenges, fights, and death. If I had ever wondered how to make Shakespeare's plays relevant to today's teens, I know now that foregrounding primary sources opens pathways to contemporary society. Pushing into early modern writers and artists to learn how they reacted to or influenced the world around them becomes an instinctive gateway into the twenty-first century.

Document Discussions

Using primary documents as stimuli for wondering should be a measure for engagement and a step toward understanding. Curiosity and wonder interface with how sixteenth-century thinking connects to today's issues. The measure of understanding may be in the strength of our connections.

How early modern artifacts lead to discussions about today's world was exemplified when I showed my students the woodcut found in the Saviolo text (Figure 1.12). It contained a skeleton on the ground with two men standing next to it: a ragged man and a rich man.

The message ran around the circumference of the picture:

> Oh wormes meat: O Froath, O Vanitie. Why art thou so insolent?

"Does this language ring a bell?" I asked.

"Yeah," said Sarah. "Mercutio says that when he yells, 'A plague on both your houses!' Then he says, 'They have made worm's meat of me!'"

"So that's where it comes from," said Jake.

FIGURE 1.12. The *Wormes Meate* woodcut from Saviolo's fencing manual *His Practise* appears in Book 1 as the only nontechnical illustration (sig. K3 of "The Firft Booke," 51) and as the only pictorial ornament in Book 2 (sig. Gg6 of "The Fecond Booke," 135) (qtd in Homer 174).

"He's saying you all are putting me in the ground. Killing me. And now the worms are going to have me for dinner," quipped Sarah.

"Not exactly the best thought," said a voice from the back.

"Well, we're all afraid of that. Where we go, I mean. Nobody likes the thought," said Sarah. She looked down as though she was thinking about someone or something else. Our discussion didn't stop there, though. We left Mercutio and worm's meat behind and moved into other topics: burial, cremation, funerals, and senseless death. I went with wherever my students led me. Increased and engaging discussion was my yardstick for measuring comprehension and engagement.

Early Modern Poisons and Drugs

As we approached acts 4 and 5, I wanted my students to reflect more on the relevance of Shakespeare's world to today's popular culture. Drugs and potions, particularly those that have unusual lore connected with them, are hot topics.

An interesting, accessible article, "Would Shakespeare's Poisons and Drugs Work in Reality?" (Hammond), was our entry point into Juliet's plea and Friar Laurence's plan. The potion's promise to "shut up the day of life" and "appear like death" (4.1.101, 103) intrigued my students. Was this real? We watched two versions of Juliet's soliloquy when she fearfully considers the consequences of drinking the "distilling liquor." Many students wonder what drug could make her sleep for a defined amount of time. How could Juliet's parents think her dead when her heart was still beating? How could they *really* pull off this ruse? We looked at other documents from Gerard's *Herball*. Sleeping nightshade, or *Atropa belladonna*, according to Claudia Hammond (quoting Gerard), may have been the answer because "a small quantity leads to madness, while a moderate amount causes a 'dead sleepe' and too much can kill." Other possibilities are leopard's bane, which was thought to kill animals but not humans. Students much preferred the idea of the mandrake because of its early modern lore. As a medicine, it had both soporific and aphrodisiac powers. "Is that why she woke up with so much love for Romeo?" a student asked. The most humorous, however, was the idea the plant sprung from the seed of a hanged man, but that is not all. According to early modern lore, the plant actually screams when pulled out of the ground, which reminded a few students of the same scenario in Harry Potter. In the 1579 document *Bulleins Bulwarke of Defence*, the author claims the scream not only causes the plant's death, but also "the feare thereof kylleth the dogge or beast, whych pulled it out of the earth" (Bullein 41). Early modern audiences would not have touched the mandrake because of the poison found in the leaves that permeates the skin. They might have imagined the Friar using a harnessed dog to do the job, followed by a careful grinding of the root that "beareth the image of a man" (41). Philip Barrough's document warns users that sleep-inducing drugs are dangerous because of the dose, which if given in excess, can kill. André du Laurens agrees and adds "wee must take heed to deale with very good aduise, for feare that in stead of desiring to procure rest vnto the sillie melancholie wretch, wee cast him into an endlesse sleepe" (qtd. in Pollard, *Drugs* 67).[7] Plants, and their sleep-inducing, death-like constitutions, were a constant source of discussion and intrigue among my students. Did they find plant lore relevant? Absolutely. They knew today's drugs, whether synthetic or natural, generated stories passed from person to person and also had the power to help or to kill.

Students developed listening skills by comparing audio performances of scenes. Ellen Terry and Emily Trask perform Juliet's act 4 soliloquy in which she laments her plight, fearful of taking the Friar's potion. After listening and writing about both performances, students discussed which actress expressed Juliet's fears in the way they envisioned the text. Next, they worked with a partner in a close reading activity where they reread the soliloquy, making lists of the fears Juliet expresses about taking the potion. At this stage in our unit of study, I was both amazed and gratified at how eagerly the students now dove into Shakespeare's text. Despite the length of her speech, a full forty-four lines, students had already listened twice and had read the plant lore's warning about the mandrake's screams. Juliet's fears "That living mortals, hearing them, run mad" (4.3.48) seemed totally justified. Discussions led to writing, which many students were anxious to share. Zac said, "Juliet is listing things that could happen if she takes this potion. She wants to know if it would work."

Table 1.1 lists early modern documents about poison, potions, and death that are featured in excerpted form for high school students on the *Teaching Shakespeare* website (shakespearedocuments.info) and can be used as a basis for writing and discussion.

Having looked up from her writer's notebook, Ainsley argued that Juliet was doubting the potion would work and doubting Romeo would save her. "She's scared," she said.

Gradual Release

By the end of the play, students were reading the early modern documents without the same confusion they had when they had only one act under their belts. Their confidence in getting the gist of early modern documents, knowing that they might not understand every word, was increasing their confidence in reading Shakespeare's language too. At this point, formatively assessing their

TABLE 1.1. Documents about poison, potions, and death.

Text comparisons of afterlife	*Book of Common Prayer,*[8] 1549; *The Bible*; John Calvin's works from the *Corpus Reformatorum*; Edward Vaughan, *A Divine Discoverie of Death*, 1612 (qtd. in Targoff 20; see also Marshall 217); John Donne's letter of consolation to Lady Kingsmill, epitaphs, 1624; Ramie Targoff, "Mortal Love: Shakespeare's *Romeo and Juliet* and the Practice of Joint Burial," *Representations*, 2012
Catalogue	John Gerard, "Sleeping Nightshade," "Mandrake," "Garden Poppies," "Black Henbane," *The Herball, or Generall Historie of Plantes*, 1597
Catalogue	William Bullein, "Mandrakes" (41–42) and "Poppy" (25), *Bulleins Bulwarke of Defence*, 1579
Woodcuts	Hans Holbein the Younger, *The Dance of Death* series, 1538 (see Pennant-Rea)
Article excerpt	Tanya Pollard, "'A Thing Like Death': Sleeping Potions and Poisons in 'Romeo and Juliet' and 'Antony and Cleopatra,'" *Renaissance Drama*, 2003
Article excerpt	Michael MacDonald and Terence R. Murphy, editors, "Suicides in the Early Modern Period," *Sleepless Souls: Suicide in the Early Modern Period*, 1996, including "Mortality Record: 'The Difeafes and Cafualities this Week,'" 1665

Note: All excerpted documents recommended in this book are also featured on the accompanying *Teaching Shakespeare* website (shakespearedocuments.info).

independence in reading both the play and other documents was critical to success on the summative assessment. Using a Gradual Release of Responsibility strategy (see Appendix C), I was moving students from teacher-facilitated collaborative support to independent reading. They worked through difficult language with more confidence and skill. Instead of students reading with a partner, they formed groups of four, but this time each read different documents on the same theme.

I introduced a new idea: how to "read" documents, specifically visual texts, through a cultural lens. First, I asked the question, "Why were Romeo and Juliet buried side by side?"

"Because that's how they did it back then?" Jenna asked, eyebrows raised.

"Well, let's see what other writers said about burials, beliefs, and the afterlife." Students read several quotes from Renaissance authors who had competing ideas about what happens after people die. In John Calvin's *Corpus Reformatorum*, he claims "husbands and wives will then be torn apart from one another" (see, e.g., Thompson), whereas Alexander Hume believes "we shall see them face to face." John Donne, in an effort to console a grieving widow, shares a personal thought: "God hath another purpose to make them up again."[9]

We also discussed how to analyze visual texts through a close reading of Hans Holbein's wood engravings of death intervening in everyday life (Figure 1.13; see also Pennant-Rea). Matthew suggested that Holbein thought death could be anywhere—it didn't matter if you were rich or poor: "He could show up when you were doing something else."

"Who are you talking about?" asked Lydia.

"Death! He's like a person in those pictures."

FIGURE 1.13. *The Nobleman, The Old Woman,* and *Fool*: Three of nine Hans Holbein wood engravings of death intervening in everyday life.

"That's called *personification*," said someone quietly in the back of the room.

"Right," said Lydia, "but we don't really see that in *Romeo and Juliet*. I mean, Shakespeare didn't have Death come and get either of them."

"Is it the same way we think of death today?" I asked. One student suggested *The Book Thief* by Markus Zusak as an example of how death is the narrator of the story. Another girl mentioned *The Fault in Our Stars* and *Me Before You*, where death is the expected outcome, causing tears and questions about why someone so young has to die.

Jenna raised her hand. "Did the audience cry when they saw *Romeo and Juliet*?"

Moving Toward the Assessment

Even though summative assessments test what has been learned, ongoing, formative checks throughout a unit of study help students practice without penalty. But when do we begin *talking* to students about what they should be able to *do* when act 5 comes to a tragic close? It makes sense that teachers *and* students understand how each piece of their learning fits the end goal.

Begin with the end. On the first day of the unit, I gave my students this assessment prompt:

> Analyze how Shakespeare develops a theme, drawing evidence from primary documents, including *Romeo and Juliet*, to reflect on how early modern cultural issues are relevant today.

We broke it down into sections and worked toward understanding each week. Students wondered about themes. After each act, we listed the cultural ideas we saw embedded in Shakespeare's play and in other plays, poems, sermons, pamphlets, recipes, woodcuts, and paintings. Each act was also infused with pre-writes, quick-writes, warm-ups, summaries, poetry, silent discussions, and reflections. Writing or talking about themes was a daily activity.

Steps to the Assessment

- Varied and multiple writing about themes and how they integrate the play
- Focused close reading opportunities to find evidence of text to support themes
- Reflections and discussions about how themes are relevant today

Students also wondered about evidence. We looked for textual details in text that supported a variety of themes. We studied clues from visual text. We inserted quotes from documents to support opinions. We read. We discussed. We wrote.

The interest in how Shakespeare continues to be relevant grew out of the document approach. Students wanted to talk about today's issues too. They could relate to ongoing feuds, family problems, unnecessary violence, sudden attraction, emotional outbursts, and tragic endings.

As a final activity to think about the end of the play, we watched the 2013 film version of act 5, scene 3 (Carlei), followed by *silent annotations* (see Appendix B). I divided the text into eight sections and created small groups of three or four. I had glued each of the eight sections to large "sticky note" chart paper and hung them in the hall.[10] Students in each group used markers of different colors and went out to the hall to stand in front of their excerpt. For ten minutes, students silently read the text and, based on close reading and the film clip, silently annotated with explications, sketches, definitions, and questions (see Figures 1.14 and 1.15). After ten minutes, I allotted two minutes to discuss the excerpt and decide how to present their thinking in a one-minute "flash" presentation.

FIGURE 1.14. Silent annotation activity: Three students explicating an act 5 excerpt.

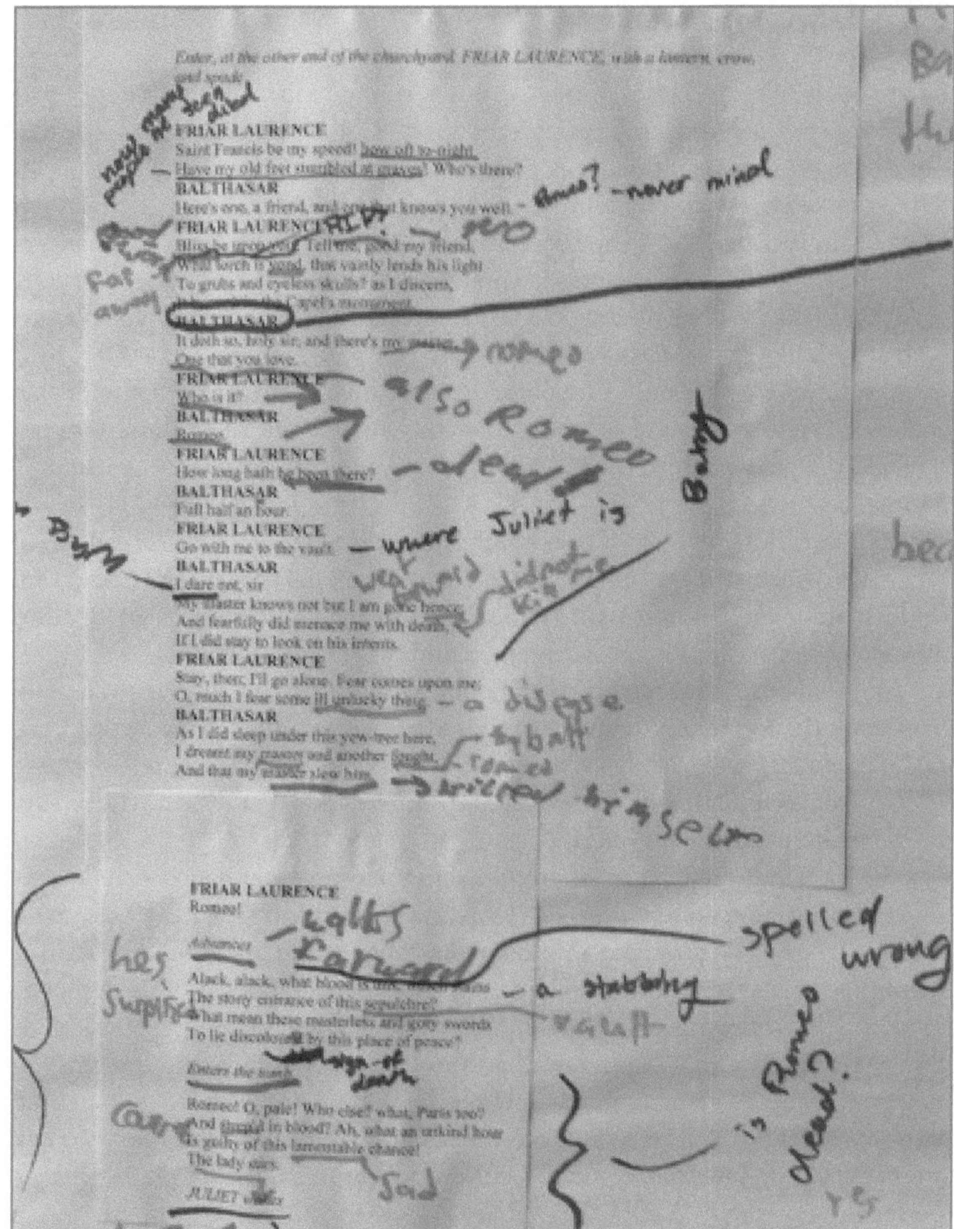

Enter, at the other end of the churchyard, FRIAR LAURENCE, with a lantern, crow, and spade

FRIAR LAURENCE
Saint Francis be my speed! how oft to-night
Have my old feet stumbled at graves! Who's there?
BALTHASAR
Here's one, a friend, and one that knows you well.
FRIAR LAURENCE
Bliss be upon you! Tell me, good my friend,
What torch is yond, that vainly lends his light
To grubs and eyeless skulls? as I discern,
It burneth in the Capel's monument.
BALTHASAR
It doth so, holy sir; and there's my master,
One that you love.
FRIAR LAURENCE
Who is it?
BALTHASAR
Romeo.
FRIAR LAURENCE
How long hath he been there?
BALTHASAR
Full half an hour.
FRIAR LAURENCE
Go with me to the vault.
BALTHASAR
I dare not, sir
My master knows not but I am gone hence;
And fearfully did menace me with death,
If I did stay to look on his intents.
FRIAR LAURENCE
Stay, then; I'll go alone. Fear comes upon me:
O, much I fear some ill unlucky thing.
BALTHASAR
As I did sleep under this yew-tree here,
I dreamt my master and another fought,
And that my master slew him.

FRIAR LAURENCE
Romeo!
Advances
Alack, alack, what blood is this, which stains
The stony entrance of this sepulchre?
What mean these masterless and gory swords
To lie discolour'd by this place of peace?
Enters the tomb
Romeo! O, pale! Who else? what, Paris too?
And steep'd in blood? Ah, what an unkind hour
Is guilty of this lamentable chance!
The lady stirs.
JULIET wakes

FIGURE 1.15. Annotations of act 5, scene 3 excerpt.

The hallway exploded with voices. After two minutes, all students were invited to the first group, and we began our Document Walk (see Appendixes B and C). Each group explained their annotated section of text before sending us off to the next group.

Final Reflections

After we finished the last couplet of the play, students reflected on our process. Conner said, "the story was pretty good" and "I liked the way we read it because, if we just read it one way, it would have been boring."

Kyla liked the story but admitted she "would have liked to watch the movie more." Olivia disagreed: "The process we read it was perfect for me. I came to class really wanting to read and see what was coming next."

Spencer said, "I like how we went through the book in class. I haven't ever read a book like this in class, and it's hard to compare to other books."

Elle, an avid reader, said, "It may be because love stories are so common, but I thought the first half was sort of predictable. Two people fall in love after one day and things keep stopping them from being together. That's not unusual for a romance."

"But they don't live happily ever after," Marissa commented. "I really liked when we watched it but also when we read it aloud. Watching it made me understand what was happening better because I could visually see it. Reading aloud was fun because it got us involved and reading to each other."

Anna was excited about "taking the time to talk about it. I also liked all of the background information that we learned. My favorite part was the sword fighting and actually seeing some of the culture that wasn't just a picture."

"We felt as though we were a part of it," Eden said. "For me, the documents made Shakespeare more exciting."

Students indicated the most helpful activity to prepare them for the assessment was the independent practice. Two days before the assessment, I set up the room as it would be arranged—in rows—and they wrote for an hour on a document they had never seen: "The Ladder of Love," from Book 4 of Castiglione's *The Courtier*, which was published in 1528 and translated into English in 1561. In this one-page excerpt, Castiglione claims outer beauty is holy and the gateway to inner beauty. Students immediately thought about how Romeo's first attraction was outer beauty but soon loved Juliet's inner self. It was then easy to write about how they saw that in today's culture where social media made physical perfection everyone's dream.

The following day, I broke down one student's essay into chunks, pointing out its organization, supporting evidence, and conclusions (Figure 1.16).

After projecting several student essays, pointing out strong vocabulary and organization, we made a list of *transportable writing moves*. What did these student writers do to convey their ideas? What transitions did they use? Which active verbs drove the sentences? In other words, which writing techniques

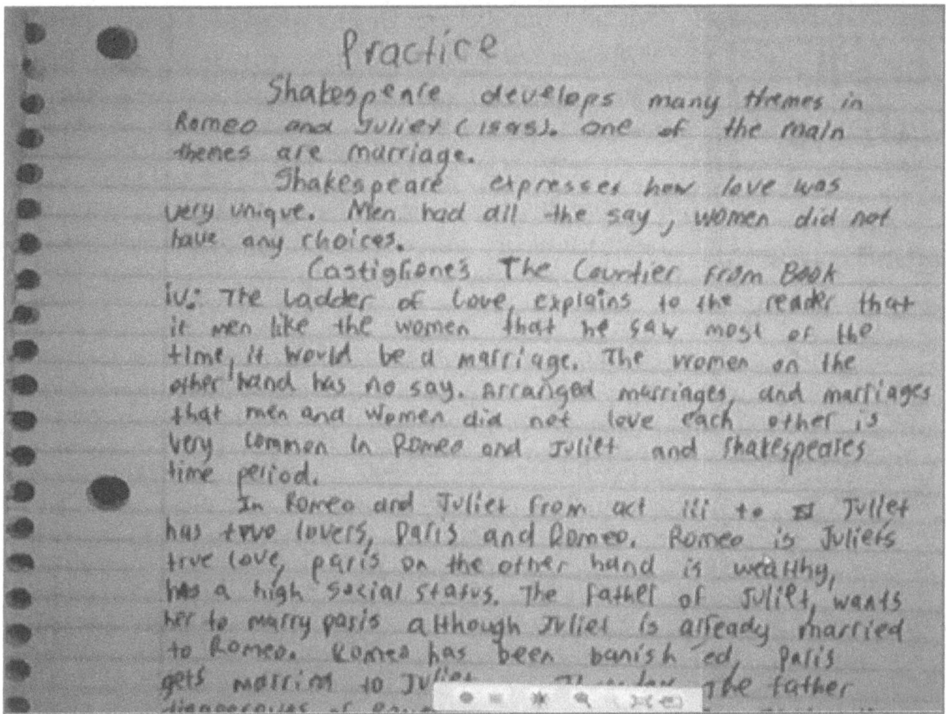

Practice

Shakespeare develops many themes in Romeo and Juliet (1595). one of the main themes are marriage.

Shakespeare expresses how love was very unique. Men had all the say, women did not have any choices.

Castiglione's The Courtier from Book iv: The Ladder of Love, explains to the reader that if men like the women that he saw most of the time, it would be a marriage. The women on the other hand has no say. Arranged marriages, and marriages that men and women did not love each other is very common in Romeo and Juliet and Shakespeares time period.

In Romeo and Juliet from act iii to IV Juliet has two lovers, Paris and Romeo. Romeo is Juliets true love, paris on the other hand is wealthy, has a high social status. The father of Juliet, wants her to marry paris although Juliet is already married to Romeo. Romeo has been banish ed, Paris gets marrim to Ju ... the father

FIGURE 1.16. Student formative practice on how Shakespeare develops cultural themes in *Romeo and Juliet.*

could they use in their own essays, moves that good writers incorporate? Students made lists in their notebooks and reviewed their essays from the day before. After rereading their own essays, they rewrote their weakest sections and shared the revisions with their writing groups. Feeling ready, most students left our classroom with a thumbs-up self-assessment.

For the final assessment, students had a choice. They chose a document to write about and, using the skills they had developed for the past five weeks, wrote about how that writer's ideas either contrasted or paralleled themes found in *Romeo and Juliet*. One document, Sir Francis Bacon's "Of Marriage and Single Life," written in 1553, was an essay that developed gender, marriage, sexuality, liberty, identity, and relationship themes. Bacon claimed single men "are more cruel and hardhearted because their tenderness is not so often called upon" (1554; see also Bacon, *The Essays* 34). In a homily against disobedience and willful rebellion, Thomas Cramner considers rebellion a sin against God and believes rebels are violating not only their country but also their parents. This document could be used to support violence, death, religion, goodness and evil, family relationships, spirituality, or gender. The third document, based on

FIGURE 1.17. *Everyone Living Shall Die Presently* (Day 82)

a visual from Richard Day's *A Booke of Christian Prayers* (1578), contains the service for burial and touches on death, burial, religion, love, compassion, and empathy (see also Figure 1.17).

After the minister speaks, the collection of people surrounding the casket ask the Father to raise the living from the death of sin "unto the life of righteousness" in hopes that when "we shall depart this life, we may rest in him, as our hope is this our brother doth."

Students knew they could choose either a document or a visual found in any document, a viable option for struggling readers. Organizing their desktops with books, foldables, documents, and writer's notebooks, students fell into an easy silence. I noticed they often paused to stare off into the distance or close their eyes but other than the sound of pages turning and pens moving, the entire hour was filled with thinking and writing.

Analyzing Assessment Data

I couldn't wait to read their writing. Nick wrote about rebellion, because "Romeo and Juliet are rebels. They defy everything that their parents desire for them." Despite the connotation of the word *rebel*, Nick insightfully thought about how neither Romeo nor Juliet considered the ramifications of their parents' feud, choosing instead to be together. Other rebellious characters Nick wrote about were the nurse, who disobeys her master, Lord Capulet. Although Nick acknowledged "people defy authority [to] fight for what they believe in," he discussed Cranmer's document by delineating how breaking rules recklessly is not the same as fighting for a cause. He added that Friar Laurence is a holy man but one who also rebels against the senseless family feuding. He is a rebellious co-conspirator by marrying Romeo and Juliet against his own better judgment and gives Juliet a potion disregarding the danger of his actions. Nick finished his essay by ruminating on our own rebellions, such as multiple protests in 1960s' America to bring the troops home from Vietnam.

Micah wrote about the theme of death, explaining it can take you anytime and anywhere, using act 3 as his source for how Shakespeare incorporates this idea. Noting that the *Booke of Christian Prayers* portrays death religiously and therefore "a good thing," Micah understood that people were expected to welcome death as a ticket into heaven, rather than as an enemy, which he thought "plays a huge role in the ending."

Cody spent considerable time writing about how the early modern theme of violence is still relevant today. He discussed terrorists, such as members of ISIS, as having had a "huge impact on our world by bombing, shooting, and stealing." "It's terrible," he wrote. He added other levels of violence inherent in gangs, noting, first, "for some gangs, to be able to join, you have to beat someone up just to be a part of it no matter [if] it is women or male" and, second, in online bullying, "so much they take their own lives."

Collaborative Course Teams

Our ninth-grade English team functioned well together during our maiden voyage with primary documents. Discussions about the hundreds of students who studied *Romeo and Juliet* using the document approach provided new learning. First, we confirmed the value of classroom observations to learn new strategies, especially when followed by debriefings. Questions that forced our thinking about process were beneficial as we collaborated on how to increase student success.

Document Discussions

If someone tells me I have to overhaul everything, I freeze up. If someone says, "Here, you're welcome to all of this you want, and you may want to start small," then I feel empowered and on my own I feel driven to try it all at once.

Second, we realized more documents would provide alternative choices, especially visual texts. Students loved analyzing sketches, paintings, frontispieces, and portraits to reflect on both early modern and contemporary thinking. We discussed how to add more opportunities for student inquiry, including research of both early modern and contemporary documents. One idea was to add a twenty-first-century document outlining the average ages of marriage to contrast with the early modern table we studied, "Mean Age at First Marriage in England by Fifty-Year Periods, 1550–1849" (Laslett Table 1.2; see also Young 470). We developed a shared Team Drive (Google) to house all the documents and organized them by acts and themes. Finally, our own discoveries about Shakespeare's world became a source of great joy. We know the process will open doors to our own discoveries about Shakespeare.

Whether you insert a few strategically throughout the unit to gauge the reaction or dive into a new approach "feet first," positive student reaction is always our primary thermometer for measuring how primary sources enliven and enrich our teaching of Shakespeare. I suggest that you peruse the documents described in these and other chapters and decide when and where they fit in your current curriculum. If it works well, add a few each year. Try some group activities, add some quick-writes, and open discussions on text comparisons between Shakespeare and his contemporaries. In short, allow documents to permeate what you presently do and let it mushroom. I know it will.

You may be a teacher who is reading this chapter because you are or will be teaching *Romeo and Juliet*. If so, keep reading. I promise that many of the strategies and documents used with other plays and students are versatile and adaptable. In the next chapter, you will join another "virtual" classroom by witnessing the joy and challenges of teaching *Hamlet* to struggling readers in English 11 class.

If you with patient eyes attend, "our toil shall strive to mend."

2

Unfolding *Hamlet*

I know I'm not alone when I admit *Hamlet* is my favorite play, and probably Shakespeare's greatest work, so you can imagine my dismay when two students entered my English 11 classroom on the first day of the unit and asked to leave. "We would rather do an online course instead," said one young man.

"I don't understand," I answered. "Why?"

"Well, we don't really care about Shakespeare or his life."

Many of my English 11 students were self-proclaimed reluctant readers who had little reading stamina beyond fifteen minutes. As part of a school district immersed in a language arts workshop model, we take pride in a K–12 reading culture developed over time. Our high school English department agrees upon common practices and vows to hold ourselves and our course teams accountable to best practices in the field.

English Department Agreements

- We will write every day and incorporate writer's notebooks in our classes.
- We will use ten to fifteen minutes of class for choice reading.
- We will confer with students about their reading/writing during choice reading time, taking notes on our discussions.
- We will use the readers/writers workshop model as the *how* for our teaching.
- We will build classroom libraries with engaging books for students to read.
- We will *book-talk* books each day to create excitement about reading and to share our reading lives.

To this end, our English hallway is quiet during the beginning of each hour, the only sound the turning pages and hushed tones of students conferring with teachers about their reading lives. Despite our commitment to literacy, some students struggle, their disinterest in "that old stuff" exploding with shards of boredom. I vowed not to let *Hamlet* be my greatest teaching tragedy.

I have always taught with the resolve to open hearts, using *Hamlet* as the key, similar to Azar Nafisi when she describes reading imaginative literature as a sensual experience:

> If you don't enter that world, hold your breath with the characters and become involved in their destiny, you won't be able to empathize, and empathy is at the heart of the novel. This is how you read a novel: you inhale the experience. So start breathing. (111)

I know this to be true. Despite the challenges, I depended on Shakespeare's writing to invite these young skeptics to empathize with a young Dane who loses his father, who watches his mother carry on with his uncle, and who hides his own fear, hatred, and love until he is able to right these torrid wrongs.

My classes, having read *Romeo and Juliet* two years earlier, willingly shared their previous experiences with Shakespeare's plays. Their comments mirrored former students, divulging a range of feelings about anything written four hundred years ago.

Document Discussions

Using documents in the classroom helps students personally interact with the text through cultural lenses that open dialogue about race, gender, class, and politics. Excerpts situate Shakespeare's work within his society and help students understand the sixteenth-century diverse audiences who stood in front of the Globe's stage.

Some students relayed factual information as they remembered, such as believing Shakespeare "put tragedy plays on the map" or "wrote a long time ago." Other students expressed dismay, describing the language as "boring" or "tiresome," while others didn't understand "why we have to keep classic literature alive." Some, however, admitted how they didn't understand the language but enjoyed the story.

Initial concerns about reading Shakespeare stemmed from deep-seated inadequacies about their reading lives, admissions they brought to light during conferring time at my café table in the corner of the classroom. During daily book talks, I often shared young adult fiction based on Shakespeare's works (see also Appendix F), such as *Saving Hamlet* by Molly Booth and *To Be or Not To Be: A Chooseable-Path Adventure* by Ryan North. After students settled into reading, I began student conferences by asking them if they considered themselves readers.

"Not at all." Cam said. "I just can't seem to find anything I like."

Destiny admitted, "I don't read much and, when I do, I get distracted."

Josh said, "I enjoy reading, but I only read during this time in class. I can't do it at home."

Some students, however, loved reading and were excited about their favorite books. Jennah loved *Insomnia* by Stephen King. Alex said his girlfriend got him into *The One and Only Ivan* (by Katherine Applegate). Lindsey loved the idea of "poem books" and was into *Crank* by Ellen Hopkins. Most wanted class time to read even though many of them did not see themselves as readers. Most suggested they were not readers because they "didn't have time" or they were "too slow" or "not into it," but all were riveted when I talked about the books I loved and the stories they told.

Reading conferences also provide ongoing opportunities to develop relationships with my students and is an important tool I use to convince them that Shakespeare has something to offer. I create parallels between *Hamlet*'s world and ours—sagas of greed, of longing, of family, of betrayal. Linking the early modern period with today's world through documents that situate the writing of *Hamlet* within a tumultuous, throbbing early modern society was my best hook.

When beginning any whole-class novel or play, I often struggle with how to begin. Two short clips, one a short biography ("William Shakespeare – Playwright | Mini Bio") and another from the National Endowment for the Arts, provided glimpses into early modern culture and background on Shakespeare's life in London in the late sixteenth century. Students *turned and talked* (see Appendix B) with an elbow partner about engaging societal issues, such as education, marriage, theater, monarchy, language, or the plague. I had used a similar strategy with the ninth-grade students, but I wondered if juniors who had read at least one other play would ask the same types of questions or if their inquiries might probe deeper. If their "wonderings" were more thoughtful—more provocative—would they glean more from this tragedy? As we listed themes and questions on the board, I noted similarities to their younger counterparts:

Why did Shakespeare leave to go to London?
Why couldn't purple be worn?
Why are his plays so popular now?

After their lists took shape, I noticed a change. Their thinking turned more philosophical. I realized that ninth-grade students wondered about factual information whereas eleventh-grade students began dabbling under the surface (see Table 2.1). It is possible that some may have remembered background information from previous years, but most, regardless of reading ability, structured their questions with more complexity. Ninth-grade students were specifically interested in details, such as how murders were staged. They wanted to know if they used real or fake blood, real or trick knives, or if actors knew how to sword fight. The older students gravitated toward process questions, inquiries that reached beyond specific plays to contextualize and understand how culture shaped his writing. The question about whether there were people from England in America at this time denoted an insufficient grasp of history, but also reflected an interest in the world beyond Shakespeare, similar to the questions about the present location of his scripts and the ramifications of leaving home to train for

TABLE 2.1. A comparison of ninth- and eleventh-grade questions about Shakespeare and his world.

Ninth-grade questions	Eleventh-grade questions
Why are the Montagues and Capulets so angry with each other?	What was Shakespeare's inspiration?
Why are Romeo and Juliet so quick to commit suicide?	Was there nothing done to change how sixteenth-century people live?
Why do Romeo and Juliet get married after a few days?	How did Shakespeare's plays get recognized and become so famous?
If the Queen liked the plays, how did they get shut down?	How can you be among the poorest in your town but still be a leader?
Did Shakespeare have a similar story to Romeo and Juliet?	How was Shakespeare so informed about history and so literate if he never finished school?
Are there plays still missing?	Why didn't they keep better records?
Why didn't Shakespeare's wife go to London with him?	What is his best play? How did they hold auditions?
How did they make the murders look real?	How were plays staged?
Why was Shakespeare so popular?	What made Shakespeare want to start writing plays?
What was Shakespeare's favorite play?	Where are the scripts for each actor?
Why did theaters close so much?	Were there English people in America in this period?
Why were girls not allowed to act?	Why did boys leave their homes to prepare for adult life?
Why did people let others steal their stories?	Why are Shakespeare's plays considered better than everyone else's when he took ideas from other people?
Why did Shakespeare write in poetry style?	Who was Shakespeare's inspiration?
Why did Shakespeare want to be a mystery?	Is Shakespeare his actual name?

vocations. The older students' interests reached beyond specific plays to contextualize and understand how culture shapes writing.

Cognitive psychologists have analyzed the impact of supplemental information on student achievement. In one study, two types of information—extraneous and catalytic—were provided to students, as compared to content that was delivered without articles, anecdotes, or audiovisuals, to determine the effect on learning (Tislar). Both *extraneous* information, interesting but not directly related, and *catalytic*, related yet not necessary, unsurprisingly improves comprehension.

Document Discussions

Adding documents helps students place Shakespeare into an historical context, using a multi-disciplinary approach. Hamlet's melancholy and "antic disposition" makes more sense when students read Richard Amyas's 1659 *An Antidote against Melancholy*, or view the 1646 "Picture of an English Antick" from the Thomason Tracts series.

Sixteenth- and seventeenth-century primary documents are both extraneous and catalytic when used in conjunction with Shakespeare's plays, such as Thomas Nash's 1597 *Terrors of the Night* in which he questions why kinsfolk appear to us in the likeness of a father or mother, and then answers that we would listen to them "with a naturall kind of loue" (348). Nash's ideas, catalytic, explain Hamlet's obsessive desire to find out the story behind his father's death by confronting his ghost, which contextualizes the play within early modern beliefs about the afterlife. Other documents, such as Simon Fish's *Supplication of the Poor Commons* (Brinkelow and Fish; Fish), are extraneous—interesting background information but not directly related to *Hamlet*. In his treatise to King Henry VIII, Fish pleas for a just Catholic clergy on behalf of the poor. The information foregrounds religious strife but explains neither the ghost's presence nor Hamlet's reaction.

Student interest in cultural and historical issues, based on the act 1 documents about early modern ghosts, impressed me on two counts: first, students wanted to know more "interesting" information, and, second, they were drawn to Shakespeare's world through the stories the documents told. Later responses would confirm their interest in both catalytic and extraneous primary documents as the narratives that breathed life into *Hamlet*.

> **Document Discussions**
>
> Documents are the bridges between early modern society, Shakespeare's writing, and contemporary thinking. Students build narratives to connect with their own life stories that create links from the past to the present.

Based on the questions students asked, you might think that my classes were filled with philosophical discussions about Shakespeare's life, followed by easy pathways into the play. Far from it. I struggled daily with alleviating anxiety about reading *Hamlet*. Experience in the classroom helped tremendously, yes, but best practices are based on research, so I went to the organization that is the single most valuable resource available to American secondary teachers: the National Council of the Teachers of English. It was fortuitous that I attended the national conference during the *Hamlet* unit and had marked all the Shakespeare workshops I could find, many sponsored and led by the Folger Shakespeare Library staff. The first session was attended by well over two hundred teachers, who, upon arrival, received lines from *Romeo and Juliet*, *Macbeth*, *Twelfth Night*, and *Hamlet*. We roamed the room, reciting lines using different cadence, volume, and tone. We then convened in small groups where we combined our lines and created motions to carry the meaning. I was encouraged to be up on my feet interacting with peers who also were learning how to interpret Shakespeare's text and to teach his work with fidelity.

In addition to creating an environment for students to experience language through movement, I introduced the juniors to Shakespeare scholars as another inroad to primary documents and their possible influence on Shakespeare as a playwright. Emma Smith, in her podcast *Hamlet*, introduces the source text "Amleth" (from *Gesta Danorum*, a French adaptation printed in 1570) by Saxo Grammaticus, as well as the *Ur-Hamlet*, possibly written by either Thomas Kyd or William Shakespeare. Smith's central question—"Why is *Hamlet* called 'Hamlet'?"—may seem slightly ludicrous to teachers. My students, however, perked up. They had heard of Hamnet, Shakespeare's son who died in 1596, and had asked about whether or not the play was named for him. Smith addresses the question directly by explaining that the name *Hamlet* was in print before Shakespeare wrote his version. The idea that Shakespeare could have taken at least some of his ideas from Thomas Kyd's blood tragedy, *The Spanish Tragedy*, was also intriguing because students understood "remakes" or "spin-offs." They easily related to a writer's appeal to fear, the ingredient that pumps the blood and races the heart. "How would you define a 'blood tragedy'?" I asked.

"Lots of blood," said Erik.

"And knives," added Lucas.

"And villains," said Leah. "But why would Shakespeare take someone's ideas who was writing at the same time? Wouldn't everyone know?"

"Thomas Kyd wrote *The Spanish Tragedy* between the 1580s and the early 1590s, so, yes, it was just before *Hamlet* came out. The two plays had some close similarities: a ghost, a character named Horatio, a crazy female, and the main character who waits for the right moment to take revenge."

"So, basically, Shakespeare didn't make up this play," said Jaden.

"That's right, but, when Shakespeare wrote, no copyright laws existed like they do today. Playwrights and poets borrowed and even took lines from each other without fear of recrimination." I knew my students would find Smith's information interesting, and I also knew they would not be able to listen intently for more than seven to ten minutes. To alleviate the problem, I created a graphic organizer of Smith's podcast with information provided in some shapes but not in others. Students first copied the *diminishing map* (see Appendix C) in their notebooks while I briefed them about Smith's ideas. Next, I played the podcast, modeling my own thinking as I filled in blank sections while they followed suit in their own maps; during the second half, students listened and made their own meaning while I roamed the room, taking notes on their thinking.[11]

The second step included "partner talk" where they alternately read sections of their graphic organizers. Through reading, listening, and writing, students learned how primary documents informed us about Shakespeare's world. They were also experiencing a variety of written genres, such as poetry, pamphlets, sketches, sermons, letters, and catalogues. Primary documents revealed an early modern society that situated *The Tragedy of Hamlet* and became not only a springboard for reading the play but also a device for staying afloat. After approximately one week, students had not yet begun reading the play.

First, I wanted to set the stage for what was happening in the castle at Elsinore, the preface to Marcellus's appraisal about the state of Denmark (1.4.90). Forming partner groups, students read the first twelve lines from strips of paper, playing the parts of Bernardo and

Ideas for Learning Character Relationships

- Create family tree using name strips.
- Block short scenes.
- Arrange student desks by grouping closely related characters.
- Create sociograms.
- Use short-writes after scenes to describe how characters relate to each other.
- Place character signs at each corner of the room and ask student "players" to move to the most closely related character.
- Draw character maps.
- Tape quotes under characters names on wall.

Francisco. To stage these lines, each group determined who was on guard and who was coming to change guard. Why would Francisco say, "Nay, answer *me?* Stand and unfold yourself" (1.1.2)? Using plastic swords, several groups acted out these lines in front of the class, putting their own spin on whether Francisco was indignant, sarcastic, or scared. Allowing students to get up out of their seats and read parts aloud does not guarantee an understanding of Shakespeare's language, but the physical movements helped students visualize the meaning.[12] Something was definitely rotten in Denmark.

Sometimes I blocked the action, directed attention, or changed seating to help students understand character relationships. In act 1, scene 2, I placed stools in the front of the room to visually demonstrate character loyalties (Figure 2.1). Claudius, Gertrude, and Hamlet were in the middle, flanked on Claudius's side by Polonius and Laertes. Cornelius and Voltimand, messengers at Claudius's bidding, sat behind. Horatio, Hamlet's best friend, sat near, with the guards—Bernardo and Marcellus—who told Hamlet about his father's ghost, sat behind.

Using audio versions for longer speeches, students then read their parts with the instructions to listen for the royal "we" when Claudius speaks; for the use of "you" and "thou" when he addresses Laertes and Hamlet; the king's admonishment of Hamlet's grieving process and what it means to be a man; Hamlet's disgust over his mother's "o'er hasty marriage"; and the King's and the Queen's request that Hamlet not return to Wittenberg.

Students needed to see and experience character relationships and alignments.

My purpose for using specific seating arrangements was twofold: first, students needed to see and experience character relationships and alignments.

They viewed Hamlet next to his mother and Laertes next to Polonius on the King's side as his chief counselor. Horatio was associated with Hamlet by sitting next to him with the guards nearby. The visualization of this grouping would be important when they encountered the ghost of Hamlet's father.

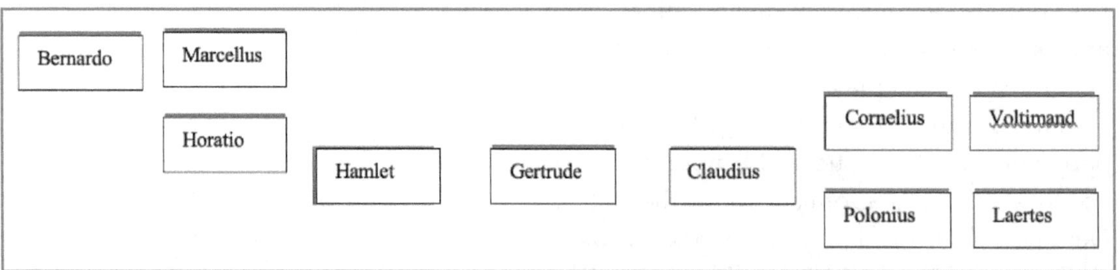

FIGURE 2.1. Stools placed to depict character relationships helps students visualize and remember the names.

Second, I hoped to pique their fascination with the cultural and historical information that would surface in early modern primary documents. After reading several scenes, students wrote about their growing knowledge of Elizabethan culture. Alex noted, "People believe the king is the highest power. They believe he is the next thing to a god. Everyone looks to impress the king." Austin learned "the language is very important. You don't want to say one thing and mean another." Scout wrote, "the 'parents' or guardians seem to be very strict toward [their] children," referring to Polonius's advice to both Ophelia and Laertes. Josh wrote, "The old Elizabethan culture seems very boring to me. That old culture had a bunch of traditions that everyone had to follow like everyone was the same and there was no fun. Everyone had to be the same religion and wear the same clothes." Savannah noted the differences between "you" and "thou," stating "thou" could be an indication of closeness or even an insult. I asked Savannah what she meant about her comment. "Well, look at how Polonius uses 'thou' with Laertes and 'you' with Ophelia. It's as if he is putting her down for her behavior with Hamlet, even though she hasn't done anything wrong!"

Students were now commenting on new information and using it to help them understand Shakespeare's language choices.

Document Discussions

Categorizing documents by theme, such as ghosts and the afterlife, helps students understand discrepant viewpoints about a cultural more. They soon learn that early modern writing, including *Hamlet*, often reveals the deep divides among people.

Introducing Documents

Although documents can be placed strategically throughout the play, I share several documents about a specific theme, chosen to coincide with each act. If you have taught *Hamlet* before, you probably agree that the ghost's story explains why he is "doomed for a certain term to walk the night" and why he is "forbid to tell the secrets of [his] prison house" (1.5.15, 18–19), making this scene the culminating event of act 1. Some students understood the concept of purgatory as "where you go before you can get into heaven" and some remembered the Catholic and Protestant deep divide, but they did not know the specific conditions under which Shakespeare was writing. After watching Kenneth Branagh's portrayal of the ghost scene Act I, Scene V), students had more questions:

- Were ghosts a big thing back then, or was it just Shakespeare who used the ghost idea?
- Were people scared of ghosts?
- Was Shakespeare in trouble with Queen Elizabeth I for having a ghost on stage?
- Was Shakespeare sad because his son had died just five years earlier, so he wanted to write a play about him?

The appearance of the ghost in act 1 was the perfect entryway to documents.

Each student received eight primary documents but were assigned one to read and share in a Jigsaw activity. The following steps, which include multiple readings, helped prepare students for a successful group experience:

- Step 1: *Think-Aloud*—teacher shares thinking about language and explains fix-up strategies, such as rereading and self-questioning
- Step 2: *first reading*—students independently read assigned document to practice fix-up strategies
- Step 3: *second reading*—students read a second time in groups to find author's slant on topic (seven groups, four students per group)
- Step 4: *third reading*—students read third time to generate specifics to share in Jigsaw activity (see Appendix C)

Step 1: Think-Aloud

Before students began reading, I used a document camera for my Think-Aloud (see Appendix B). First, I read the excerpt from Thomas Kyd's *The Spanish Tragedy*, where the ghost of Andrea is both visitor and commentator on the play. I reflected on how this excerpt looked similar to *Hamlet*. It was a play in poem form. I read through a short section and asked myself questions as I was reading, to demonstrate what I do when I'm feeling lost in the reading. *Fix-up* strategies, such as rereading or self-questioning, would be a useful strategy for students on their first reading. In this section, the ghost of Andrea seemed oddly familiar:

> When I was slain, my soul descended straight
> To pass the flowing stream of Acheron;
> But churlish Charon, only boatman there,
> Said that, my rites of burial not performed,
> I might not sit amongst his passengers. (1.1.18–22)

Document Discussions

Students do not need to read the entire play for an excerpt to become a viable primary document on how ghosts are used in early modern plays.

As I read, I involved my students as a formative check on understanding and engagement. "Does this sound like the ghost in *Hamlet?*" I asked.

"Well, yeah," said Tanner, "because Shakespeare's ghost says he has to walk during the night and burn during the day until his sins are gone. And this ghost can't go to the underworld because of his burial. So, something is keeping the ghost on earth. That's kind of like *Hamlet*'s ghost, right?" Within only a few moments, Tanner made a text-to-text connection about sixteenth-century thinking about ghosts.

Step 2: First Reading

Students numbered off ("1" to "7") and read a corresponding document. I encouraged them not to let historical spelling be a barrier. "For the first read-through, see what you can comprehend," I suggested. I listed the fix-up strategies on the board to remind them of what to do if they got stuck.

At this point, they were reading for the gist, an overall picture of their document. I hoped they remembered how I had scanned my document in the Think-Aloud to note the overall structure and genre. Was it a letter? An essay? A poem? A graph? A portrait? Did it have divided sections that would help separate ideas? Could I write a one-line summary about each section, or make checkmarks in the margins to mark important points?

I gave them time to read silently to make sense of the primary sources on ghosts.

Fix-Up Strategies

1. Slow down.
2. Reread.
3. Use context clues.
4. Make connections.
5. Visualize.
6. Whisper read.
7. Self-question.
8. Discuss.
9. Annotate.
10. Summarize.

Steps 3 and 4: Second and Third Readings

During Steps 3 and 4, I roamed from group to group, jotting notes, answering questions, and directing attention to specific sections of the text. Some groups understood the early modern language, but others needed me to walk through documents with them. In the small-group reading, Jane Owen's *Antidote against Purgatory* (Figure 2.2), I directed students to the second paragraph where Owen

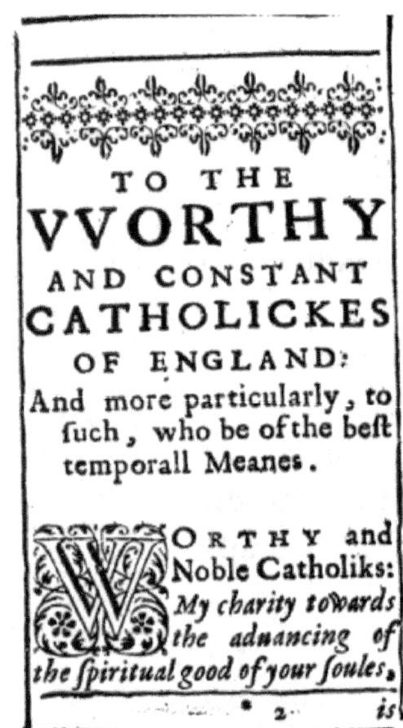
TO THE

VVORTHY

AND CONSTANT

CATHOLICKES

OF ENGLAND:

And more particularly, to ſuch, who be of the beſt temporall Meanes.

VVORTHY and Noble Catholiks: *My charity towards the aduancing of the ſpirituall good of your ſoules,* is

2

FIGURE 2.2. "To the Vvorthy and Constant Catholickes of England": Jane Owen's *Antidote against Purgatory* (2).

states her cause: "I could wish you (*worthy Catholickes*) that you would haue a feeling apprehension of the paynes of *Purgatory*."

Students noted that purgatory was scary and that Catholics were not popular at the time, remembering that we had discussed the national religion under Queen Elizabeth I during our first few days of early modern period discussions.

"What points does Owen make that would help her case against purgatory?" I asked. Students went back to the text.

"It says God is cruel and will turn to punishments," said Jaden.

"It also says that every person is flying toward death," said Scout. "So that must be why people are supposed to do 'Good Workes.' Those two words are capitalized, so they must be important."

I wanted to be sure this group understood Owen's feelings about the Catholic religion and why she was steering her readers away from the punishments of purgatory. "Is Jane Owen trying to help Catholics in her treatise?" I asked.

One girl spoke up immediately. "Well, she must like them because she calls them 'worthy' and 'deare' in the last paragraph."

"If Catholics believed in purgatory, why would she claim that purgatory is bad?" I asked.

"Maybe she doesn't want them to walk the earth forever like Hamlet's father," said one of the boys. The seeds of how the documents related to Shakespeare's play were beginning to sprout.

Checking in with small groups was important for me to gauge the support they needed and would be time well spent.

Sharing Documents

Jigsaw Discussions

After reading and discussing in small groups, students joined larger groups with students who read different documents. It was important that struggling readers had a clear idea about exactly what they would share. According to Timothy Hedeen, using a *jigsaw* technique provides a structure for sharing information. As pieces of a larger entity, each participant shares one document and listens to other presentations. Together, they decide how all the pieces connect. A Jigsaw activity also sets up an expectation: students know they are held accountable for their reading.

I eagerly listened in, taking notes on student language and how they reacted to one another during the process. Students began by summarizing, using the annotations they made in their small groups. I realized they needed instruction on how to move beyond simple reporting. Comparing authors' ideas to deepen understanding about *Hamlet* simply wasn't happening yet. The answer lay in writing.

Write–Think–Pair–Share

Writing helped clarify thinking, but using Turn and Talk (see Appendix B) fostered confidence and skill for large-group discussions. I noticed a change in how students moved their thinking well beyond what they had shared in smaller groups. After the Jigsaw activity, I asked students to write about how Shakespeare incorporated early modern thinking about ghosts and the afterlife in *Hamlet*. Next, each student turned to a partner to share what they had written. The room exploded with talk. I could hear the excitement in their voices and wanted to hear about their ideas.

"Tanner, what did you and your partner talk about?" Tanner, who had compared Shakespeare and Kyd's ghosts, now brought up differing perceptions about how ghosts interacted with people. His writing gave him time to reflect, and now he willingly shared bits and pieces from other student presentations. Soon, other students brought up *Hamlet*. The topic of the ghost's demeanor and form prompted questions. Was he helping Hamlet? Was he tricking Hamlet? Was he a shape-shifter and not really Hamlet's father at all?

The Write–Think–Pair–Share technique (see also Appendix C) also boosted Austin's confidence in speaking out during class discussion. Having read several short text comparisons (see Table 2.2), Austin wrote about the conflicting ideas about ghosts. He shared Ludwig Lavater's tests to determine which spirits are good and which are evil. One test requires that a spirit will show "humilitie acknowledging or confessing of his sinnes & punishments" (109). In the group discussion, he wondered about Shakespeare's ghost. "That's kind of like *Hamlet*'s ghost, right?"

"What do you mean, Austin?" I asked.

"Well Hamlet's father sounds like he feels bad because he died before he could confess his sins. So that makes him a good ghost, right?"

"You seem to understand Lavater's ideas," I answered.

"Then why is Hamlet so scared? He's obviously a good ghost and won't hurt him," Austin said.

"Very true. So why do you think Shakespeare's ghost is different?"

"Well," he said, "this makes a better story."

Students were nodding. They were beginning to grasp how early modern and contemporary writers may use the stage or other artistic works to illuminate cultural concerns.

Jake made a connection between the documents and the play by suggesting the afterlife "was presented very coldly in *Hamlet* and the primary documents." Keenan shared his thinking about Shakespeare having "a lot of rebellious feelings toward the government." He went on to say that a ghost on stage may have been a way to rebel because he was a Catholic father ghost visiting a Protestant son. Keenan was reacting to *Daemonologie,* making the connection between a monarch's persuasive writing and what Shakespeare had presented on stage.

Cassandra raised her hand. "My document had to do with purgatory, and, if you didn't do Good, then you would stay there forever. And I think Shakespeare definitely portrays some of that in his play."

Layla added, "But this ghost is stuck, not going to heaven or hell. Back when Shakespeare wrote *Hamlet,* it was against the law to disagree with the church. Believing and doing what this ghost says wouldn't have been a good idea." I

TABLE 2.2. Document genres on ghosts and the afterlife.

Essay	Francis Bacon, "Of Revenge," *The Essays, or Councils, Civil and Moral, of Sir Francis Bacon, Lord Verulam, Viscount St. Alban*, 3rd ed., 1625
Pamphlet	Jane Owen, *Antidote against Purgatory*, 1634
Text comparisons on afterlife	St. Augustine, *De Civitate Dei Contra Paganos (Concerning the City of God Against the Pagans)*, circa 413–426 CE; Thomas Aquinas, *Summa Theologica*, 1265–1274; Ludwig Lavater, *Of Ghofts and Fpirits Walking by Nyght*, 1572; Thomas Nash, *The Terrors of the Night*, 1594; King James VI, *Daemonologie*, 1597; Reginald Scot, Appendix, *The Discoverie of Witchcraft*, 1584
Poem	Robert Southwell, "The Burning Babe," 1595
Drama	Thomas Kyd, *The Spanish Tragedy*, 1587 (1.5.98); William Shakespeare, *Hamlet*, (1.5.14–26)
Notes	Harold Jenkins, editor, *Hamlet* (new Arden ed.), 1982
Treatise	Simon Fish, *A Supplicacyon for the Beggers*, 1529 Henry Brinkelow and Simon Fish, *A Supplicacyon of the Poore Commons Whereunto is Added the Supplication of Beggers* [a plea for catholic reform], 1546)
Article	Stephen Greenblatt, "The Death of Hamnet and the Making of Hamlet," *The New York Review*, 2004

Note: See also the *Teaching Shakespeare* website (shakespearedocuments.info).

was writing their responses as quickly as I could and noted that many students wanted to share connections between the documents and *Hamlet*. Some thought broadly about Shakespeare's culture, as Layla did when she mentioned common beliefs about ghosts. Keenan and others made text-to-world connections, placing themselves in the position of a playwright caught in the middle of religious strife.

Students were now getting a sense of what was happening in Shakespeare's world at the time: religious liturgy, common beliefs, and writers' slants were all brought to life through the documents they read. Students understood that we could never be sure of Shakespeare's intent, but their discussions began to center on his society and how the ideas of other writers may have been influential. The ghost of Hamlet's father became more than merely one man's idea; it was now an early modern ghost and was borne of sixteenth-century thinking.

Document Discussions

Having enough context to make comments or connections removes the hesitation in forming questions and ideas about Shakespeare's work. How students approach documents is as important as the types of documents used. Similar to any type of reading, students need background knowledge to bring to the experience.

Words, Words, Words

The act 2 documents, focused on melancholy and madness, connected to contemporary issues of depression and mental illness. Now that a greater number of characters had been introduced, students discussed the issues with more complexity. We looked at the character traits for each of the four *humors*—metabolic agents in the body believed to control temperament and affect the mind. First, I asked students to analyze the chart (Figure 2.3) and mentally place themselves in the area that described their own personalities best. I placed myself in the phlegmatic area, careful

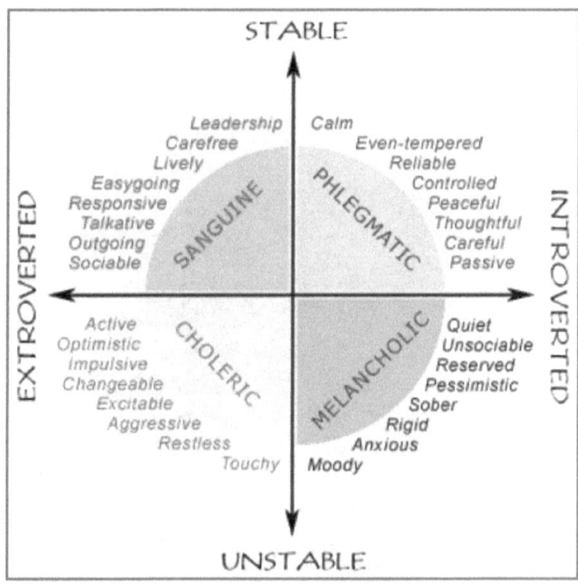

FIGURE 2.3. A chart of the four humors, in perfect balance, believed to be necessary for good health (Kay).

and even-tempered, yet I could see some traits from the sanguine side, especially when feeling sociable and easygoing. Next, students worked in small groups to place at least two of the characters in the play on the humors chart.

During act 2, many students saw Ophelia in a different light. They placed her on the unstable part of the chart in the melancholic and choleric sections because of her reaction to Hamlet when he pushes into her "closet." This was a fortuitous time to show them the picture of Thomason's 1646 printed sketch of the English *antick* (Figure 2.4), which proved the most popular document of this section.

Comparing the descriptions of an antick, especially his "apish gestures," with Ophelia's accounting of Hamlet revealed similar language. According to

The Picture of an Engliſh Antick, with a Liſt of his ridiculous Habits, and apiſh Geſtures.

Maids, where are your hearts become? Look you what here is!

1 His hat in faſhion like a cloſe-ſtoole pan.
2 Set on the top of his noddle like a coxcombe.
3 Banded with a calves tail, and a bunch of ribands.
4 A feather in his hat, hanging downe like a Fox taile.
5 Long haire, with ribands tied in it.
6 His face ſpotted.
7 His beard on the upper lip compaſſing his mouth.
8 His chin thruſt out, ſinging as he goes.
9 his band lapping over before.
10 Great bandſtrings with a ring tied.
11 A long-waſted dubblet unbuttoned half way.
12 Little skirts.
13 His ſleeves unbuttoned.
14 In one hand a ſtick, playing with it, in the other his cloke hanging.
15 His breeches unhooked, ready to drop off.
16 His ſhirt hanging out.
17 His codpeece open, tied at the top with a great bunch of riband.
18 His belt about his hips.
19 His ſword ſwapping betweene his legs like a Monkeys taile.
20 Many dozens of points at knees.
21 Above the points of either ſide two bunches of riband of ſeverall colours.
22 Boot-hoſe tops, tied about the middle of the calfe, as long as a paire of ſhirt ſleeves, double at the ends like a ruffe band.
23 The tops of his boots very large, turned down as low as his ſpurs.
24 A great paire of ſpurres, gingling like a Morrice-dancer.
25 The feet of his boots 2 inches too long.
26 Two hornes at each end of his foot, ſtradling as he goes.

FIGURE 2.4. *The Picture of an English Antick, with a List of his Ridiculous Habits, and Apish Gestures* (Thomason).

both, madness appears in physical dress as well as behavior. Shakespeare's "antic disposition" includes:

> stockings fouled,
> Ungartered, and down-gyved to his ankle,
> Pale as his shirt, knees knocking each other,
> And with a look so piteous in purport
> As if he had been loosed out of hell. (2.1.89–93)

Thomason's antick includes a long list of transgressions, such as unbuttoned sleeves, unhooked britches, open codpiece, large boots, low-slung belt, and generally slovenly appearance coupled with ridiculous behavior.

Students noted two very different interpretations of madness: Ophelia's description is more diabolical. Hamlet's behavior, according to her, is beyond ludicrous. She notes he "held me hard" and studied her face. After some length of time, he "raised a sigh so piteous and profound," it seemed to fill his entire body (lines 99, 106). Is this the same behavior Hamlet portrays to Polonius in scene 2, actions that cause Ophelia's father to describe them as "madness" in an aside to the audience? One student noticed the difference between how early moderns reacted to madness, depending on gender. In the play, Hamlet believes his behavior will be excused if he acts crazily. He tells Horatio he will "put an antic disposition on" (1.5.192), such that Horatio will "know aught" of him. Hamlet's display of madness in fact changes, depending on his company and his own degree of temper.

In many documents, females are noted as most likely to succumb to madness. In fact, after reading an excerpt from the document *A Juniper Lecture, With the Description of All Sorts of Women, Good and Bad* (J. Taylor) (Figure 2.5), Erick laughed: "Look at the picture of the man raising a stick toward his wife! He's gonna frickin' beat her!"

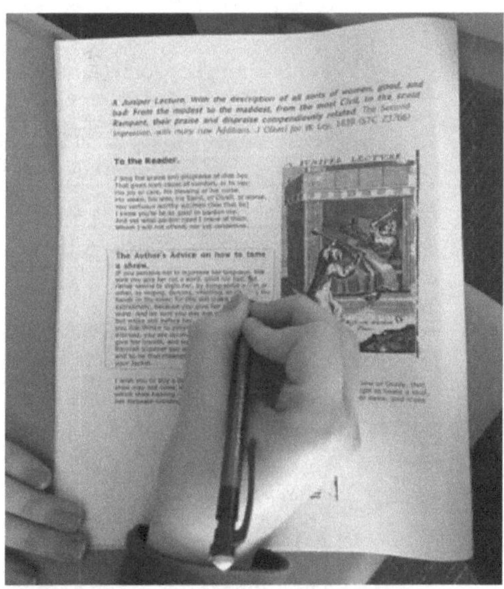

FIGURE 2.5. Student annotating *A Juniper Lecture* (J. Taylor).

Kayla read the actual text aloud:

> IF you perceive her to increase her language, bee sure you give her not a word, good nor bad, but rather seeme to slight her, by doing some action or other, as singing, dancing, whistling, or clapping thy hands on thy sides; for this will make her vexe extreamely. (J. Taylor 138)

"What does *vexe* mean?" she asked.

"I think it means that she'll get upset," said Erick. "This is crazy stuff. It also says, in the last part, that the man should buy a drum and lock it up, so he can beat it if she acts crazy! And that's supposed to help?"

Document Discussions

Providing multiple documents on one theme allows students to compare different writers, sketches, genres, and thinking around a topic. See Appendix A or the *Teaching Shakespeare* website (shakespearedocuments.info) to find excerpted documents that are age appropriate (Steelman).

I was interested in Erick's interest in this article because it was not the article he was assigned to read. Another teacher suggested that I ask students to choose a second document they had heard about in their groups and to pair with their own. The idea worked well.[13] Their writing and debriefing with the class was enlightening and engaging. Despite the suggested theme of "melancholy and madness" (see Table 2.3 for excerpted documents presenting early modern ideas on this theme), students noted other themes, and our discussion took a slight turn. Tyler mentioned how Shakespeare also developed the theme of "analyzing then solving."

TABLE 2.3. Act 2—Primary documents on melancholy and madness.

Catalogues	John Gerard, "Blacke Hellebore" and "Sweet Fruit," *The Herball, or Generall Historie of Plantes*, 1597; *The Anatomy of Melancholy*, edited by Robert Burton, 1621, pp. 308, 455–59
Text	Robert Burton, *The Anatomy of Melancholy*, 1621
Visual	George Thomason, editor, *The Picture of an English Antick*, 1646
Text	Phillip Stubbes, *The Anatomie of Abuses*, Part 1, 1583
Catalogue	Richard Amyas, *An Antidote Against Melancholy*, 1659
Lecture	John Taylor, "The Author's Advice on How to Tame a Shrew, or Vex Her," *A Juniper Lecture*, 1639
Sonnets	William Shakespeare, "Sonnet 45: The Other Two, Slight Air and Purging Fire," 1609 Ben Jonson, "On My First Sonne," 1616 (see Hunter 864)
Essay and poem	Amelia Lanyer, "To the Virtuous Reader" and "Eve's Apology in Defence of Women," *Salue Deus Rex Iudæorum*, 1611
Pamphlet frontispiece	*The Araignement and Burning of Margaret Ferne-Seede*, 1608

"Can you tell me more about that?" I asked.

"Well, the document on the black hellebore shows how they analyzed the plant that caused melancholy, then they found certain fruit that cured it. And, in the play, Hamlet analyzed the situation that the ghost of his father told him. After he analyzes, Hamlet tries to figure out how to get revenge and deal with the problem." Tyler had looked at the play through a completely different lens and one I had not considered. I pushed for more examples.

"Is that same theme in the second document you read?" I asked.

"Well, not exactly," he said. "That one was about plants and medicine. It talked a lot about plants and how some may be used to make medicine. In the play, a mixture of plants and medicine is made into a poison. Claudius uses this poison to kill Hamlet's father. So, in the play, it was meant for harm. I guess it doesn't make sense."

"Yeah," said Madisyn, "I read that one too, and the guy who wrote it, Robert Burton, said that eating fruit causes sadness, but it says only certain fruit, like when it's 'putrid.'"

"That means rotten," said Jacob.

"But certain fruit are okay," she added. "Sweet stuff, like cherries and plums. Does that mean you can go crazy if you eat rotten food?"

"Well, did they have refrigerators?" asked Jacob.

"Maybe people died from rotten food back then," she answered. "Or maybe they went crazy."

"So, how do the themes you talked about, the ones about analyzing and solving or about plants and medicine, relate to Shakespeare's play?" I asked, hoping to get them back on track.

Tyler answered quickly: "Plants can be used to hurt and to help. Either for poison or for medicine. They just have to know what they're doing. And Shakespeare used the plants he knew would kill Hamlet's father."

"Are you seeing any overlapping themes here?" I asked.

"I hadn't thought about that, but yes," Tyler said. "Actually, it's all about problem-solving or getting what you want. Is that right?"

"I think *you* made it connect. Good thinking!" I was definitely impressed.

Document Discussions

Student inquiry often creates moments for students to do more research on the period.

To Be or Not to Be

Before beginning act 3, I wanted to check in with students about how they were faring with the experience of reading Shakespeare and learning about his world through primary documents:

> "The documents are kind of hard to understand sometimes"
> "They are helpful to understand what's going on in the play"
> "They are easier to read in groups"
> "Good to see something to compare to what's in the book"
> "Women were treated a lot differently"
> "Some things to do with religion"
> "Stereotypical ghosts"
> "Nobility was easier to corrupt"
> "Plants and fruits cause and cure depression"
> "Some depression going on in the book—like today"
> "All or almost all the themes are relevant today, like violence, revenge, madness"

Using a wireless keyboard, one student listed ideas, and I could hear the excitement in their voices. Despite difficulty with some language, their knowledge base was growing and deepening. We were ready to move on to an important soliloquy, "To Be or Not to Be." Students read the part where the King tells Ophelia of his plan to have her meet with Hamlet alone. The Queen hopes Ophelia's "good beauties be the happy cause / Of Hamlet's wildness" and hopes her "virtues / Will bring him to his wonted way again" (3.1.43–45). I set up Hamlet's soliloquy by reminding students of Hamlet's preoccupation with death and which humors would be prevalent in his body at this point in the play. We began the soliloquy, reading slowly. Nate, a normally silent student, suddenly blurted, "What do you mean you 'don't wake up'?" The entire class turned toward him.

"Well, let's look at the text. Hamlet wonders if death is like sleeping or dreaming, but you don't wake up," I answered tentatively.

"I think you do," he answered quickly and firmly.

"Really? Tell me more about that idea." Nate began to talk about how babies, before they are born, are not conscious, but do eventually wake up to a conscious state. The students all stopped talking and listened. Then Nate actually stood up. This was very strange. Normally, Nate comes to class late, slumps in his chair lazily, and says little to nothing at all. He said, "Can I go up front?" I was shocked, but the class was now all sitting up straight and I heard several voices.

"Go for it, dude!"

"All right!"

"Tell it like it is!"

This was an emerging Nate whose interest I had never seen before. At the front of the class, he stood straight. "Death is temporary," he said. "We do have a temporary unconscious state, like we do when we are born. It's a matter of waiting. We eventually will wake up again." Indeed, Nate had just awakened. Perhaps it was the content of our discussion. Perhaps it was the documents. More than likely, though, Shakespeare's magic had been rumbling around in his head, and he simply had to speak. Here's a kid who rarely speaks but was totally into Hamlet's soliloquy. Crazy. Everyone, including me, clapped and hollered. I couldn't believe it.

Then our player Hamlet, Alex, read the soliloquy, followed by a short reading of the First Folio version. Next, each group took a big sticky note sheet with the soliloquy printed in the middle and a pack of markers. During the next fifteen minutes, they sketched what they thought Hamlet was saying (Figure 2.6).[14] After approximately twenty minutes, they explained their sketches.

What I found interesting is that Nate's request to stand began a new tradition in the class. Everyone wanted to stand to "report out." It became a "thing" in the class that made each person's contribution seem more profound. They spoke louder and raised their hands to participate. None of us knows how a soliloquy will change a person, a class, an experience. Nate became a viable part of the class from that day forward.

FIGURE 2.6. Small group sketching a scene in *Hamlet*.

Gender and the Relevance of Shakespeare

Our study of the documents on madness and melancholy permeated future discussions about both Ophelia and Gertrude. During act 3, scene 7, the closet scene with Hamlet and Gertrude, students read aloud until line 30 when Hamlet stabs Polonius, who is hiding behind the arras. I showed the Mel Gibson clip where Hamlet and Gertrude argue (1:19:43–1:22), and she kisses him. Students were appalled, but we talked about directors' choices and explored other possibilities to depict Hamlet's relationship with his mother as well as Gertrude's relationship with Claudius. After viewing a clip from scholar Clare Kinney's lecture "Difficult Women," students responded to Gertrude's and Ophelia's roles in the play as subjugated women who rarely express their inner thoughts. I had not yet attempted a Socratic Seminar with English 11 students, and was amazed at the results of how passionate these students were about the question, "How are gender issues relevant today?" (Figure 2.7). We used the *Hamlet* text and the primary documents on madness (Table 2.3) as our sources.

FIGURE 2.7. A small-group precursor to a Socratic Seminar allows students time to share personal thoughts.

First, they shared ideas in small groups before forming a large circle. Some of the initial comments, "Gender is not a problem today, at least not at this school," were followed by admissions of inequities. One girl broke the ice: "It might be an issue with individual cases, though."

"We don't see as much disrespect as during Shakespeare's time, but little things might come up."

"Yeah, girls can play varsity football now, volleyball too."

Document Discussions

Using a variety of approaches to *Hamlet*—such as close reading, viewing, performing, reader response, Socratic discussions (see Figure 2.8), and primary documents—allows students to experience Shakespeare through different lenses.

It wasn't long before the conversation changed direction. Jake joined in. "But, in the armed forces, standards are higher for men. They say it has to do with science," he said. I noticed he was wearing an armed forces sweatshirt. "Something about the science of men's builds, that women just don't have the strength." At this point in the conversation, a few boys became agitated. One said he was going into the Navy and, even though some females were in the armed forces, they simply were not as strong. I asked him if he would trust a female soldier next to him, and he shook his head.

Rick said that girls seem to get the upper hand. "They think they are better than boys." I could see Jadan nodding, which gave Rick more confidence. "Girls can play football and basketball too, but here boys can't even try out for volleyball. Only girls can."

"That's not fair," another male said.

"Yes, it is," said a female student. "You guys have had it your way forever."

"It's like the picture on the document of that lady who got hung because she was accused of burning her husband. It didn't matter if she did it or not. They hung her because she did something to her husband, and he may have deserved it!" The conversation was escalating.

"Or that article about the lady who was defending Eve from the Garden of Eden. It wasn't her fault that Adam didn't take care of his own business. God said he was in charge, and yet she got into all the trouble. I agree with her." One group of girls had some attitude. I was relieved and excited to see it come out during our seminar, mostly because it created the energy (albeit

FIGURE 2.8. Students discussing gender issues in a Socratic Seminar.

tinged with some negativity) that was needed for some lively discussion during a Shakespeare unit. A male student initiated the discussion about radical feminists, and I asked him to define his term. He said, "You know. Women who think they're better than men. Feminists are people who think men and women should be equal, but radical becomes women thinking they are better than men."

Document Discussions

An interesting comparison is to bring modern texts/primary sources into the unit to give more talking points and deeper questions, similar to providing them with early modern sources.

"Women were not equal back then," another female blurted. "Women had fewer perks, and it seemed like they just accepted their role at the time. It didn't seem to be as much of an issue back then—women couldn't fight back."

Another male spoke up. "Not *all* men are stronger than *all* women."

Now Mara looked at him. "Don't get me started, dude. We get the shaft around here, and you know it. Females can't wear short shorts or tank tops that show a lot of shoulder. Guys can wear just about anything. They allegedly can't sag, but no one says anything if they do."

"So guys are aroused by shoulders? That's offensive to guys and makes it sound like we are only focused on one thing," said Christopher.

Liz chimed in. "Oh, come on! What about 'wife beaters'? Now *that's* offensive! Sports bras cover more than swimsuit tops!"

I tried to redirect. "Do you see gender issues in the play?" I asked.

"It's all about sexual expectations," said one female. "Girls who flirt are called names. Like Ophelia when Hamlet is yelling at her. He says to get to a nunnery and that she's a 'breeder of sinners,' like every kid she has will be bad."

"What about other writers during the early modern period?" I asked. "Did they indicate that women had less power than men? Or was Shakespeare alone in his development of Ophelia as a character?" I could see Mara was still fuming. She is one student who misses a lot of school, but I was glad to see she came on this day.

"Girls can't do anything," she said.

"What?" interrupted a male classmate.

"Without blame," she added. "Think about how many of these readings point the finger at women." We had come far in our discussion, and I was relieved that we didn't stop after the first student said we didn't have gender issues at our school.

Students who invested themselves in discussions where the themes continue to haunt their own culture were the ones who see Shakespeare's relevance. Yes, the language is difficult. Yes, the norms seem archaic. But many students related to Hamlet's inability to act swiftly and to Ophelia's feelings of unabridged devastation. Powerlessness and the sense of lost autonomy in the face of crisis are all too often universal. Students may not have cited evidence from the text or primary documents, but I did see unabridged engagement that day. They made text-to-self connections based on their personal experiences at school, at home, and with the world around them.

Theater and Acting

Document Themes

- Act 1—ghosts and the afterlife
- Act 2—melancholy and madness
- Act 3—theater and acting
- Act 4—gardens and lore
- Act 5—espionage and treason

After we finished act 3 and discussed the "play within the play," students formed groups of six for a brief overview of the documents, all themed as theater and acting. Students read a combination of primary and secondary documents, including sketches of bear baiting and the Globe Theatre, articles on the perceived "wickedness" of stage plays, other playhouses, and an excerpt from Sir Philip Sidney's *The Defence of Poesy*, describing the difference between delight and laughter. In a quick-write (see Appendix B) written in writer's notebooks, students outlined how they might share their articles with their groups, and then joined students with similar documents. I often filled in as a student when groups were short a member. In addition to filling an otherwise hole in the conversation, my presence in groups gave me opportunities to note dynamics and to model my thinking in smaller groups.

In one class, I reviewed the fourth document, *The Shakespearean Stage* (Gurr). We discussed how the Puritans were upset that tragedy, which included murder, was used for entertainment. Shakespeare's plays often ended with a *jig*, a chaotic and bawdy dance performed by all the actors and considered lewd and inappropriate by the Puritans:

> The jig reached the height of its fame with Tarlton and then Kemp . . . In the eyes of satirists it epitomized all that was disgusting in popular entertainment . . . Mostly it was the obscenity that drew attacks from the satirists but jigs did get associated with uproar generally.
>
> —Gurr (174–75)

Another document, an excerpt from Sir Philip Sidney's *The Defence of Poesy*, describes *Hecuba* as a form of entertainment. Sidney did not believe in the mingling of kings and clowns and mentioned the difference between delight and laughter: "Our comedians think there is no delight without laughter, which is very wrong" (971). Women, he notes, can be pretty, which is delightful, but not funny. When I read, "we laugh at deformed creatures, wherein certainly we cannot delight" (971), students thought this was awful. "Who would do that?" asked a student. But I noted a few raised eyebrows and wondered if some of them could relate. In small groups, students categorized the articles; one group said the second, third, and fourth documents went together because they all discussed the Puritans and why they did not like the theater.

Document Discussions

Teachers may use documents that are themed by act or by cultural ideas. When students categorize within the themes, they are using higher-order thinking to analyze author's purpose, slant, and tone.

Other comparisons were obvious, such as the articles on the Globe. With practice, making connections among the documents was becoming much easier, and students were beginning to do this on their own, especially in small groups when individuals shared how Shakespeare's contemporaries informed his writing. Listening to their own peers improved with the understanding that follow-up activities were moving from summarizing and explaining to analyzing and concluding. Writers' claims became part of our daily discussions.

Focused discussions on how themes are relevant today often became clearer when we talked about the past. It happened on the day we talked about the relevance of the theme of theater and acting. I asked about early modern Puritans who were against entertainment because it was morally wrong. "Is there anything like that today?" I asked. Jacob mentioned that parents don't want their kids watching R-rated movies or playing videogames because it might make them want to do "those things." Another student mentioned it was "like that article by Stubbes on *Anatomy of Abuses* where he said you could learn to be a hypocrite if you play the part of one on stage."

"Can you find that in the article? I asked.

Eric flipped through the document booklet and said, "Actually, I marked it. Here it is: *'If you will learne fallshood, if you will learn cosenage: if you will learn to deceiue: if you will learn to play the Hipocrit'*. . . What's *cosenage*, anyway?"

"It's a legal term," I said. "Like deceit or fraud."

"Oh, well, then that makes sense. The whole thing this guy was getting at means this is what people learn from going to the theater. And that's what freaks out parents today." Eric was making a connection between the sixteenth century and his world. Stubbes's treatise on the morality of stage plays, his warnings that actors or "players" who dress up to pretend they are someone other than who God intended them to be, may not essentially differ from those who now tout the corruption of the internet or X-rated movies. Today's forms of entertainment continue to be suspect in the tainting of God-fearing people, similar to Stubbes's claims that those who attend playhouses will learn to do the very things they see on stage: laugh, swear, mock, deceive, lie, deflower, steal, and flatter—all the sins of the wicked and doomed to "eternall damnation."

> *Abuse God no more, corrupt his people no longer with your dregges, and intermingle not his blessed word with such prophane vanities.*
>
> —The Anatomie of Abuses *(Stubbes)*

Plants and Lore

Using primary documents in conjunction with reading *Hamlet* provided the social, historical, and cultural background within which he was writing and allowed students to deepen their conversations and thus their understanding of concurrent thinking during the early modern period. The plant lore documents led us into some of the most interesting conversations we had about Ophelia's death. Was it suicide or an accident?

We began with a summary of act 4, so students could visualize Ophelia's drowning, which is not shown on stage but, instead, reported by Queen Gertrude.

> **Document Discussions**
>
> Summarizing an act provides context for working with documents before reading the play.

Exposure to early modern plant lore before reading act 4 in *Hamlet* helps students understand why Ophelia offers certain flowers and herbs to Laertes, Gertrude, and Claudius as well as a CSI approach to her drowning.

Providing the gist of the act allowed us to laser-focus on scenes 5 and 7, when Ophelia dissembles into madness and again, one hundred fifty lines later, when she offers flowers and herbs to Laertes, Gertrude, and Claudius. The act 4 documents provided a wealth of information about how plants were used during the sixteenth century and included writers, such as John Gerard, a botanist and an herbalist, who wrote *The Herball, or Generall Historie of Plantes* a few years before *Hamlet* was written; an illustrated catalogue of plants and herbs that includes their history and use; Rembert Dodoen's 1578 table of "vertues," a listing of the "nature, vertues, and dangers" of "herbes, trees, and plantes"; a recorded 1581 dispute between the Royal College of Physicians and a poor woman apothecary; and a hymn and frontispiece that depicts Queen Elizabeth I as a gatherer and goddess of flowers (see also Appendix A, Table A.8).

During scene 5, Ophelia enters the castle after her father is mistakenly yet fatally stabbed by Hamlet. She is the classic early modern "mad woman," whom Laertes describes as a "rose of May" yet compares her "young wits" with an "old man's life" (4.5.181, 183–84). In John Everett Millais's Pre-Raphaelite visual representation of Gertrude's report in scene 7 (Figure 2.9), Ophelia floats, floral coronet in her right hand, eyes and mouth open. According to Gertrude, mermaid-like, "she chanted snatches of old lauds / As one incapable of her own

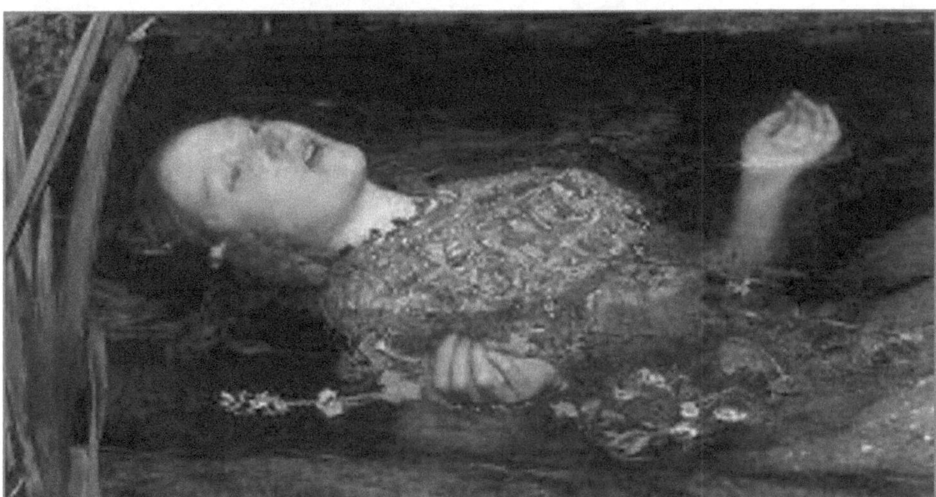

FIGURE 2.9. *Ophelia* (Millais).

distress / Or like a creature native and endued / Unto that element" (4.7.202–05). Based on her account, Gertrude saw and heard the entire tragedy. Ophelia's open eyes, mouth, and arms invites an imagined repressed young woman on the threshold of sexual awakening or self-expression, experiences she would never have enjoyed, dead or alive.

Her role in this play is one of "recipient and victim of external authority, embodied in the voices of her father, her brother, and her beloved Prince Hamlet" (Barbudo 153). Students were extremely interested in how plant lore intersected with Ophelia's behavior before she died and whether her death was accidental or planned.

Document Discussions

Students may note the sexual significance of fennel and columbine noted as *emmenagogues* or stimulants of menstrual flow.

One document juxtaposes Gerard's description of the plants Ophelia gives to Laertes, Claudius, and Gertrude with a contemporary accounting. Gerard notes that rosemary "comforteth the braine, the memorie, the inward senses, and restoreth speeth unto them that are possessed with the dumbe palsie, especially the conserve made of the floures and sugar, or any other way confected with sugar, being taken every day fasting" (1292). In the contemporary explanation, Thomas and Faircloth explain that Laertes is the most likely recipient who responds that her words are a "document in madness" (4.5.201). Authors note that rosemary is not only found in wedding bouquets but also placed on the deceased. Ophelia seems to be floating between two states as represented by her floral self-recriminations. While awake and communicative, she chooses rosemary; while floating and nonsensical, she chooses spring flowers that wilt quickly and stink, a pathetic replica of the woman Gertrude describes as "the happy cause / Of Hamlet's wildness" (3.1.42–43).

I have taught *Hamlet* many times before without using the documents that shed light on Renaissance plant lore and green imagery. Student reaction is often "Ophelia-negative." They often do not understand why she can't argue with her father and brother, why she can't reason with Hamlet, why she can't simply leave. A twenty-first-century reading is often one that creates confusion and boredom. After reading the documents, including the excerpts above, and searching Shakespeare's text for related quotes,[15] however, students had more to say. Alex mentioned that, in his document, Queen Elizabeth I had a fascination with herbals and went to different gardens. He said, "One mistress didn't have a license to practice and got in trouble but the Queen wasn't too upset about it. The play didn't have anything about that, though."

"What about when Ophelia gives Laertes the rosemary," I asked. "That was for remembrance or memory. That's a kind of medicine, isn't it?"

Document Discussions

Ophelia's death: accident or suicide?

- The spring plants she weaves into her coronet wilt quickly and smell bad.
- Some of the plants have sexual connotations, placing her focus on Hamlet, rather than her father.
- Hanging a coronet on a willow tree symbolizes unrequited love.
- Ophelia would have reached up to hang the coronet, a branch breaking in the process.
- She must have already been standing in the river and laid back with the coronet in her hand because her face is not wet and she is singing.
- Her dress is not completely wet. The water fills her skirt and pulls her down.
- Her death is accidental.

Adam chimed in. "My article talks about rosemary—that's good for memory, like you said. And pansies. That one was for thoughts. I found a quote in the play 'Therewith fantastic garlands did she make' that talks about making the wreath" (4.7.169).

Liann said, "Rue and daisies were talked about in mine. Rue was famous for its scent but gave skin irritations. It says it's associated with repentance and regret. And violets are associated with virginity and gentleness. Daisies are a symbol of purity and innocence. They give it as an antidote for anger."

"How do they make it?" I asked.

"I don't know. It doesn't say. I wonder." And that is exactly what I had hoped she would do.

During this class, I joined a group, filling in for Jake. I had Shakespeare's sonnet 15. I followed my notes and read aloud to my group that the poem relates plants to dying. "We are like plants because we grow from seed, we blossom, we die. So beauty and youth are destroyed by time. But," I added, "There's one way to be immortal. To live forever. Write poetry."

"Wow." said Ethan. "I didn't think about that."

"Right. That way you can live through your poetry . . . it's beautiful . . . so beauty can go on. And I figured I would use the quote where Ophelia says, 'they withered all when my / Father died' [4.5.188–89] because both the violets and her father are compared here, and in both cases their beauty was used up. Dead. Her words, though, have stayed, right?" They just looked at me. Dead silence. I understood that to be a "yes."

Wrapping Up

The summative assessment, a reflective response to how primary documents bridge, contextualize, and inform Shakespeare's *Hamlet*, provides students a platform for sharing their thinking. We had been practicing in "pieces," adding steps and complexity to each section of the assessment question throughout the unit. First, we wrote about themes, then added how Shakespeare developed them in *Hamlet*. Second, we analyzed documents to discover how writers, artists, clergymen, women, and botanists were interpreting society's norms. Students realized that early modern concerns defied time.

Our discussions led to diverse thinking and writing. Students wrote daily, in the form of *quick-writes* (see Appendix B) or longer, formative pieces to practice one section of the assessment question. Feedback on student writing often took place during independent reading conferences, but I also shared student writing using the document camera, using a *Think-Aloud* (Appendix B) walk-through of

Writers who read their own essays/writing aloud are providing self-feedback by hearing how language sounds in their own ears. Does it make sense? Do pauses indicate punctuation? Would another word sound better? Reading to a partner in a "one-foot voice" keeps the volume down and the content more private.

the writing. Students sometimes shared their writing with peers in a "one-foot voice" to hear their own writing spoken aloud.

During these activities, I wandered the room and sat in on conversations to provide informal feedback. The most effective feedback, according to students, was when I projected their writing to point out *transportable moves*, how other writers express ideas. One day I shared a variety of student examples of introductions with attention to how some writers use a *warm-up* sentence just before the thesis that contains one or two words from the thesis statement. "How does this 'move' help the reader?" I asked.

"It's not a surprise when we see the thesis," said one student.

"It sounds like he knows what he's doing," quipped another. Some students smiled.

"I like this 'move,'" I said, "because it makes the transition to the thesis smoother, like this writer is slowly getting us to the point, rather than jumping in suddenly at the end of the paragraph."

Another student said, "I like looking at other people's writing for better ideas when I write. I also like a diagram, because, if I didn't have something to guide me, I'd be jumping around with my thoughts and not get anything done." (See also Figure 2.10.)

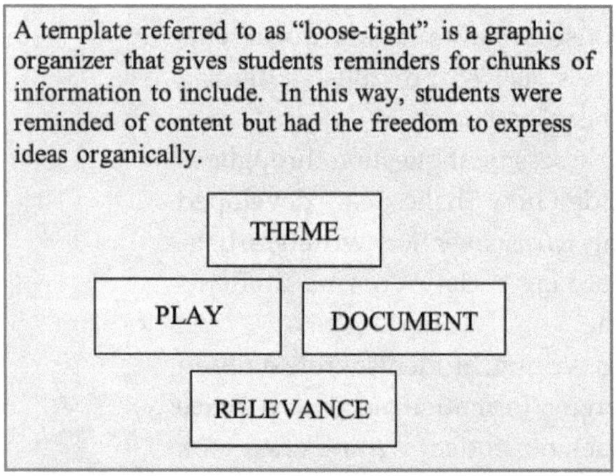

A template referred to as "loose-tight" is a graphic organizer that gives students reminders for chunks of information to include. In this way, students were reminded of content but had the freedom to express ideas organically.

THEME

PLAY

DOCUMENT

RELEVANCE

FIGURE 2.10. Loose–Tight graphic organizer for writing (see also Chapter 5).

The Final Assessment

The next day, they received three new documents[16] and chose one to read and analyze. Every student passed.

Student reflections echoed my own conclusions. None of these students had approached Shakespeare through a cultural/historical lens and many had never before read primary documents in ways that required them to think and write about how ideas from four hundred years ago might continue to be relevant today.

Answering the question "Should we read Shakespeare?" is indeed different from "How should we read Shakespeare?" The answer funnels down from student anxieties and successes with this project, and can be summed up as "not in isolation."

If we read only Shakespeare's words, we miss the melting pot of early modern society and how it must have driven him to share his world creatively and beautifully. As one student said, "The ghost of Hamlet's father became more than merely one man's idea; it was now an early modern ghost and was borne of sixteenth-century thinking."

I know now how their reading improved, how their thinking deepened, how their writing sharpened. Incorporating primary documents will be a staple in how I approach Shakespeare henceforth.

Assessment Question

Analyze how Shakespeare develops a theme, drawing evidence from primary documents, including Hamlet, *to reflect on how early modern cultural issues are relevant today.*

Learning from New Ideas

I had several "hallway meetings" with other English teachers who were using documents; those moments in the hallway when we, like quarterbacks, hand off new ideas to a downfield receiver, usually "quick and dirty" within a few minutes, and then, suddenly, the classroom doors shut and another teaching hour begins. It is often during these brief exchanges that brilliant, insightful remarks are made about the success or failure of a lesson, or a warning is given that can help fend off an inadvertent tackle. Other feedback took the form of email, passing the ball in the form of questions and answers that turned into a discussion about teaching Shakespeare.

Question: What are the advantages of using the actual documents? Can we just have discussions or watch video clips about what early modern life was like?
Answer: Some teachers will prefer to do it that way. In other words, they may read the documents and either rewrite or blend the information into their lessons they believe would help students understand the play better and what I refer to as *catalytic* information.

Question: Do documents always come at the END of each act? Could they be used *before* or *during* the reading of a particular scene to have "background knowledge" to comprehend Shakespeare's language?
Answer: Initially, I envisioned students perusing many documents that reveal discrepant viewpoints on the similar issues after each act. After working with

documents over the year, it makes more sense to show the *English Antick* when Hamlet puts on an antic disposition, or showing Queen Elizabeth I's gown [see Figure 2.11] when Rosencrantz and Guildenstern come to spy.

QUESTION: Which documents would you use in future units of study about *Hamlet* and how would you use them?
ANSWER: I was very interested in the elements of a revenge tragedy, as this would be useful for students to *chart* each element as it appears in the play. "William Shakespeare and the Representation of Female Madness" might be a good secondary document as a set-up for Ophelia's behavior in act 4.

QUESTION: Which documents fit with your approach to *Hamlet*?
ANSWER: I would definitely include the information about the Globe and use "Ophelia's Flowers" as a student handout. I would also consider going over sonnet 15 as a mini-lesson.

QUESTION: Which documents bring in new information to add to your teaching?
ANSWER: I would definitely use (a color version of) the *Rainbow Portrait*. Spying is a key element throughout the play, so I would show this as soon as we get Polonius sending Reynaldo to spy on Laertes in act 2, and then use it as a reference for the *many* other incidents of spying: Polonius and the King spying on Ophelia and Hamlet, Rosencrantz and Guildenstern spying on Hamlet, Polonius spying on the Queen and Hamlet.

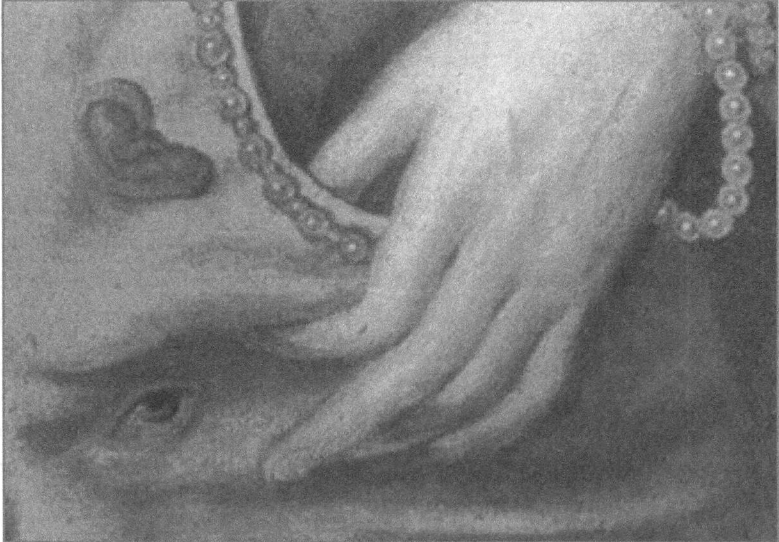

FIGURE 2.11. Close-up of Queen Elizabeth I's dress, showing eyes and ears embroidery.

Student Evaluations

Ninety-three percent of the students believed the primary documents to be either "somewhat" or "extremely" important in their study of Shakespeare.

In the end, student responses are usually honest, forthright, and helpful. The students who studied *The Tragedy of Hamlet* redirected my path many times. Only three students out of the fifty I taught had not read a Shakespeare play before, so most had, at the very least, experienced *Romeo and Juliet*. The results I received on the student survey revealed that over half the students knew the language to be difficult and thus boring. From prior experience, 67 percent of the students believed they would have to read some or all of it on their own. Only 33 percent believed they would succeed on this unit and only two students agreed they would learn to love Shakespeare. After having read the play, their answers mirrored other grade levels in that 20 percent now loved Shakespeare and only 24 percent believed the play to be boring. One of the telling factors was how the students viewed their own success: after reading the play, 69 percent thought they had achieved success on this unit as opposed to the 33 percent who thought they would be successful before having read the play (Table 2.4).

Student reflections emphasized how primary documents enriched the Shakespeare experience. Learning about a culture was the best part of the unit. They mentioned the differences between the sixteenth century and today's world, but also noted, "It's just not that different and helps us think about how things are similar to back in his time."

Table 2.4. Student survey: Responses to statements before and after reading *Hamlet*.

Survey statements	Before	After
The play will be/was difficult to read.	64%	38%
The story will be/was boring.	62%	24%
I will have/had to read some or all on my own.	67%	27%
The teacher will explain/explained the play to me.	42%	64%
I will have/had to take a test on this play.	69%	33%
The play will be/was fun to read.	24%	49%
I will learn/learned to love Shakespeare.	4%	20%
I will succeed/succeeded on this unit.	33%	69%

3

Teaching *Macbeth* in the AP World

In *Daemonologie*, a dissertation that precedes Shakespeare's *Macbeth*, King James VI uses dramatic form to admonish his readers about the dangers of necromancy and to articulate religious reasons for persecuting witches. Why then, students ask, would Shakespeare write a play with witches appearing in the very first scene? And why are *Macbeth*'s witches so much more compelling compared to the source? I was eager for my AP students to explore early modern societal touchstones about the supernatural, resistance, and gender—intriguing topics for most high school students.

> **Document Discussions**
>
> This chapter taps into two different issues: teachers looking to elevate the document approach for AP students and those who teach *Macbeth* in general classes.

When I added a few document excerpts, such as Shakespeare's noted source, Raphael Holinshed's *Chronicles*, in addition to King James's *Daemonologie*, to shed light on witchcraft motifs, students were drawn like magnets. During act 1, scene 3, in response to Banquo's request for his own prophecy, the third witch briefly states, "Thou shalt get kings, though thou be none" (1.3.70)—a mere eight single-syllable words, compared to Holinshed's sixty-nine-word full accounting of Banquo's future (see Figure I.2 in the Introduction). "By compacting Holinshed's words, what do you think Shakespeare's words do?" I asked.

"Maybe Shakespeare wanted it shorter?" Jeffrey's voice indicated he wasn't sure.

"Well, if it's shorter and uses one-syllable words, it could be stronger," offered another student. "You know, more powerful."

"Or maybe," added Jeffrey, "Shakespeare's version sounds a little more mysterious. If you don't describe as much, the reader has to figure it out."

"Yeah," said Claire. "We don't know if we can trust them. We really don't."

Through only a few primary documents, I had provided a quick snapshot of early modern culture, illuminating Shakespeare's tragedy as more than a single story. By moving primary documents to center stage, rather than placing a scant few peripherally, I now hoped to give other writers equal footing and to expose students to a host of early modern writers who spoke to similar issues—religion, government, family life, and medicine, all topics relevant to twenty-first-century students—but through different genres and temperaments. The richness of their arguments and the eloquence of their writing would no doubt surface in *The Tragedy of Macbeth*, allowing us entrance into Shakespeare's play with potent discussion points.

A new approach to teaching Shakespeare includes an exploration of primary documents from the Renaissance period, which will provide a rich historical, cultural context and gain you entrance to his poetry and plays. Rather than study Macbeth *in isolation, my ultimate goal is that you will expand and embolden your thinking to include other writers and genres as evidence of early modern controversy. Let's discover together why his work still matters.*

My excitement about primary documents was balanced by my students' practical natures. Would it be too difficult to handle? Students knew we would tackle the primary documents, including *Macbeth*, together, but they also understood they would do considerable reading and writing outside of class. So, how manageable were primary documents?

My hope was that these eleventh- and twelfth-grade AP students would find their passion within my dog-eared *Macbeth* books, relying on primary sources to understand Shakespeare's cultural backdrop. Were women as strong as Lady Macbeth? Were kings as vulnerable as Duncan? Did early modern society generally follow prophetic advice? Did witches simply appear? And did any of this connect to the present day?

They had read my overview of the project, but they had realistic questions that begged concrete answers.

I was surprised to learn that thirteen out of one hundred nine students had never read or studied a Shakespeare play. Most of these students came from other schools or states and somehow fell through a Shakespeare crack or two. Over the years, many AP students have reported that, despite having read *Romeo and Juliet* as ninth-graders, most had relied on *SparkNotes* to clarify language if they were reading independently. Pre-twentieth-century literature was daunting, they complained, admitting they often simply gave up. And, yes, they were extremely anxious about the work and how they would measure up against their aspiring, confident peers.

Document Discussions

To launch documents with students who have relied on other sources to "translate" Shakespeare's plays, begin with documents that answer student-generated questions. Visuals of what Holinshed's witches looked like will inspire discussions about why and how Shakespeare changed their appearances.

On the first day of the unit, one student, often self-reliant, took control of the document camera, scribing notes on previous knowledge about Shakespeare and his world. The class discussion began slowly but grew as students remembered information from their ninth-grade year. The first question had to do with Shakespeare's birth and death. The conversation pivoted first on one topic, then another, as students voiced past memories. They were aware that Shakespeare wrote sonnets and that he was married and had a son who died. They knew about the Globe Theatre and that females did not act at all. They knew about the plague and its effect on theater closings. What they did not know was the thinking about cultural norms. They might have known, for example, that Hamnet died when he was eleven years old, but they knew nothing about the burial or the customs surrounding death during the early modern period. Religious liturgy, the afterlife, and grief—historical/cultural beliefs that created parameters for behavior—were unknown to these twenty-first-century students. Once the discussion began, however, students couldn't stop talking or asking. Initially, they wanted to know if the knowledge they had was accurate, but, eventually, their questions focused on Shakespeare's world: "What was it like back then?"

After sharing prior knowledge, students spent one class period researching their own queries, situating Shakespeare within a culture where other writers and artists also commented on early modern issues. Was Shakespeare using current scandals as his topics for writing? Was he a feminist? A racist? Did people like his poetry? Did he get into trouble for his writing? After perusing various websites for background on sixteenth- and seventeenth-century England (Lambert; Greenblatt *Core Selections Ebook*), we examined a list of themes they saw emerging either in his plays or pop culture—big ideas we could track throughout our exploration of primary documents, including *The Tragedy of Macbeth*. Initial thinking included broad topics, such as love, jealousy, death, betrayal, conflict, murder, kinship, and gender; universal themes that students knew would emerge in literature across time and place, but not necessarily the same issues and themes that would bubble up from eleventh-century Scotland, such as tanistry and primogeniture or honor and war. This was new territory for my high school students. Understanding Shakespeare's writing as a discourse situated in a historical period encouraged them to explore how history establishes pathways into contemporary thinking in ways that seemed natural and inevitable but also complex and influential.

Document Discussions

Using primary sources illuminates how texts are not written in isolation. Instead, they are a product of culture and provide readers with knowledge about the human condition. Reading *Macbeth* provides multiple narratives about politics, relationships, gender, history, power, and greed.

My goal was twofold: I wanted to show students how *Macbeth* was not simply a text in isolation but one man's thinking permeated by other cultural perspectives. Second, I hoped they would reflect on their own culture to determine how contemporary cultural themes are rooted in historiographies. Perhaps golden threads from Macbeth's Scotland would weave an early modern tapestry, one in which James I reigned as "divine" monarch. By uncovering the hidden complexities of the past through works that reflected the human condition, perhaps today's students would better understand and thus revalue the complexities of their own lives.

Taking First Steps Together

The first steps into a Shakespeare play are crucial. I have used various techniques to segue into *Macbeth*, especially those activities that engage students in language. Regardless of the pedagogical approach, the idea is to get them up on their feet to experience the cadence and beauty of the words, incorporating movement and gestures to help carry the meaning.

Document Discussions

Using primary sources prompts deeper questions about big ideas. Rather than looking for facts, students probe questions that may not have precise answers. Instead, research, writing, and discussion focus on exploration of gray areas where possibilities often live.

Since the first set of documents included both digital and visual texts on witches and religion, I began with small-group performances of act 1, scene 1, with the three witches on the heath. After sharing unique and varied imaginings of the "weird sisters"—nurses, hags, drag queens, garbage collectors—students planned and practiced. Some performances included costumes, hats, and hoodies. To be more creative, Ashley, Kerra, and Josh wore matching blue hospital aid uniforms. Other groups brought blankets to be used as capes, and another had a Spice Girls twist with wild hair and fishnet stockings. Jerod brought a pot, which he placed at the front of the room while Eddie threw in stuffed animals, plastic worms, and fingers. The most ingenious idea was performed as cats, meowing the entire script and imitating the cadence and intonation of the witches' words. By having fun with the opening scene, students engaged immediately with Shakespeare's language—a key ingredient for our starting point.

After some discussion on the dynamics between the Macbeths and a close reading of Lady Macbeth's solicitation of the spirits to "unsex" her and to fill her with "direst cruelty" (1.5.48–50), students were ready, albeit slightly hesitant, to dive into their first set of documents on witchcraft and religion. Many had never read primary documents before and didn't know what they were. Regardless of prior exposures, I spent time frontloading the experience, sharing my own *self-talk* on the strategies I used to overcome barriers as I walked through a few documents.

Document Discussions

Students benefit from reading an entire act before each set of documents, but some teachers prefer to place them strategically throughout the text. The best strategy is to try different methods to see which best fits your teaching style.

It is true AP students are strong readers and writers, but my classes are usually varied and therefore warrant a *gradual release of responsibility* (see Appendix C). I would therefore provide substantial support in the form of modeling, scaffolded activities, and discussion before expecting independent practice. Regardless of age and ability, students need *fix-up* strategies, ideas for maintaining momentum and engagement, and were assured that eventually their skills would improve.

My skills were improving too. I found better ways to present documents and felt more comfortable in my Think-Alouds. My introductory mini-lessons usually included modeling my thinking interspersed with formative checks for understanding before students worked collaboratively. Rereading was a must. Because most of the documents are one- or two-page excerpts, students are willing to read multiple times: once independently to annotate and gather big ideas, another time in small groups, and a third time during the larger group debriefing where students share findings and reread sections they find interesting (Figure 3.1).

During small-group collaborations, I generally spend time in specific groups to provide support before students participate in *each teach*. I have tried variations of Jigsaws or Each Teach activities (see Appendix C), gradually releasing independence in discussions. In one variation, after students formed their Jigsaw groups, they were assigned a document to read. Next, they moved to smaller groups, meeting with one other student from each of the other Jigsaw groups who had read the same document. This step was pivotal, especially to students who needed extra support after their initial reading. Together, these

FIGURE 3.1. Students reading and annotating various accounts of early modern witch hunts.

small groups reread their documents, stopping to review annotations and to discuss reactions. As I roamed the room, I noted the methods they used to make sense of text: brief outlines, bulleted points, arrows, headings, and sketchnotes,[17] creating meaning that could be shared and modeled for peers. Many students enjoyed sketching and made use of their own artistic abilities to help them express the basic tenets of documents. These crucial small groups took precedence and were instrumental in the success of the larger Jigsaw discussions.

Document Discussions

Listening to students discuss primary documents is magical. I found that, if students have multiple opportunities for small-group discussions, my presence within the group to "listen in" rarely affected the content or the direction. After the Jigsaw discussions in which students shared their documents, we engaged in a large-group debriefing. This was not exactly the same as sharing for feedback, understanding, or additional information. Rather, student discussions on primary documents were treasure troves. As unique gems were uncovered, students discovered the gleams of other nuggets as they became more visible.

In essence, the more they read and discussed, the more they understood. Initially, students waited while each group member shared the major points of their documents. It didn't take long for the summarizing to end and the real crossfire to begin. Carson jumped in when Jake shared King James's *Daemonologie* (see Table 3.1). The form of the excerpted document, Jake explained, was a play with two characters, Philomathes, a skeptic on magic, who asked Epistemon, a teacher, whether there was any such thing as witches. "The teacher in this play says there are two kinds—*necromancy*, which is witchcraft, I guess, and *sorcery*. I just don't know the difference because the teacher, Epistemon, says they're both bad."

"After I read mine, I read that one too," said Carson, eliciting some surprised expressions. "And, on the second page, it says something about astrology. It's the skeptic who says that not everything comes from the devil. And the teacher agrees that astrology is different but only if you're learning about the *course* of the seasons and weather. It's different if you're influenced *too much* by them."

"But how much is too much?" asked Jake.

"I'm not sure, but I think it has to do with conjuring the devil. The skeptic goes right from talking about the naturalness of weather and asks about the unnaturalness of circles and conjurations."

TABLE 3.1. Primary documents about witchcraft and the supernatural.

An Act against Conjuration, Witchcraft, and Dealing with Evil and Wicked Spirits	James I, King of England, 1604
A Briefe Description of the Notorious Life of John Lambe, otherwise called Doctor Lambe, Together with His Ignominious Death	1628
"Calves Snout or Snapdragon"	John Gerard, *The Herball, or Generall Historie of Plantes*, 1597
Daemonologie, in the Forme of a Dialogue, Divided into Three Books	James VI, King of Scotland, 1597
"Demonic Possession," *Histoires Prodigieuses*	Reproduced in James Shapiro's *The Year of Lear: Shakespeare in 1606*, 2015, p. 65
A Discourse on the Damned Art of Witchcraft So Farre Forth As It Is Reuealed in the Scriptures, and Manifest by True Experience	Perkins, 1610
"The North Berwick Witch Trials"	James Carmichael, *Newes from Scotland*, 1592
Text comparisons on Lady Macbeth: Demonic or evil?	Dawn Saliba, *King James and the Theatre of Witches: Subversion upon the Jacobean Stage*, 2013; James Carmichael, *Newes from Scotland*, 1592; Daniel Swift, *Shakespeare's Common Prayers: The Book of Common Prayer and the Elizabethan Age*, 2013
Caption	Documents used with act 1 of Macbeth

Note: Excerpted documents suggested here are available via the *Teaching Shakespeare* website (shakespearedocuments.info).

I was fascinated not only with how they were teaching each other, but also with how they were moving beyond their own reading.

Eliot shared the document on snapdragons, focusing on the fact that people would wear them to ward off witches but mentioned Gerard's instructions for soaking the plant to use as a compress for "dim eyes" (000). "That seems weird, doesn't it? I mean, warding off witches and bad eyes just aren't even close!"

Jake brought up the fact that he had a secondary document, an excerpt from the 2015 *The Year of Lear* by James Shapiro (68–69). He said, "This one was a lot easier to read and was about the trial of Anne Gunter. I guess, back then, neighbors and relatives would come to your house to watch your symptoms to see if you were possessed. That happened to her, and she went to trial, and that went on for eight hours!"

"What year was that?" Camille asked.

"It says here about 1605."

"When was Macbeth was written?"

"1605?" asked Ashley. She looked at me.

"Close," I said. "It was thought to have been first performed for King James in 1606."

"Looks like witches were on everyone's minds," Jake said.

"Could be." But now they were wondering about what witches looked like, if people thought witches could be someone living next door. Jake showed the group Pierre Boaistuau's *Demonic Possession* (see Figure 3.2), a picture of the 1598 woodcut included in Shapiro's text (*Year of Lear* 65), which prompted the discussion on whether or not Shapiro's description and Boaistuau's woodcut depicted the same "wyrd" sisters in Shakespeare's play. Students were nonplussed. "Let's go back to the text," I ventured.

"Banquo says in scene 3," said Cassie, "that they are withered and wild and 'not like th'inhabitants o'th'earth' [lines 41–42]."

"And don't they have beards?" a male student asked. The group laughed.

"So, no, they don't really seem the same as in the witch trials. Shakespeare's witches are women, the same as in the Berwick Trials." (See also Figure 3.3.)

"But the picture from *The Scotland News* showed regular women, like it could have been anyone in the community," Jake concluded.

Cassie looked up from her document. "But look at the guy in the *Demonic Possession* picture. He's got something coming out of his mouth. It looks like fire."

"Or a forked tongue," said another student. Students were starting to see that Shakespeare may have been capitalizing on *Newes from Scotland* but made

FIGURE 3.2. *Demonic Possession* (Boaistuau).

FIGURE 3.3. An illustration of the North Berwick witch trials from a woodcut in *Newes from Scotland* (Carmichael).

changes for his own purposes. In *Macbeth*, they noted, the witches were rarely seen alone and mostly in threes. Their looks, their words, and their actions seemed mysterious yet believable.

"I wonder why Shakespeare changed them?" Ashley asked. I realized that other scholars could add information to their immediate questions, such as James Sharpe's research on early modern conceptions of witches' meetings. We discussed the word *sabbat*,[18] which students thought could be how Shakespeare first presents the three witches on the heath.

"The idea of the sabbat was at its peak just after *Macbeth* was written, so it was probably something his audiences may have heard about," I said. "Other researchers," I added, "believe that covens, orgies, and sabbats were not part of English trials at all, and these 'witch hunts' were rather low key in comparison to other countries like Scotland."

"So that's why the document on the North Berwick Witch Trials was from *News from Scotland*," said Jake. "But wouldn't the word spread to England?" he asked.

"It doesn't say that in the document," said Camille, "but since James VI was in Scotland and probably knew about it, he brought the news to England with him. And that's when *Macbeth* was performed, right?"[19]

"Wait a minute! *Macbeth* takes place in Scotland! Now it's making sense!" said Jake.

"But what about the snapdragon plant?" asked Eliot.

"You and your snapdragon plant," laughed Cassie.

"But wasn't the guy who found that plant thinking about how to keep witches away too? And he was English."

I decided to add a little more to the pot. "Also, remember that England was a Protestant state, so another reason that witch hunts were not as prevalent could have been who was writing at the time and about what. Many sermons focused on evangelizing or correcting anti-Christian behavior."

"But there were witch hunts, right?" asked Ashley.

"Yes, the Essex witch hunts, which took place before they happened here in America but a good forty years or so after Shakespeare wrote *Macbeth.*" I could see Tray flipping through the documents to look at some of the visuals but then looking up before adding to the discussion.

"I was just looking at some of these contraptions they used to get people to confess they were witches. This Dr. Flan and Agnes Sampson were average people, good citizens. They refused to confess, and so Dr. Flan was tortured by the boot. They put this vice on him and turned the screw until he went unconscious. And they were chained to a wall and couldn't sleep. Then they were strangled after going through all that torture. I can't believe it," he said.

"So, based on all that you've read, what are you thinking about Shakespeare's witches?" I asked.

"Pretty tame."

"The witches in the play aren't really the same witches we're reading about in the documents," Jake concluded.

"That's interesting, Jake," I said. "I'd like you to do some thinking around that idea. If you are seeing differences between the play and the documents, how do you negotiate that information? Let's do some writing about how the documents might help in your understanding of how Shakespeare includes ideas about witchcraft and the supernatural." Students wrote for fifteen minutes and were eager to share their thinking in both small groups and then with the entire class.

Document Discussions

Writing helps students form thoughts around primary documents and their influence on Shakespeare's plays.

I had to coax Brodie a little. I could see he had written almost a page, and I saw that he didn't say much in his small group. I decided to push him out of his comfort zone a little. "So, Brodie, what did you write about?"

"I don't personally feel the documents gave me a better understanding of the story itself, but they have given me the contextual information to compare it."

"I agree," said Ashley. "The documents to me make *Macbeth* more confusing. If witches were basically the darkest beings on earth besides Satan, why did the characters believe them and listen to their prophecies? Wouldn't someone with as much influence as Macbeth be able to easily put them in jail where everyone thought they belonged? Wouldn't it be dangerous for Lady Macbeth to call upon the spirits to help her since she could be accused?"

"Are you saying Lady Macbeth is a witch?" I asked.

Cassie spoke up quickly. "Lady Macbeth is conjuring like a witch, and witchcraft is regarded as the devil's magic, which makes sense due to Lady Macbeth's conjuring being more powerful. Remember, she asked the spirits to 'unsex her.'"

"If Lady Macbeth had prayed to the devil outside of her home, she would have been accused of being a witch, although she couldn't be one because she is of the 'earthly realm,'" added Hailey.

"But people of everyday life also seemed to get into the hysteria and accusations whether they were true or not," said Kaylee.

Zach's hand went up. "The documents really help to set the time period and what was actually going on with witchcraft. And, anyway, Shakespeare wrote about controversial topics, right?"

"I feel like the documents help me understand the time period better," said Payton. "I was confused earlier about how they treated witches, but some of the documents helped me understand better. I think talking to the other people helped."

> *Shakespeare was no longer a single voice of genius; instead, he was one instrument in an orchestrated dialogue that students were learning to understand and appreciate.*

"Yeah, it's like we're learning about a new culture. Now I get how they dealt with witchcraft and how society rejected it," said Jenae.

"What confuses me," said Caitlyn, "is why Macbeth would be seen with these three witches, because of the harm they could cause. This is serious and so were the criminal accusations that went along with the practice of black magic."

The discussion grew. I had never heard so many students speak up before. Students, generally quiet, were not only engaged, but also forthright. Yes, students did at times express confusion as they were working through multiple early modern voices, often with competing ideas. They wondered how to connect ideas as they explored individual writers and varying genres, such as treatises, catalogues, essays, sermons, and letters. Shakespeare was no longer a single voice of genius; instead, he was one instrument in an orchestrated dialogue that students were learning to understand and appreciate.

Government and Freedom

After a few weeks, students were much more comfortable with reading documents, synthesizing ideas, and discussing issues. We were ready for documents related to government and freedom. To increase facility and independence, I used a *shared reading* strategy (see Appendix C), adding annotating and questioning to my *Think-Aloud* (Appendix B). I chose one of the more difficult documents: an excerpt of John Milton's *Areopagitica*, his 1644 speech to Parliament, opining the need for free speech (Figures 3.4–3.6). At the time, all written documents, including scripts, were licensed and registered with the stationers and censors before flooding the market with dangerous "opinions."

AREOPAGITICA;
A
SPEECH
OF
Mr. JOHN MILTON
For the Liberty of VNLICENC'D
PRINTING,
To the PARLAMENT of ENGLAND.

Euripid. Hicetid.

This is true Liberty when free born men
Having to advise the public may speak free,
Which he who can, and will, deserv's high praise,
Who neither can nor will, may hold his peace;
What can be juster in a State then this?
Euripid. Hicetid.

LONDON,
Printed in the Yeare, 1644.

FIGURE 3.4. *Title page of Areopagitica; A Speech of Mr. John Milton for the Liberty of Vnlicenc'd Printing, to the Parlament of England* (Milton).

In 1606, when *Macbeth* was first performed in court, the Master of Revels had authorization over all scripts "to ensure that the Court received the best possible entertainment, and that no one would be upset too greatly by anything they saw" (Crystal 195; see also Gurr 293). Using the document camera, I annotated my copy and modeled a Think-Aloud on seven basic premises he made to drive home his points (Figures 3.5 and 3.6). "First," I remarked, "note in the first paragraph how Milton uses the analogy of confused seeds that bear an apple where both good and evil are mixed. He calls them 'two together.' Milton makes the analogy of the Garden of Eden when 'Adam fell about hereinto of knowing good and evill, that is to say of knowing good by evill.'

"In other words, we cannot know goodness without its twin. I'm going to number what I think his major points are while I'm reading and annotating and draw boxes around each section to help me keep his ideas straight in my mind."

I went on to my second point, indicating where, in the text, Milton asserts "wisdome can there be to choose."

Annotating

"Is he talking about free will?" asked Ross.

"Yes, and good question! That takes me to what I believe is Milton's third point. He claims God gives us free will to choose goodness and posits evil can be learned without books."

"So," continued Ross, "he's saying that censoring books won't do it. I mean, people will still do evil stuff."

"Right," I said. "He seems to lay out his argument logically in a way that is almost step by step. He's appealing to logos here." Students were nodding. I marked the fourth point in my document about learned men needing books as tools for teaching. "See what he is doing?" I went on. "He is placing good, but specifically evil, outside the realm of books. If he can convince Parliament that learned men—and we have to assume those 'learned men' are sitting in front of

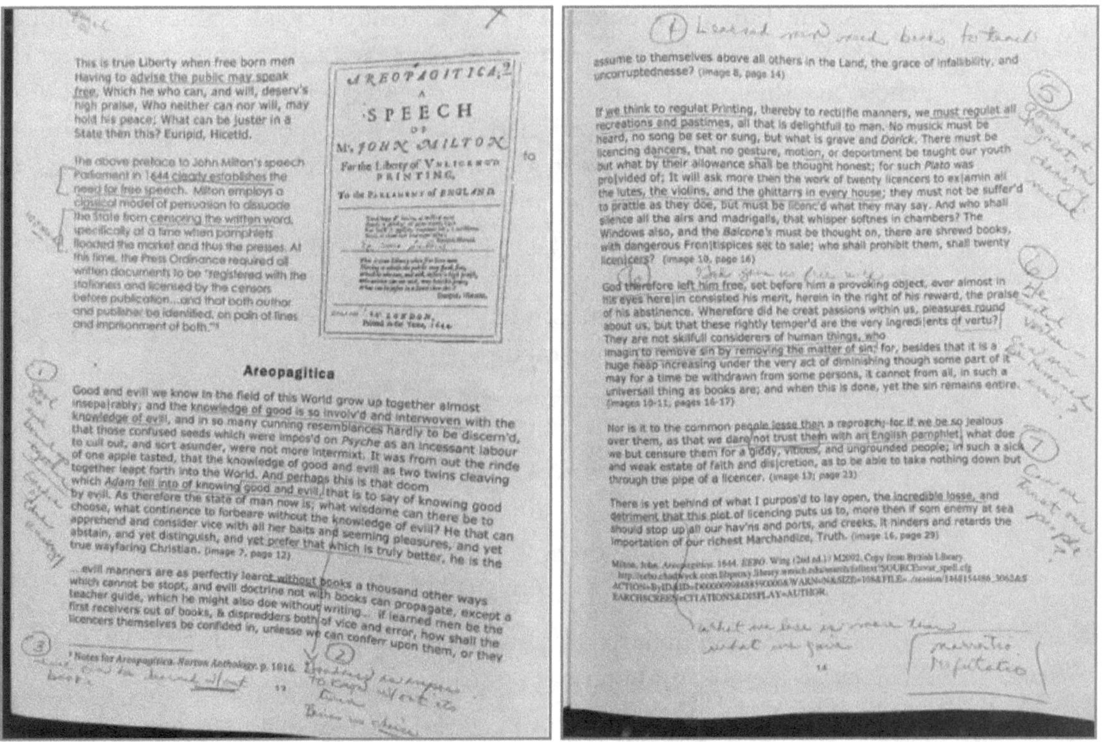

This is true Liberty when free born men Having to advise the public may speak free, Which he who can, and will, deserv's high praise, Who neither can nor will, may hold his peace; What can be juster in a State then this? Euripid, Hicetid.

The above preface to John Milton's speech to Parliament in 1644 clearly establishes the need for free speech. Milton employs a classical model of persuasion to dissuade the State from censoring the written word, specifically at a time when pamphlets flooded the market and thus the presses. At this time, the Press Ordinance required all written documents to be "registered with the stationers and licensed by the censors before publication...and that both author and publisher be identified, on pain of fines and imprisonment of both."[1]

AREOPAGITICA; A SPEECH OF Mr. JOHN MILTON For the Liberty of UNLICENC'D PRINTING, To the PARLAMENT of ENGLAND.

LONDON, Printed in the Yeare, 1644.

Areopagitica

Good and evill we know in the field of this World grow up together almost insepa|rably; and the knowledge of good is so involv'd and interwoven with the knowledge of evill, and in so many cunning resemblances hardly to be discern'd, that those confused seeds which were impos'd on *Psyche* as an incessant labour to cull out, and sort asunder, were not more intermixt. It was from out the rinde of one apple tasted, that the knowledge of good and evill as two twins cleaving together leapt forth into the World. And perhaps this is that doom which *Adam* fell into of knowing good and evill, that is to say of knowing good by evill. As therefore the state of man now is; what wisdome can there be to choose, what continence to forbeare without the knowledge of evill? He that can apprehend and consider vice with all her baits and seeming pleasures, and yet abstain, and yet distinguish, and yet prefer that which is truly better, he is the true wayfaring Christian. (image 7, page 12)

...evill manners are as perfectly learnt without books a thousand other ways which cannot be stopt, and evill doctrine not with books can propagate, except a teacher guide, which he might also doe without writing... If learned men be the first receivers out of books, & dispredders both of vice and error, how shall the licencers themselves be confided in, unlesse we can conferr upon them, or they

[1] Notes for Areopagitica. Norton Anthology. p. 1016.

12

assume to themselves above all others in the Land, the grace of infallibility, and uncorruptednesse? (image 8, page 14)

If we think to regulat Printing, thereby to rectifie manners, we must regulat all recreations and pastimes, all that is delightfull to man. No musick must be heard, no song be set or sung, but what is grave and *Dorick*. There must be licencing dancers, that no gesture, motion, or deportment be taught our youth but what by their allowance shall be thought honest; for such *Plato* was pro|vided of; It will ask more then the work of twenty licencers to ex|amin all the lutes, the violins, and the ghittarrs in every house; they must not be suffer'd to prattle as they doe, but must be licenc'd what they may say. And who shall silence all the airs and madrigalls, that whisper softnes in chambers? The Windows also, and the *Balcone's* must be thought on, there are shrewd books, with dangerous Fron|tispices set to sale; who shall prohibit them, shall twenty licen|cers? (image 10, page 16)

God therefore left him free, set before him a provoking object, ever almost in his eyes here|in consisted his merit, herein the right of his reward, the praise of his abstinence. Wherefore did he creat passions within us, pleasures round about us, but that these rightly temper'd are the very ingredi|ents of vertu? They are not skilfull considerers of human things, who imagin to remove sin by removing the matter of sin; for, besides that it is a huge heap increasing under the very act of diminishing though some part of it may for a time be withdrawn from some persons, it cannot from all, in such a universall thing as books are; and when this is done, yet the sin remains entire. (images 10-11, pages 16-17)

Nor is it to the common people lesse then a reproach; for if we be so jealous over them, as that we dare not trust them with an English pamphlet, what doe we but censure them for a giddy, vitious, and ungrounded people; in such a sick and weak estate of faith and dis|cretion, as to be able to take nothing down but through the pipe of a licencer. (image 13, page 23)

There is yet behind of what I purpos'd to lay open, the incredible losse, and detriment that this plot of licencing puts us to, more then if som enemy at sea should stop up all our hav'ns and ports, and creeks. It hinders and retards the importation of our richest Marchandize, Truth. (image 16, page 29)

14

FIGURES 3.5 and 3.6. *Shared reading*, a primary document teaching strategy, is here illustrated through annotated excerpts from *Areopagitica* (Milton) (see also Appendix C).

him—need books for learning, which is his fourth point, he can include them in his argument by convincing them of *their* need not to indulge censorship."

"Nice job," said Alyssa. I loved the idea that students felt they could either ask questions or make commentary as I was talking because it showed they were engaged and thinking through Milton's ideas.

"I know, right? His fifth point, though, his *refutatio,* borders on ludicrous. Look at this section where he says, 'If we think to regulat Printing, thereby to rectifie manners, we must regulat all recreations and pastimes, all that is delightfull to man.' Then he makes a list of other things that would also be regulated. Music. Dance. Gestures. Motion. Lutes. Violins. Of course, that seems ridiculous, right? So why would he do that?"

Questioning

"Maybe he wanted them to see how dumb this was," said Sophie.

"But he had a smart audience," said Emily. "I think he just wanted them to see how far this could go. The government getting into your business. Like Big Brother."

Students watched me work my way through the text, breaking it into manageable bits, looking for avenues to comprehension through categorizing and synthesizing. But now I could see they were ready to read. Together, we flipped through the rest of the documents, scanning the titles, authors, and graphics. I chose five different documents that represented discrepant viewpoints. First, students numbered off by five. I had arranged the room with three groups of ten desks. Each group had five in a row, each row facing the other.[20] Students sat opposite someone who had the same article.

After independently reading and annotating assigned documents, students discussed their understandings with their facing partner, then shifted to the right to share with a different student until, after four shifts, they had talked about their own document several times.

Shift and Share Strategy

1. Choose five documents on a theme.
2. Arrange desks in three groups of ten each. Each group has five desks in two rows facing each other.
3. Students sit across from someone reading the same document.
4. Begin independent reading and annotating.
5. Share learning with partner.
6. Shift one row to the right to share document with new partner.
7. Shift and share four times.
8. Debrief in small/large groups.

The Shift and Share strategy (see also Figures 3.7 and 3.8) worked well. First, it allowed time to read, annotate, and share before deciding how to articulate the author's ideas with someone who had never read the document. Second, the strategy provided repeated opportunities to "say something" about an author's slant on a topic, building confidence and skill.

Student pairs walked slowly and carefully through their shared documents, and I observed how, together, they patiently fought through difficult language while searching for meaning. Finally, they were ready to share their thinking. The two parallel lines afforded the opportunity for one line easily to shift to the right, such that students had the opportunity to debrief their articles with four different students.

During each class, I participated, which proved to be a worthwhile experience and valuable for them to see me as a learner. As we listened to interpretations, it helped me evaluate their understanding.

I was especially impressed with Haley, who read the secondary document "Spectral Communities and Ghosts of Sovereignty" (Kottman) on the theatricality of the king. She mentioned the fact that Macbeth failed in the theatricality of kingship because he did not recognize the importance of the "show" of hosting.

FIGURE 3.7. In this Shift and Share activity (see also Appendix C), students are sharing documents on government and freedom.

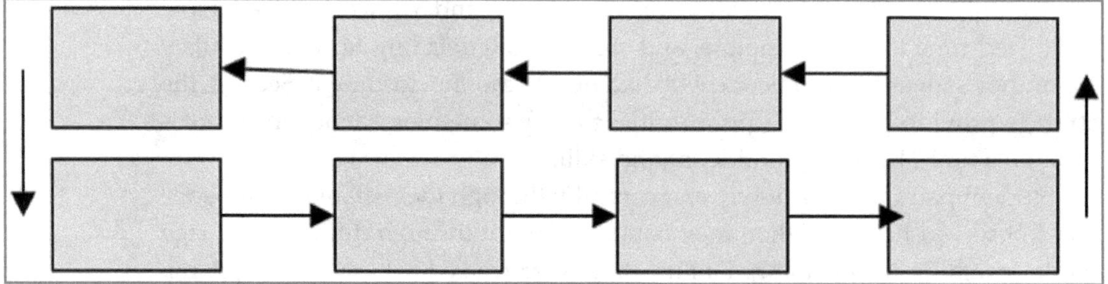

FIGURE 3.8. A model for the Shift and Share group activity for reading documents.

That was his downfall. She said she had no trouble reading the document and "got a lot out of it." I shared Rebecca Lemon's article, "Sovereignty and Treason in *Macbeth*," which included words of advice from Machiavelli's *The Prince*. It is a secondary document that houses a primary document excerpt, in which Lemon explains that neither Duncan nor Macbeth measured up to Machiavelli's idea of kingship. I mentioned that Machiavelli believed princes should elicit fear and respect from their subjects. Macbeth elicited fear but was not respected.

"Duncan definitely was respected but did not elicit fear. In fact, he was too trusting of those around him." Haley immediately saw some similarities in our two documents.

"So, basically both documents say that neither of them were good kings," she said.

"That's what I'm thinking," I answered.

"What do you think of these two documents?" I asked.

"Well, secondary documents are easier to read and give some good information."

I agreed.

Simply reading the documents would have been tedious without a variety of arrows in my quiver. I had tried Jigsaw, Roaming Team Leader, and Shift and Share, but I knew better than to create a template for each day's approach to the play and documents. Some days, we looked at several documents at one time. Sometimes, I projected a sketch while we read a scene, and sometimes we looked at several short passages to analyze complex attitudes about a topic. We often used writing to clarify our thinking about our reading.

Documents and the Performance Approach

I never considered combining the study of documents with a performance approach. Actually, I wasn't the one who made the suggestion. It was the students themselves. During act 5, students formed triads to experiment with blocking the sleepwalking scene with Lady Macbeth, the doctor, and the gentlewoman. Students playing Lady Macbeth had battery-operated candles but needed to figure out how they would deal with that prop when she says, "Out, damned spot, out I say!" (5.1.37). Discussions included comments about how Lady M. would walk in the darkened room. Would she seem crazy or lucid? Would she stumble around with her eyes open? Would the doctor seem amazed or knowing? Was the gentlewoman worried or simply annoyed?

> Her pain is absolutely paramount. And I think that is what she dies of—she has nothing left. There's nothing left for her to live for, and that's the tragedy of it.
>
> —Judi Dench on playing Lady Macbeth

While small groups discussed how to play this scene, I listened in on several conversations. Jason told his group that Macbeth is with the doctor two scenes later asking what has ailed his wife and seems to think that rhubarb will purge her of her ailments. He went directly to John Gerard's *Herball* excerpt to find out the "vertues" of rhubarb. "It says here to slice and boil the roots," said Jason, "and then to add honey to the mix."

"That actually sounds good," said Emily.

"Are you joking?" said Carissa.

"I like rhubarb!"

"Well, it says you drink eight to ten spoonfuls before a fit, but that's not really what's happening here," said Jason, who was now back in the *Macbeth* book. "She's walking around in her sleep but not shaking."

"But, it's actually Macbeth who asks about the rhubarb. It's like he has heard about it because he says to the doctor, 'Hear'st thou of them?'"

"So, could this be a new discovery in medicine?" I asked. Their discussion was getting my full attention. I had never before seen students research background when they were performing a scene.

"Well, maybe," said Carissa, "because the doctor says something about it being a royal preparation. Maybe that means it's being used at court."

"But then this other guy in the other document says that peonies are used for dreams. So, then which one do you use?" asked Jason.

"It's probably just like today when you go to the doctor, and they don't know exactly what to give you." It was fascinating listening to conversations emerge from unlikely places. I did not expect that students would check the documents while problem-solving how to block a scene. This was important "talk," especially now when students were thinking about the upcoming assessment and wondering, *What shall I write about?*

Writing about Primary Documents

Document Discussions

Reading and writing about document excerpts prepare AP students for writing the prose or rhetorical analyses. Many of the devices we discuss, such as word choice, tone, and selection of detail, work well with both fiction and nonfiction.

Students wrote daily about *Macbeth* and other primary sources that spoke to faith, fear, paranoia, and trust. Documents undergirded discussions and writing about the regicide, ambicide, and hosticide, all of which described Macbeth's relationship with King Duncan. Carissa wrote about the idea of faith and how the people had to have faith in each other and in their God, which meant their king as well. She cited *The Divine Right and Irresistibility of Kings and Supreme Magistrates* when she wrote about how the people must account to the King if they believe in God. "If that trust is broken, so is their country," she said.

This type of writing serves many purposes. By writing short pieces, either in their critical-reading journals or as quick-writes to be turned in, students have opportunities to stop and reflect on learning. While they write, I often write with them. During and after our writing sessions, I gain considerable information about group and individual progress, alerting me to next steps in either reteaching or moving forward. The students also gain information about themselves as learners. Writing helps clarify thinking and provides practice for sharpening their writing skills. It could be said that every word they write moves them closer to success on the AP exam, but more importantly, it helps them decompress. I have found that after intensive reading and discussion, taking five minutes to relax and reflect allows all of us time to "be."

The Document Workshop

We finished *Macbeth* and had written numerous responses to early modern cultural issues based on our reading and discussions of Shakespeare and his contemporaries. The final assessment was a researched essay in which students explored historical/cultural issues and analyzed how primary documents, including *Macbeth*, speak to these issues. One of the most important features of the essay was the relevance factor. How does a four-hundred-year-old play traverse time, landing in our laps with such ferocity? Students had already made connections with some of today's political unrest, specifically the presidential election, and they realized how complicated sociopolitical issues often escalated into frenzied debates. They had discussed and written about how greed, misunderstanding, and dishonestly can have devastating results—not so different from what happened to the Macbeths.

In English language arts, we often talk about *workshop* approaches. Nancie Atwell describes the *writing workshop*. Sheridan Blau uses the word *workshop* to talk about literature discussion. It makes sense to call the approach I am using a *document workshop*. This type of workshop is not relegated solely to reading the play and writing responses to specific scenes or other authors. It spans the entire unit of study as well as the assessment process. In truth, I believe in an assessment that capitalizes on the skills they develop while we read *Macbeth*, an assessment that allows students the freedom to explore independently and collaboratively. I thought long and hard about how to extend the process of reading *Macbeth* using primary documents to create an assessment experience. Thus, the document workshop was how I approached the entire project, incorporating three key elements: inquiry, collaboration, and debriefing (Figure 3.9).

Using a document workshop approach created multiple dimensions in understanding *Macbeth*. Rather than focus their writing solely on the events in the play, students were now abuzz with documents they had researched. They watched tutorials, reread excerpts, and researched documents, each at a different place in the process. The "urgency" of knowing they had to produce a piece of writing about emerging themes based on early modern issues was palpable. I don't think I have ever taught *Macbeth* when students were so seriously and yet so passionately working.

I first noticed that students had various approaches to settling on topics. Some began with the play itself, jotting down quotes from scenes they found interesting, such as the sleepwalking scene in act 5. From there, one student

Inquiry	Collaboration	Debriefing
Students explore interest areas, brainstorm historical/cultural themes, and question social norms. Reading a wide variety of documents while reading *Macbeth* situates the play within a tumultuous and complex society. Some issues raise questions about twenty-first-century thinking and lead them in diverse directions, prompting more research.	Working in dynamic writing groups provides opportunities for seeking, finding, and providing support. Building teamwork is a skill that not all students find completely natural. Students often understand and find comfort in the organized chaos of classroom "think tanks," relying on and taking advantage of a noisy yet productive environment.	Reflection can provide the markers for how far we have come and how much we have learned. Students need time to discuss their learning, so they can move forward with more direction and confidence. They also need time to debrief their writing, making a document workshop a viable platform for peer discussions and teacher conferences.

FIGURE 3.9. Inquiry, collaboration, and debriefing elements of the document workshop approach.

reviewed the documents they already knew about and then spent some time talking to their writer's group about the Macbeths' insomnia. Rick discovered the element of sleep deprivation (see Table 3.2), deciding that it probably had some effect on the Macbeths. He said, "I could look at when they stopped sleeping and then see how their behavior started changing. There must be something about sleeping. I guess I never thought about people having trouble sleeping back then."

As a class, we had already read one document about natural medicines for dreaming or for fits. One of his group members suggested he research contemporary thinking about high levels of stress and sleep disorders.

Other students knew exactly which subject they wanted to research. Claire was interested in children and wanted to look further into the scene where Lady Macduff and her young family are murdered in act 4, scene 2. She went to her group for help. One member suggested she begin with the secondary document on civility, which gave some background on private and public life. "It might give you a starting point, something to do with families."

TABLE 3.2. Documents on insomnia and angst.

An Alarme to Wake Church Sleepers	1646
Microcosmographia: A Description of the Body of Man	1615
The Sicke Womans Private Looking Glasse	1636
O England Looke Upon This Monstrous Thing (woodcut of a body politic Puritan nightmare) (*The Kingdomes Monster*)	1643

"Think about what happened in the play when Macduff finds out his family is murdered," I added, having just joined their group. "Remember, Malcolm told Macduff, "Let grief / Convert to anger" (4.3.268–69).

"Revenge!" she said, smiling. This was not the original direction she had anticipated, but her curiosity was now piqued.

Any type of workshop where students are working both independently and collaboratively can result in reteaching and delays. The one challenge I had was to plan for the variability in learning styles and pacing balanced with a project deadline. For this reason, I decided to record mini-lessons, which could be accessed on the class website, allowing students to view them from home or on a bus on their way to a game, taking advantage of the emerging "flipped classroom" approach.[21] The recorded lessons were a tool for those students who chose to move ahead quickly or to hear a lesson more than once. Other resources included a sample writing schedule to help students who needed a plan to finish on time as well as suggested and linked websites for further research.

The beauty of the document workshop approach was that students were all at different stages of writing—researching, drafting, rewriting, proofreading—creating opportunities for them to discuss their processes with one another. The classroom, filled with the aromas of coffee and tea, was where students came together to discuss the play, sources, writing, and struggles. As facilitator, I conferred with students individually and in small groups, encouraging them to give themselves permission to experiment. I call this type of writing *dynamic*, and repeatedly expressed my mantra: "Let your essay grow out of your thinking. Let go of the predictable, 'five-paragraph essay.' You know how to write, and you know what you want to say. Write, and see where it takes you." Initially, hesitantly, they did. Eventually, confidence grew.

One historical topic that proved to be especially interesting to students was the Gunpowder Plot of 1605 in which Guy Fawkes was involved, which created quite a stir within the classroom—especially when they read the excerpt from "Remember, Remember" in Shapiro's *The Year of Lear* (119). The story of Guy Fawkes and the 1606 engraving of his tortured and ravaged body pulled on a wattled hurdle to his death allowed students to contemplate the full scope of regicide (Figure 3.10).

My students believed Shakespeare's world, filled with horror at the attempt on the life of King James I, provided a reason to write *Macbeth*.

"I know he probably got his ideas from other sources, but, come on, he must have known his play was gonna be a hit," said Jeremiah.

"Who wouldn't want to see a play about a murder attempt and then watch everybody involved get punished so horribly?" said another.

FIGURE 3.10. Execution of Guy Fawkes and associates (from *Verratheren in England*)

Students analyzed the frontispiece of *Mischeefes Mysterie: OR, Treafons Mafter-Peece, The Powder-Plot* (Herring) (see Figure 3.11), which depicted a huge eagle delivering the letter to Robert Cecil, 1st Earl of Salisbury, who handed it to James I, warning him of the impending explosion that would take his life.

The subsequent proclamation of Guy Fawkes Day to commemorate the incident created its own wake when an anonymous 1678 pamphlet warned citizens that the celebration was wreaking havoc with the religious community. The Pope's likeness had been doused in flames during a Fawkes celebration.

"This makes total sense to me now," said Hope. "I've never heard of this before, and why not? Reading *Macbeth* is one thing. But finding out about the Guy Fawkes incident is something totally different. It's no wonder Shakespeare wrote this play. Now it almost seems like a warning."

"I know," said Rachael. "People then watched all this happening. When you see all the people standing around when Fawkes was dragged in, you can see all the people who seemed like they were cheering or shaking their fists at him."

"I wonder what happened when *Macbeth* was actually performed for the first time. They must have thought, 'Yeah, this is what happens,' and it really did," said Hope. She shook her head.

Students recognized the images they found during their research on Guy Fawkes, particularly the ones associated with the movie *V for Vendetta.* As I was working with writing groups, occasionally I heard students laughing about some of the graphics they had uncovered, such as the recognizable masks worn by anonymous activists or "anons," internet-based groups that, in public, don Guy Fawkes masks. Some of their discussions, however, turned more serious when they talked about the state of our nation. Students now saw how historical events could be discussed in English classes while reading imaginative literature. "This isn't just about the setting of a story," said Jenna. I agreed. Perhaps this was not a multidisciplinary course, but it was a multidisciplinary approach.

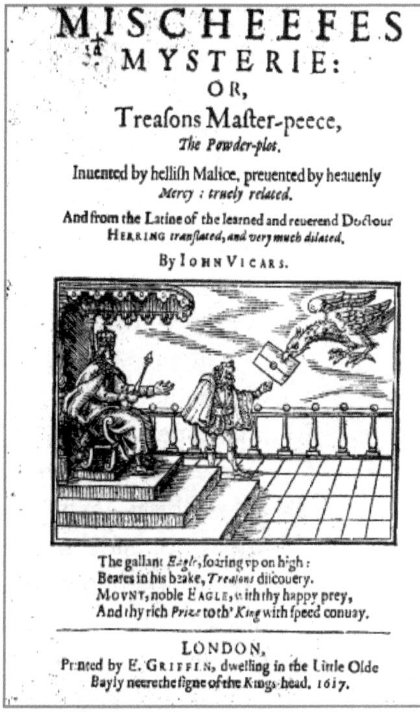

MISCHEEFES
MYSTERIE:
OR,
Treaſons Maſter-peece,
The Powder-plot.
Inuented by helliſh Malice, preuented by heauenly *Mercy: truely related.*
And from the Latine of the learned and reuerend Doctour HERRING *tranſlated, and very much dilated.*
By IOHN VICARS.

The gallant *Eagle*, ſoaring vp on high:
Beares in his beake, *Treaſons* diſcouery.
MOVNT, noble EAGLE, with thy happy prey,
And thy rich *Prize* to th' *King* with ſpeed conuay.

LONDON,
Printed by E. GRIFFIN, dwelling in the Little Olde Bayly neere the ſigne of the Kings-head. 1617.

FIGURE 3.11. Frontispiece of *Mischeefes Mysterie: OR, Treafons Mafter-Peece, The Powder-Plot* (Herring).

Culture and Context Matter

Using the document approach to *Macbeth* wasn't all Shakespeare heaven. Through the challenges, what I deemed most important was reading and discussing early modern documents, the historical and cultural backdrop of the play. According to leading scholar Stephen Greenblatt, a culture's ideology can often seem vague unless we see it as both *constraint* and *mobility* ("Culture"). These dissonant terms work together in the relationship between Shakespeare's *Macbeth* and early modern culture. Analysis of any text can and should move beyond the boundaries of characterization and action, establishing links with cultural practices. In other words, our understanding moves beyond the text and into the realm of culture, which is limited by social norms. Deep meaning, therefore, cannot be found solely through narrowly defined close reading. Readers need to "reconstruct the situation in which they were produced" ("Culture" 13). Greenblatt's vision of how meaning is created is reflexive in that the meaning of the text is best understood within the context of the culture, and the culture is best understood within the context of the text. What my students found interesting was how Shakespeare often probed the constraints of his own cultural norms, allowing viewers—both sixteenth- and twenty-first-century—to vicariously experience life when boundaries are pushed.

To illustrate, consider Mary, who chose to write her essay on how Shakespeare develops the theme of gender in *Macbeth*. As we discussed ideas from the text, her initial thinking included how Lady Macbeth is depicted—strong, arrogant, and fearless. Macbeth calls her "my dearest partner of greatness" (1.5.11). Searching to find evidence for a thesis that Shakespeare's female characters are inconsistent with early modern normative gender roles, Mary initially analyzed the relationships among the males and females in the play, specifically Macbeth and Lady Macbeth, deducing that Shakespeare must have "desired female dominance in a world where there was none" and that he was dissatisfied with women's "power of influence." Mary was clearly interested in the play and especially in gender inequities but seemed to be painting herself into a corner without anything else to write. After consulting a secondary document, Mary Ellen Lamb's 1998 article, "Gender, Sex, and Subordination in England: 1500–1800," on the subordination of women, student Mary was able to add information about men's perception of women as household managers and caretakers. She also learned about how Shakespeare included cross-dressing in his plays to represent comedically how women compensated for their powerlessness.

At this point in Mary's process, she was accumulating facts from both the play and an outside, secondary source. But Mary's thinking deepened and impassioned when she discovered William Whately's marriage sermon. Whately's description of the inferior female brought her thinking about gender inequality to a new level. She had not considered the early modern female perspective.

Mary first quoted Whately's sermon that "the duty of a wife is to 'confesse her inferiority' and then to 'carry her selfe as inferiour'" (49). Certainly, Mary had learned from secondary documents about the sixteenth-century British life that women were considered inferior, but it was not until she read Whately's sermon that she realized the necessity of women's acknowledgement and acceptance of a subservient role for marital happiness (36). She writes, "if she [a married woman] does not recognize this, then she will live woefully." Her understanding of early modern marriage through the words of a 1619 Puritan cleric allowed her to interact with Shakespeare's play on a different plane. She now saw Lady Macbeth as someone who was willing to risk everything, even her marriage as Macbeth's "dearest partner of greatness" (1.5.11), by throwing off her cloak of femininity when she pleads with spirits to unsex her.

Documents and Empathy

Most English teachers understand that the most powerful part of reading imaginative literature resides in the empathy characters evoke, especially those characters we do not understand. Reading *Macbeth* is a case in point. Is it possible to feel something akin to pity for the man who mercilessly murders his king, his best friend, women and children, his loyal allies? According to Paula Marantz Cohen, our polarized world is reason enough "to pause and think about where others are coming from" (*Of Human Kindness* 4). Empathy may be the only inroad to understanding others, especially when the *other* is not always someone else.

Reading Shakespeare can be an exercise in understanding humanity, but it may not be possible to embrace the full extent of Macbeth's psyche without the additional historiographies other voices provide. Shakespeare was not necessarily reenacting Guy Fawkes's attempt to kill King James, but he was undoubtedly living during a time when regicide was worth the risk. One student, Carson, learned about the Gunpowder Plot conspirators (Figure 3.13): how they rented a building where they intended to, first, tunnel to the House of Lords and, second, plant the gunpowder, which would ultimately kill King James I, who was purportedly attending a session of Parliament.

Secondary documents provided the purpose: a common hatred for James's treatment of English Catholics. Carson's exploration of primary documents, such Henry Garnet's "Treatise of Equivocation" and Robert Parsons's "A Treatise Tending to Mitigation towards Catholic Subjects in England," illuminated

FIGURE 3.12. *The Gunpowder Plot Conspirators, 1605* (de Passe).

how Catholics resorted to equivocations to escape religious persecution. What she had not considered was "the other side of the story." She may not have considered the effects of the plot on James I as revealed in a letter written by the Venetian ambassador in England, which shed a surprising perspective on the post-plot state of the monarchy. In his letter, he describes a terrified King, one who will not leave his premises, who will not appear publicly, who will not allow visitors.

> The king is in terror; he does not appear nor does he take his meals in public as usual. He lives in the innermost rooms, with only Scotchmen about him. The lords of the Council are also alarmed and confused by the plot itself and the king's suspicions; the city is in great uncertainty; Catholics fear heretics and vice-versa; both are armed; foreigners live in terror of their houses being sacked by the mob that is convinced that some, if not all, foreign Princes are at the bottom of the plot. The King and Council have very prudently thought it advisable to quiet the popular feelings by issuing a proclamation, in which they declare that no foreign Sovereign had any part in the conspiracy. God grant that this be sufficient but as it is everyone had his own share of alarm. (November 21, "Elizabeth" 293; qtd. in A. Kinney 112)

The letter's tone, sympathetic and vulnerable, certainly contrasts with James's confident need to maintain power, as shown in his address to Parliament four days after the incident or in his proclamation written to reassure his subjects by thanking God for his life and then proclaiming November 5 as a religious holiday.

Reading documents offering a variety of perspectives often presents narratives that may, on the surface, seem unequivocal. The Gunpowder Plot is not a single story and neither is our ability to situate Shakespeare's *Macbeth* in the middle of such turmoil. Primary documents expanded Carson's perspective on both perpetrators and victims in a strategic plot against a government. A multitextual approach invites multiple perspectives. We are richer knowing them all.

Teaching Shakespeare in the AP World

I hope I have conveyed to you, through my high school classroom stories about teaching with primary documents, that most of my students loved learning about what it was like to live in tumultuous, throbbing early modern society. If you imagine that all AP students, notably the most talented readers and writers in our schools, are all invested in "archaic" text before they enter AP Literature classrooms, you may not be *completely* correct. In fact, there were many who needed coaxing, encouraging, and downright pushing. But I will say that most, within very short order, became excited about learning more than what Shakespeare wrote within the covers of his own plays. Our writing and the subsequent discussions we had about why Shakespeare still matters were some of the most lively and interesting.

Teaching Shakespeare with primary documents was one of the most invigorating experiences not only for my students, but also for me. It was work. No doubt. But I could see student thinking expand and deepen in ways I have never seen before in all the years of my teaching. Providing the rich resources of diverse early modern thinkers to understand the influences surrounding Shakespeare's writing will continue to be a staple in my teaching.

4

Middle School Magic and *Midsummer*

Each year, when I take students to the Chicago Shakespeare Theater on Navy Pier, I often see rows and rows of middle school students who absolutely adore Shakespeare "live." Yet, a survey of English teachers in my area, West Michigan, revealed that fewer than 10 percent actually include any Shakespeare plays in their district's middle school curriculum. The reason was clear. Shakespeare's language is just too hard. Our middle school English language arts teachers, including a special education "push-in" teacher, decided to take the plunge. Together, we jumped in to see where the current would take us.

The Power of Story

My first day of teaching eighth grade in the middle school was a bit of a culture shock. Let's face it—I am a veteran high school teacher who was teaching middle school students about Shakespeare's world, and I had plenty to learn. I decided to enter the sixteenth century with an exploration of twenty-first-century pop culture, including novels, movies, videogames, and TV shows. Perhaps then we could look into the past to see if people had changed as much as four hundred years might indicate. Our district's core beliefs about reading included student-selected reading time each day, and I knew the enormous impact contemporary young adult novels had on my students. I needed to find a way into *Midsummer* that unlocked the same narrative power.

Traveling into the Past

We approached our journey as an exciting destination. If we were to enjoy the play together, I needed to share the experience with my guests' comfort levels in mind, considering their sense of adventure, their level of anxiety, and their thirst for knowledge. Without the same confidence and ability levels as their high school counterparts, younger students would have fewer tools to navigate figurative language. They needed multiple senses to experience the language and multiple readings to understand the plotlines. As in any trip, I had a clear idea of our destination but needed to navigate detours, staying within the speed limit yet taking backroads and shortcuts as necessary. These eighth graders wanted to have fun, and I hoped they would love Shakespeare as well as other early modern artists. I wanted them to feel free to sightsee a little, stopping when they needed more time or summarizing scenes when they needed to cruise faster. Flexibility was key.

To enter the world of London during the sixteenth century, we viewed an animated clip about Shakespeare, his writing, and the Globe.[22] Next, students made a T-chart to compare what they learned about the sixteenth century from the video clip with what they already knew about their own world. As we listed their sixteenth-century topics of interest, such as the theater, I introduced a T-chart to track thinking (Figure 4.1). "Let's talk about what it must have been like to go to one of Shakespeare's plays in the Globe Theatre, the one you saw in the clip," I said. "What did you notice about the Globe from the picture you saw?"

"It's round," said Richard.

"It has no roof!" said Zach.

"So, it must be hot in the summer," said Jaiden.

"And maybe hard to hear the actors," said Adam, "with all those people."

"That's a long time to stand," said Rebecca. "What did they do if they had to go to the bathroom?"

"Just pee!" yelled Messiah. I noticed that he had his hand up constantly. His body language told me he was interested in theater and especially interested in what it must have been like to go to a play during the sixteenth century.

"Actually," I said, "Messiah is correct. Most of the plays lasted at least two hours, and many of the groundlings, or the people who didn't have much money, had to stand in front of the stage for that long. And, yes, the men did pee where they could, I suppose. But the women couldn't do that easily. Sometimes they had buckets they tied under their dresses for that purpose."

"Ooh! That's gross!" said Ivy to her table partner but certainly loud enough for all of us to hear.

"There's no way!" said Brishene, laughing. Clearly, the students were "hooked" and wanted to know more.

Sixteenth Century	Twenty-First Century
Theater -little scenery -light	Theater -elaborate sets -dark

FIGURE 4.1. T-chart comparing sixteenth- and twenty-first-century theaters.

Introducing the Play

I had two jobs ahead of me: helping students understand the characters and their dilemmas and introducing the documents and their purposes.

We began by creating foldables to categorize the three worlds in *Midsummer* (Figure 4.2). On one side, students made three columns, one for the royal world, one for the rustic world, and one for the green world. As we approached each scene, we made lists of those characters who would "live" in that dimension; students practiced pronunciations of names and learned each character by his or her role. The royal world, for example, was made up of characters introduced in act 1, scene 1: Theseus, Hippolyta, Egeus, Hermia, Lysander, Demetrius, and Helena.

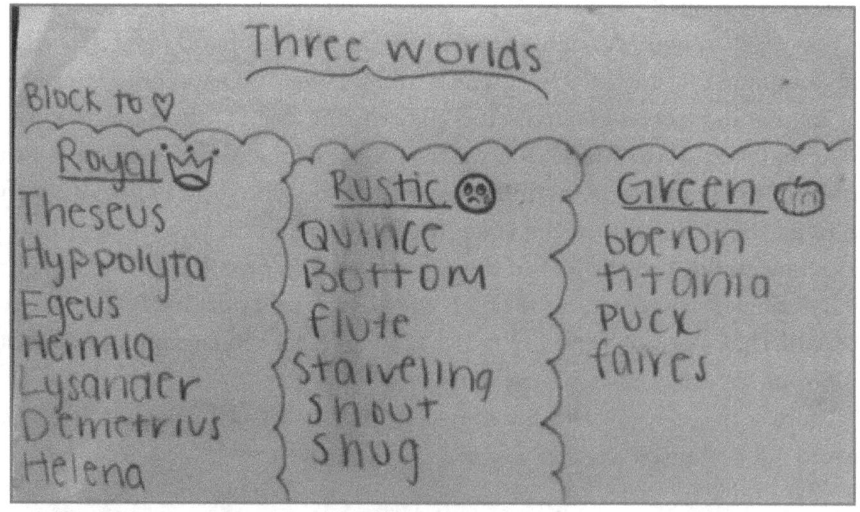

FIGURE 4.2. Student foldable:"Three Worlds."

Most students understood the differences among the three worlds and simplified the description to the *rich*, the *poor*, and the *magical*. Hannah, from the corner of the room, thought the green world was "more nature where plants and things were all green."

"Right," I said, "And, at night, when things were very dark, there might be a little magic." To capitalize on their interest in storytelling and to sensitize their ears to early modern language, I began telling the story of a royal couple, Hippolyta and Theseus, who are waiting to be wed. "How they met was not exactly the norm," I said, "because Theseus actually took Hippolyta as a prize when he won a war against the Amazons."

> These lines would have met with the approval of an Elizabethan audience imbued with patriarchal values: rebellious and disruptive womanhood, in the person of a warrior queen who had tried to overthrow one of the oldest civilizations, has been forced to submit to the "natural" order and is in the process of being returned to the civilized fold through marriage. (A. Taylor 49)

This was a perfect time to introduce the first primary document, an engraving by Levinus Hulsius from the German edition of Sir Walter Raleigh's *The Discovery of Guiana*. To understand the relationship of Theseus and Hippolyta, we read Theseus's words to his bride to be: "I woo'd thee with my sword, / and won thy love, doing thee injuries; / But I will wed thee in another key" (lines 17–19).

"Let's take a look at this engraving and think about what Theseus means when he tells Hippolyta that he won her love doing her injury," I said. "What do you think he means?"

"He hurt her?" one boy asked.

"How could he win her love if he hurt her?" another boy demanded from the back.

"Well, let's take a look at this engraving to see if we can find some answers. What do you notice in this picture [Figure 4.3]?"

The students were quiet, scrutinizing the detail in the darkened room. Finally, Messiah spoke up. "It looks like the ladies have the arrows, and they strung up two men and hung them upside down from a tree!"

"But they must be dead because they have arrows in their stomachs," said Austin.

"Or lower," said Messiah.

"And there's a fire to burn them to death just in case," said another. "So, who are these people?"

FIGURE 4.3. 1497 engraving from Raleigh's *The Discovery of Guiana* depicting Amazons practicing archery on their prisoners and preparing to roast their victims (23–24).

"According to Sir Walter Raleigh's writing, the Amazonians, female tribes from South America, were women warriors," I answered. "This text was written approximately five years before Shakespeare's play, so it's possible he would have heard about the reports from Raleigh to Queen Elizabeth I. In the play, Theseus attacks the Amazons and takes Hippolyta for his own. When he says, 'I will wed thee with another key,' what do you think he means?"

"Well, he probably doesn't mean a real key."

"Maybe like he's not going to hurt her now, just marry her. Now he loves her," said Harper. Students were connecting the primary document with the text, trying to make sense of both. Clearly, visual text would provide "another key" into narrative for these middle school students as they strove to imagine stories from pictures.

> **Document Discussions**
>
> Beginning with paintings, sketches, engravings, catalogues, and frontispieces is effective because middle school students have the opportunity to take their time in analyzing details. Visual texts provide common narratives that link Shakespeare's plays and twenty-first-century imaginative literature.

Despite inexperience with sixteenth-century documents from Europe, many of these middle school students had worked with primary documents before in social studies classes. I capitalized on their prior experiences to show them how primary sources would help us situate *Midsummer* in Shakespeare's world. After the initial run-through of the plot and several lines from scene 1, students did a quick-write[23] on one character "pair": Theseus and Hippolyta, Hermia and Lysander, or Demetrius and Helena (Figure 4.4). They wrote about these characters' situations, and many students, both male and female, included personal anecdotes about parents or past experiences. Jordan said, "Love is something that I understand." Morgan wondered what would happen to Hermia, Ava questioned why Demetrius didn't love Helena, and Hannah noted the conflict with all the females in the play.

FIGURE 4.4. Quick-writes provide time to reflect (see also Appendix B).

Madalynn wrote about the unfairness of how girls were treated and made the connection between Hermia's father rejecting her and Demetrius rejecting Helena. Madelyn's final comment was about Queen Elizabeth I: "How can a girl have little value and still become queen?" Her comment made me think, because I hadn't considered that middle school students would note gender inequities in a text-to-world connection. Their growing interest in early modern culture was changing how they perceived the action within the play. I wondered if primary documents might explain how the love relationships in the play, imbued with gender inequalities, mirrored the cultural norms during the time Shakespeare was writing.

Gender Trouble

The first primary document, the treatise *Of Domesticall Dvties: Eight Treatifes* (Gouge) (Figure 4.5), was powerful in that it clearly outlined a wife's duties.

The excerpt begins by quoting Ephesians 5:22–24:

> Wives, submit yourselves unto your husbands, as unto the Lord. For the husband is the head of the wife, even as Christ is the head of the church, and he is the Savior of the body. Therefore, as the Church is subject to Christ, so let wives be subject to their husbands in everything.

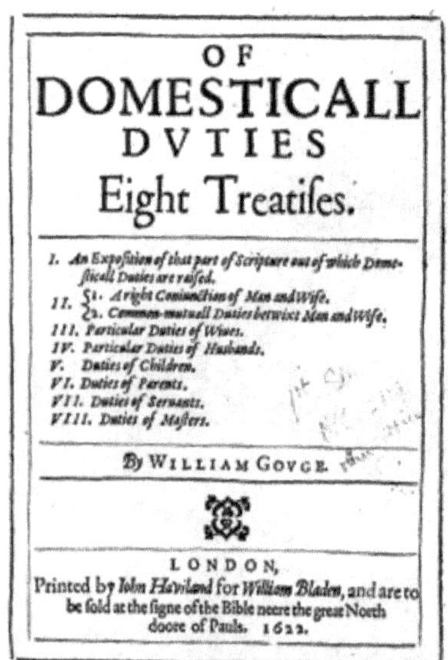

OF
DOMESTICALL
DVTIES
Eight Treatiſes.

I. An Expoſition of that part of Scripture out of which Domeſticall Duties are raiſed.
II. 1. A right Coniunction of Man and Wife.
2. Common-mutuall Duties betwixt Man and Wife.
III. Particular Duties of Wiues.
IV. Particular Duties of Husbands.
V. Duties of Children.
VI. Duties of Parents.
VII. Duties of Seruants.
VIII. Duties of Maſters.

By WILLIAM GOVGE.

LONDON,
Printed by Iohn Hauiland for William Bladen, and are to be ſold at the ſigne of the Bible neere the great North doore of Pauls. 1622.

FIGURE 4.5. Title page of *Of Domesticall Dvties: Eight Treatifes* (Gouge), including the third treatise: "Particular Duties of Wives."

I let that sink in for a few minutes after I read it aloud. The next section began with a heading that I asked Brigitte to read aloud: "Of an Husband's Superiority over a Wife, to Be Acknowledged by a Wife." "What is that saying?" I asked.

Brigitte thought a minute. "Well," she answered slowly, "I guess it's saying that, if you're married, then the husband gets to says what's what because he is superior."

"Anything else?" I asked.

John raised his hand. "I don't know what that other word is. Acknowl. . ."

"The word is *acknowledge*, and, in this case, it's a verb. Does anyone know what it means?"

Messiah spoke up. "It means the woman or the wife knows it. Like she thinks it's okay because she doesn't do anything to stop it."

"Okay, good," I answered. "Let's look at some of these duties that are outlined here. The date is 1622, so that's almost twenty-seven years after Shakespeare wrote *Midsummer*. But let's see if it makes sense. Do you think women would have had fewer or more rights when Shakespeare was writing *before* the *Domesticall Dvties* was written?"

Document Discussions

Whole-class discussions about documents are often strategic. Reading short sections first, followed by quick-writes or partner-talks, helps to provide a safe space. If students sit in groups of four, they can take turns sharing the group's ideas. Using Popsicle sticks, playing cards, or color wheels to have students report out are ways to begin.

"Less," said Brishene. This girl sat right up front, and I could tell from her expressions during class she wanted to talk but held back. Often, her hand would go up and then right back down.

"Brishene, why don't you read a few of these duties. Will you read number three?"

"'The titles and names whereby an husband is set forth do imply a superiority and authority in him, as Lord.' Does that mean she calls him *Lord*?" she asked, wide eyed. "Is he like a God?"

"Yes and no. It gives the male that right but only implies title, rather than religious significance. Think of it as being lord of a household as a master. Why don't you also read number one to see what else you can find out?"

"'God hath said of the man to the woman, He shall rule over thee.' Is that right?" she asked. "Did God really say that? Because it lists the Bible verse."

"Remember, this is William Gouge's interpretation of The Bible at that time. He is the author of this treatise. And a treatise is like an argument, the type of essay we have been studying. It focuses on a specific subject and argues a point. This treatise tells us not only about Gouge's ideas but also about others' views. Mostly men were writing during the early modern period and often wrote about proper behavior for a man and a woman. Do you think Shakespeare's characters behave in the same way as Gouge describes?"

Brishene nodded her head. "Egeus would like his daughter to do what he says, but she doesn't want to. The guys, even Theseus, seem to think they can boss all the girls around, but I don't think they like it."

Students had a copy of the excerpted primary document, but I also had a copy on the screen in the front of the room, so they could see my annotations, and I could point out specific language or direct their reading (Figure 4.6).

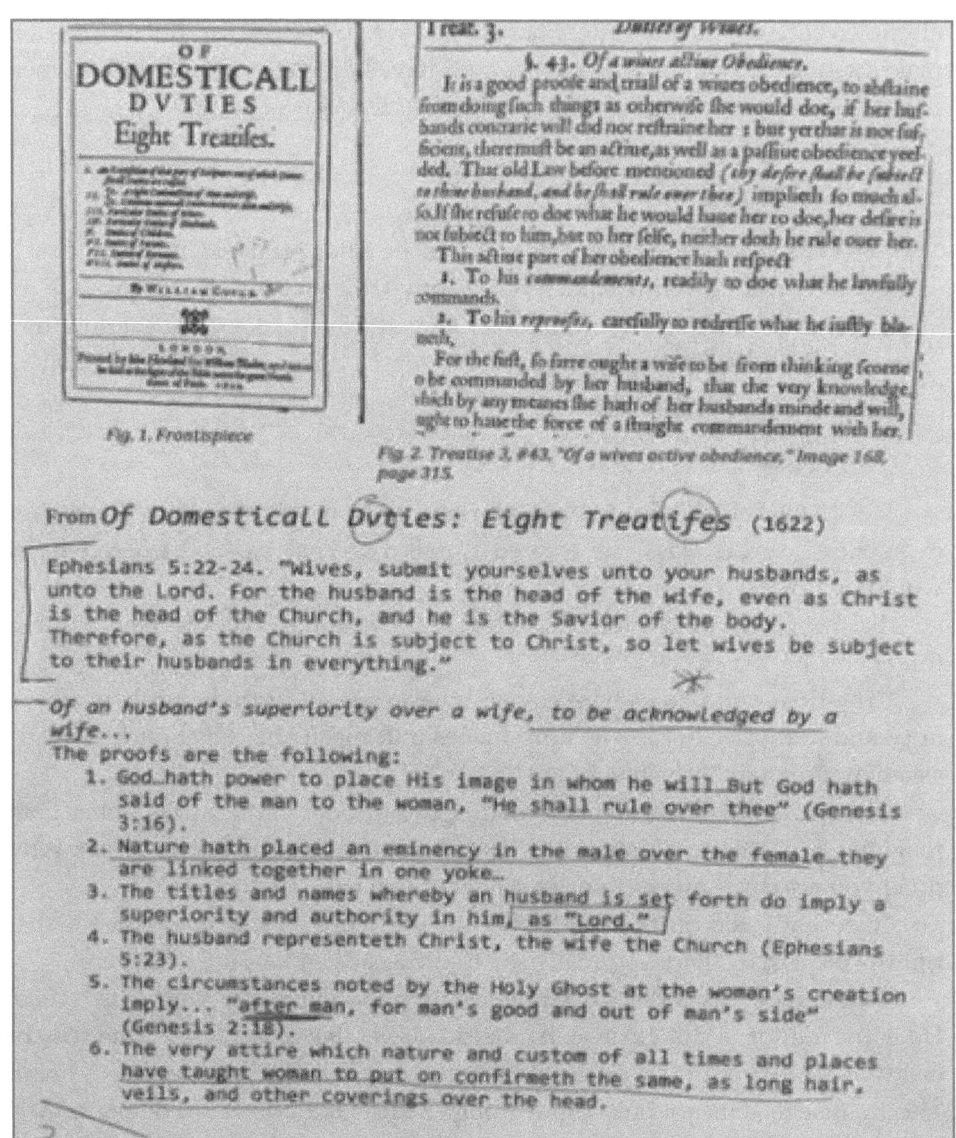

OF
DOMESTICALL
DVTIES
Eight Treatifes.

By William Gouge.

LONDON

Fig. 1. Frontispiece

Treat. 3. Duties of Wiues.

§. 43. Of a wiues actiue Obedience.

It is a good proofe and triall of a wiues obedience, to abftaine from doing fuch things as otherwife fhe would doe, if her hufbands contrarie will did not reftraine her: but yet that is not fufficient, there muft be an actiue, as well as a paffiue obedience yeelded. That old Law before mentioned (*thy defire fhall be fubiect to thine husband, and he fhall rule ouer thee*) implieth fo much alfo. If fhe refufe to doe what he would haue her to doe, her defire is not fubiect to him, but to her felfe, neither doth he rule ouer her.

This actiue part of her obedience hath refpect

1. To his *commandements*, readily to doe what he lawfully commands.

2. To his *reproofes*, carefully to redreffe what he iuftly blameth.

For the firft, fo farre ought a wife to be from thinking fcorne to be commanded by her husband, that the very knowledge which by any meanes fhe hath of her husbands minde and will, ought to haue the force of a ftraight commandement with her.

Fig. 2. Treatise 3, #43, "Of a wives active obedience," Image 168, page 315.

From *Of Domesticall Dvties: Eight Treatifes* (1622)

Ephesians 5:22-24. "Wives, submit yourselves unto your husbands, as unto the Lord. For the husband is the head of the wife, even as Christ is the head of the Church, and he is the Savior of the body. Therefore, as the Church is subject to Christ, so let wives be subject to their husbands in everything."

Of an husband's superiority over a wife, to be acknowledged by a wife...

The proofs are the following:

1. God…hath power to place His image in whom he will…But God hath said of the man to the woman, "He shall rule over thee" (Genesis 3:16).
2. Nature hath placed an eminency in the male over the female…they are linked together in one yoke…
3. The titles and names whereby an husband is set forth do imply a superiority and authority in him, as "Lord."
4. The husband representeth Christ, the wife the Church (Ephesians 5:23).
5. The circumstances noted by the Holy Ghost at the woman's creation imply... "after man, for man's good and out of man's side" (Genesis 2:18).
6. The very attire which nature and custom of all times and places have taught woman to put on confirmeth the same, as long hair, veils, and other coverings over the head.

FIGURE 4.6. Teacher annotations of *Of Domesticall Dvties* (Gouge).

"Look at the top of the page in the box where it says '43. Of a wiues actiue obedience.' The spelling here is different, right? Sometimes a *u* takes the place of a *v*, and an *s* looks like an elongated *f*. You might also see an *i* for a *j*. So, follow along while I read. 'If fhe refufe to doe what he would haue her to doe, her defire is not fubiect to him, but to her felfe . . . to his commandements, readily to doe what he lawfully commands.' So, does a wife have to do what her husband commands?" I asked.

Hannah, in the back corner, nodded. I made eye contact with her. "What do you think?"

"It sounds like she has to," Hannah answered. "I mean, it says the word *law*."

"Do you think the law extends to fathers and daughters too?" I asked.

"Probably," she said.

These thirteen-year-olds now understood why Hermia and Lysander felt the need to run away when faced with a disagreeable father whose dogged will to have his daughter marry Demetrius would not be quelled.

Writing Stamina

To begin the next class period, I wanted students to reflect on their learning about family relationships through primary documents. This would be our first quick-write about documents, and I was hoping they would go beyond the five minutes I gave them on the first day of class. I explained that primary documents could be anything that was written during a specific time period. Their job was to write about how Shakespeare develops the theme of family relationships by analyzing at least two documents, including the play. Other documents could be visual texts, such as Hulsius's engraving of the Amazon women, the scold's bridle, or the digital text *Of Domesticall Dvties* (Gouge)—the *Teaching Shakespeare* website (shakespearedocuments.info) features accessible, digitized copies of numerous such engravings, sketches, and treatises for students to download and use.

These were complex sixteenth-century texts, and students were indeed rising to the challenge.

Our first writing was no easy task. These were complex sixteenth-century texts, and students were indeed rising to the challenge.

As a formative assessment of what they were learning, the writing was also an opportunity to build stamina. I gave them ten minutes, and every single student made it to five minutes this time. Approximately half of the group worked the entire time, and half stopped writing between six and seven minutes (Figures 4.7 and 4.8). We made progress! One student wrote:

> Family is a theme in mid-summer dream by showing how women should act for example egeus want Hermia to marry demetrius but she has other Plans . . . She has been in love with lysander and wants to marry him. So She wants to defi her father Which Back then is illegal in one of the line Theseus says "To you your father should be as a god." In *Domesticall Duties* Women are not as important as men back then so they made rules.

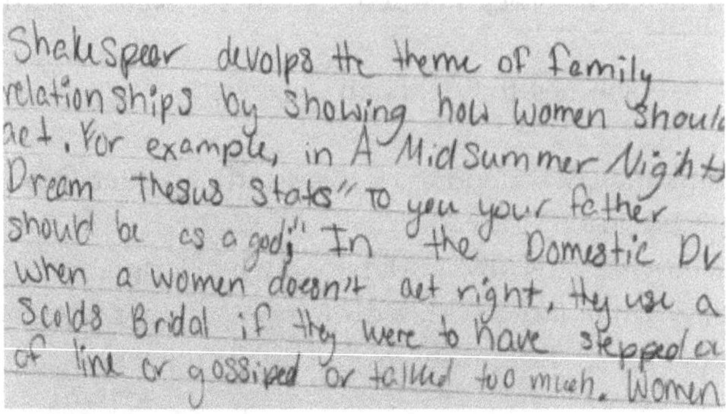

Shakspear devolps the theme of family relationships by showing how women should act. For example, in A Midsummer Nights Dream Thesus stats "To you your father should be as a god;" In the Domestic Dr when a women doesn't act right, they use a Scolds Bridal if they were to have stepped out of line or gossiped or talked too much. Women

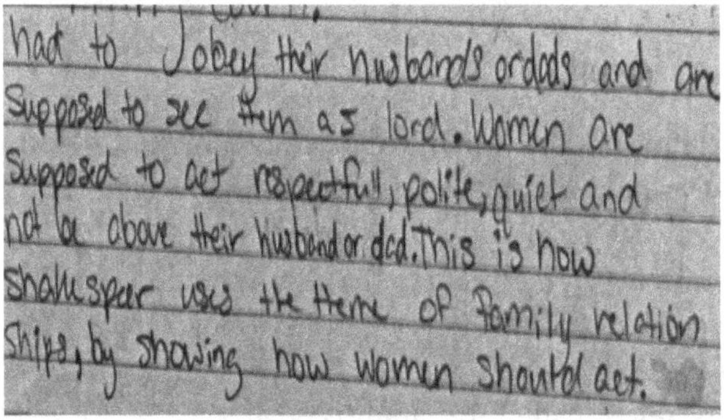

had to obey their husbands ordeds and are supposed to see them as lord. Women are supposed to act respectfull, polite, quiet and not be above their husband or dad. This is how Shakspear uses the theme of family relation ships, by showing how women should act.

FIGURES 4.7 and 4.8. Student writing on how early modern writers develop the theme of family relationships.

Another student wrote about women obeying their husbands and fathers and having to act respectfully, politely, quietly without being "above" the male members of their families. Both students zeroed in on what they were learning about family dynamics during the sixteenth century through the writings of two writers, Shakespeare and Gouge. Instinctively, they were connecting Hermia's reaction to her father's demands to their own by focusing on this portion of the play, but they reported the information factually, rather than emotionally. What struck me most was how focused they were on the language of both documents, citing both Egeus's words to his daughter and Gouge's language in his treatise. This was only a few days into our work together, and already they were moving beyond the plot of the play into the realm of Shakespeare's cultural backdrop. I saw neither questioning eyes, nor furrowed foreheads, nor frantic whispers. Only writing. It was a beautiful sight.

At this point, I realized something about middle school students and their reactions to Shakespeare or any other early modern text: students needed a visual component to anchor thinking.

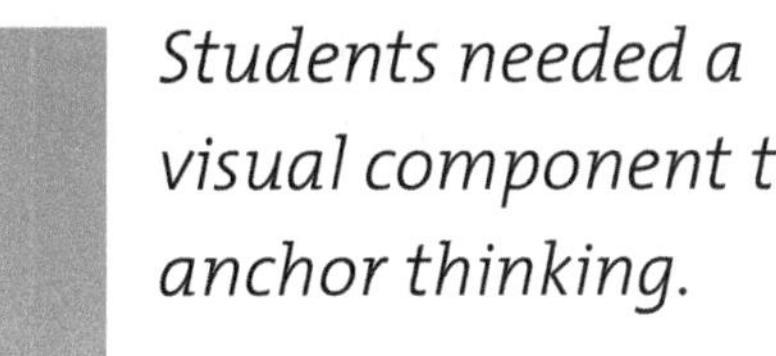

These students live and breathe visual text daily, both images and visual representations of font, lettering, and spelling, and I needed to make good use of and begin with the text types they knew best. Instead of using the digital text of *Pyramus and Thisbe*, the story from scene 2 as enacted by the rude mechanicals, I incorporated a visual text of Thisbe finding her love, Pyramus, after he kills himself. With this on the screen as a backdrop, I told them the story. This age group forced me to think about every move I made in the classroom and the strategies I have tried over the years; I needed to incorporate them strategically.[24] I used my lesson plans as a base but had to be flexible enough to change, edit, omit, and add—much like the techniques I teach students in the revision process. The same holds true for lesson plans; they need to be dynamic, fluid, and open ended. In fact, using documents in act 1 forced me to rethink how to approach act 2.

Focusing on conflict and resolution, we began with visual text and moved to pertinent highlighted portions of digital text. Act 2 of *Midsummer* explodes with conflict: Titania's and Oberon's stormy spat, Oberon's retaliatory plan, Puck's innocent misadventure, Helena's futile attempt, and Lysander's delusional blunder. During this act, resolution seems ineffectual, but students can relate to how life is full of misunderstandings.

Act 2—Primary Documents on Conflict and Resolution

Visual texts

- Samuel Rowlands, *Well Met Gossip: OR, Tis Merrie When Gossips Meete*, John Deane, 1619, frontispiece
- Hans Holbein, *The Ambassadors*, 1533, National Gallery, London, painting
- "The Merry Milk-Maid: Being, Her Longing-Desire after Matrimony, That She Might Be One of the Honourable Society of Gossips," 1690, song
- Antonio Tempesta, *Thisbe Killing Herself*, 1606, etching

Digital texts

- *The Gossips Braule, OR, The Women Weare the Breeches. A Mock Comedy*, 1654, play
- Desiderius Erasmus, *A Maid Hating Marriage*, 1523, play
- *The Schoolhouse of Women*, 1541, poem
- Sir Walter Raleigh, "The Lie," 1608, poem
- "A Letter of the Lady Jane, Sent unto her Father," 1554
- Ovid, *Metamorphoses*, 8 CE, poem (translated by A. S. Kline, 2000)

All of these primary documents, and many more besides, can be found in the accompanying website *Teaching Shakespeare* (shakespearedocuments.info).

Magic and the Green World

I began act 2 by showing contemporary interpretations of Puck as a trickster archetype, similar to Bugs Bunny. First, I asked them to name tricksters from movies, such as Johnny Depp playing Captain Jack Sparrow or *The Mask* played by Jim Carrey. Their lists were extensive, adding characters and movies, such as Kevin from *Home Alone*, Stewie from *Family Guy*, Swiper from *Dora the Explorer*, Billy Madison, Tom and Jerry, and SpongeBob.

"Based on your list, how would you describe the trickster's personality?" I asked.

"A trickster plays tricks," said Zach. Everyone laughed.

"Good one," said Messiah. "He's funny, but he lies."

"He's crafty," said Harper.

"But in a good way," said Richard.

"Is he mean?" I asked.

"No!" came shouts from the room.

We listened to the *Flocabulary* hip-hop version of one Fairy's description of Robin Goodfellow and the pranks he plays on common folk ("*A Midsummer Night's Dream*: Act 2, Scene 1"), such as "mislead[ing] night-wanderers" or "fright[ening] the maidens of the villager" (2.1.36, 40). Robin Goodfellow—or Puck, as he is called in the play—did not seem mean in any way, but his picture, sketched in 1639, elicited mixed responses (Figure 4.9).

"Let's look for a full sixty seconds at this picture in silence, noting the details. We will share after the full minute is up." I dimmed the lights and started the timer. They stared. The minute, I'm sure, seemed interminable, but they remained quiet. "What do you notice?" I asked.

"He's huge!" said one boy from the back.

"He has boobs!" said another, and we all laughed.

"He has ears like a rabbit," said a girl.

"But he's carrying a broom. But what's that thing in his right hand? A candle? Or a knife?"

"It's definitely a knife. Look at the end of it."

"Someone is blowing a horn."

"Maybe that's why the people are dancing around him."

"They're pretty small."

"Ok, let's focus on the bottom half of the picture. What do you notice there?" I asked.

FIGURE 4.9. Illustration from the title page of *Robin Good-Fellow, His Mad Prankes and Merry Jests.*

"He has feet like an animal. Like hoofs."

"Is he a devil?"

The room was silent.

The more the students noticed, the more they realized that Shakespeare had indeed changed the early modern image of Robin Goodfellow into a trickster character who does Oberon's spiteful bidding but without malice. Instead of a devilish adult, Shakespeare's changes introduce a friendly Peter Pan type.

Students seemed engaged, but I often felt as if I were pulling these students through the information, because I was not sure, from day to day, which documents or parts of the play would elicit true excitement.

Document Discussions

Adapting to the document approach often includes adaptive responses to diversity, engagement, and skill. Frontloading documents with stories, pop culture references, and audio/visuals builds prior knowledge and engagement with early modern documents.

Was Shakespeare too difficult for middle school students? Sometimes they put their heads down as if to say, "I don't want to do this." Vassar stretched out over two chairs without much interest in writing. Yet he had the most to say, remembered everything I said, and seemed to "get it." Jordan was quiet but willing to risk answering questions. Hannah remembered details. Messiah had a mind like a sieve and had his hand up for every question but would not write more than a word or two.

I had an idea. I asked them to turn to the next page in their writer's notebooks to "get ready to write." I said, "I'm going to show you a clip, and then I want you to write anything that comes to mind for five minutes." Using Michael Hoffman's 1999 version of *Midsummer*, I showed the fight between Titania and Oberon, then the part when Oberon instructs Puck to find the flower that Cupid shoots with an arrow. Students watched Oberon place a drop of magic flower juice in Titania's eyes to make her fall in love with the next "person" she sees. When the clip ended, I said, "Before you begin writing, I'd like to give you just a little more information about early modern fairies. The green world, or the place where fairies lived, provided a 'free zone' for girls, especially girls who were a little rebellious. Do you see any rebellious females so far in *Midsummer*?" Several hands went up.

"Hannah?"

"Well, Hermia. She doesn't want to marry Demetrius, so she runs away."

"Right. Anyone else?"

"How about Helena?" asked Jordan. "She isn't just sitting around waiting for Demetrius. She goes to the woods to find him and get him back."

"What about Titania?" asked Chloe. "She's a fairy, though, but she is saying no to Oberon."

"Good point. She is a fairy, and in fact may be just a product of the imagination. What that means is that she is not really in human form—she doesn't think like a human—so she is free to think in new ways about all the rules of society. Does that make sense?"

I looked around and could see a few nods of assent. Their eyes were still focused on me, so I continued. "In the next act, Titania will say, 'I am a spirit of no common rate' [3.1.154], so that must mean she is a special fairy. And we know that because of what you just said, Chloe. She defies Oberon's demand for the changeling boy."

"So, is she going to help Hermia?" asked Chloe.

"Well, let's see what happens next. But just know this: during Shakespeare's time, the early modern period, people believed fairies to be ruled by a female. Also, the green world is a bit of a safe zone for females who are trying to go against the males who are trying to keep them in a subservient role. So, as you are writing, think about how Shakespeare might be telling a story that incorporates some of the ideas people had about magic or the supernatural."

> Fairy beliefs were part of an oral tradition largely attributed to and preserved by women, whether in witchcraft depositions or in fireside tales. (Buccola 60)

They wrote. Most wrote the full five minutes. Vassar, Jaiden, and Quinden stared out the window. Ryann said she had a headache. Then, I pulled something out of thin air: "Trade with the next person next to you, and we'll try a *silent* discussion. If you wrote more than two sentences, raise your hand." Those who raised their hands traded notebooks with someone near, but I noticed something interesting. Those who had not written much looked around. Their faces told me they wanted to participate. This was something new and could be something fun to do with their writing.

"Read your new partner's writing and add two sentences of your own to share your thinking with them." Then, when they returned notebooks and read their neighbor's writing, they chose three words to describe the movie clip in a *whip-around* (see Appendix B) where each student reads a quick response. Most participated, but I was still surprised at how this task was impossible for Vassar, Richard, and Messiah. I needed to find out why.

"Writing Floats on a Sea of Talk"

At the end of act 2, we looked at a few primary documents that spoke to the conflict students noted in the play. They were especially aware of the emerging problem between Helena and Hermia because of Puck's mistaken identity as he tries to make use of his love potion or "love-in-idleness." We looked at the visual of the gossip's bridle again as well as the frontispiece from *The Gossips Braule*, a mock comedic play with female characters who do not "know their places." According to Paster and Howard, a *gossip* had many meanings, including a godparent, a same-sex friendship, or "female intimates who attended childbirth" (218) who then passed a gossip's cup to celebrate. The most familiar meaning, however, is that of idle chatter or the person, usually female, who participates. I shared this new definition and asked, "Can you think of any characters who might fit the description of a gossip?"

"Well, Helena and Hermia are supposed to be friends," said Megan.

"Yeah, but it's not working," said a voice in the back.

"Let's see if we can find out more about that word *gossip*," I said, "especially the part about girls not knowing their places."

Students had a copy of the excerpt from *A Maid Hating Marriage* (also referred to as *The Marriage Hater*) (Erasmus 140–48; Paster and Howard 227–31), a play written in 1523, but I decided I needed to recap the story first: "In this play, two young people, Catherine and her male friend Eubulus, are discussing Catherine's dilemma with her parents." I pulled up the play on the projector and asked students to draw boxes around or highlight specific passages they could refer to later, specifically the ones where Catherine shares her desire to become a nun and her parents' wishes for her to marry instead.

Document Discussions

One idea for working with documents with middle school students is to project the document and highlight sections. Students engage more closely with several, short passages, rather than with one long piece of text.

In one section, the students read the parent's response as described by Catherine: "They gave me a promise that when I had attained to seventeen years of age, they would submit to my desire."

"Catherine waited. And waited. She turned seventeen, but her parents changed their minds and broke their promise. They told her she had to marry."

"That's not fair," said Brishene. "She should just run away, so they can't find her."

"Girls that age could not always do that," I said. "They had no money of their own and probably nowhere to go. What do you think Eubulus advised?"

"He wants to marry her himself," said Messiah.

"Well, let's see what he says. 'I would advise thee to adventure upon no new thing against thy parents' minds . . . To neglect father and mother upon some occasion for Christ's sake is a pious thing . . . thou mayest put thyself in the power of a counterfeit father instead of a true one.' So, does Eubulus agree with Catherine?"

"No!" said a few voices from the side of the room.

"What is his worry?" I asked.

"She might get tricked. But how could that happen if it's the church?" These students were asking provocative questions, but I still felt as though I was leading the discussion without allowing them to make meaning from the text themselves. James Britton's words, "writing floats on a sea of talk," were in my brain (29). I needed to loosen or to let go of my own reins on their learning and allow these curious students time to share their ideas with each other before they wrote, but I also needed to stay pointed toward the written assessment, scaffolding our progress toward an essay that finds evidence from primary documents regarding how Shakespeare develops relevant historical themes.

First, I drew a graphic organizer (Figure 4.10) to help the students focus on the elements of the question. Next, using the theme of female power, I decided to write an unfinished sample essay, one that I could project on the screen for two purposes. First, I wanted to introduce the idea of *transportable writing moves*, those techniques writers use that can be transported to our own writing. Students often ask, "How do I write an introduction?" or "How do I write about evidence in an interesting way?" Students often have ideas but do not know how to put them in words on the paper. We all know writing takes practice, but these students needed some models from other writers. They often do not consider themselves writers, but I wanted to show them how much they could learn from each other. I began with the introduction.

Themes

- family and obligations
- conflict and resolution
- fairies and supernatural
- work and rank
- celebrations and entertainment

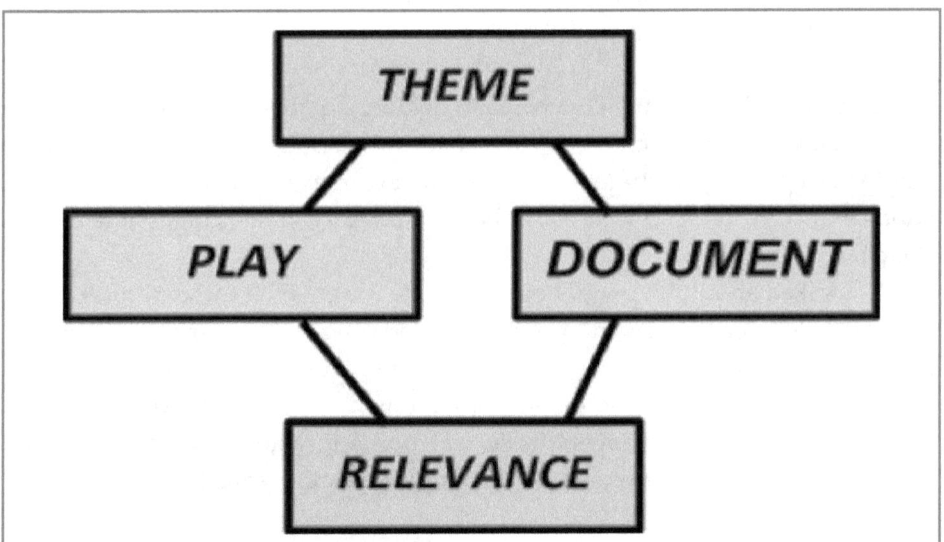

FIGURE 4.10. Graphic organizer for writing.

"Notice how the first paragraph is structured," I said. "This writer introduced the theme, female power, in the first sentence and talked about it in a general way. What did the writer do in the next sentence?"

> The theme of female power is one that is in many books and movies today. Females have not always had equal power with males, and during the early modern period, this was no exception. Males were able to decide who would marry their daughters and what their wives would do. William Shakespeare, poet and actor, develops the theme of female power in *A Midsummer Night's Dream*, drawing upon what was happening in his culture.

Morgan raised her hand. "It's saying that girls didn't have power then, and they don't now."

"Right, Morgan, and we can see what female power is by showing what it isn't: males decide who marries their daughters and told their wives what to do. So, as the writer, I'm saying that the females in *A Midsummer Night's Dream* may not have power over their own lives. If the thesis is what you want to say about the idea of female power, what am I trying to prove?"

Joslyn raised her hand. "That Shakespeare wrote about what it was like to be a girl back then?"

> The introduction is often one of the hardest parts of an essay. I tell my students to start somewhere in the middle, explore ideas, and take me on an intellectual journey trying to answer a question that seems important to you. (Carey-Webb interview)

"Right," I said. "So now I have to find evidence of this same theme in *primary documents*, which are documents from that time period, right? The play we are reading is a primary document, so I need to find an example there and one from another document—and that could be a visual text, a painting, engraving, or sketch."

As I talked about the play, I began to write the essay at the computer, which was projected on the screen. Yes, it was nerve-wracking, writing in front of these students, making mistakes, correcting them, taking risks. I thought these students would start talking to each other, bored, and possibly drown out my words. But that didn't happen. They watched and listened without saying a word. I wrote the next two paragraphs, thinking aloud while I was writing.

In Shakespeare's play, not all the characters have power and those who try to gain power are punished. For example, Egeus does not allow his daughter Hermia to marry the man she would like to marry, Lysander. She must run away to gain power, and, even then, she has trouble trying to figure out how to make it work. Titania also tries to obtain power in her relationship with Oberon, but, when she asserts herself, he finds a way to punish her: he asks Puck to find a flower, love-in-idleness, so he can squeeze the juice from this flower in Titania's eyes when she is sleeping. Once she wakes up, she will fall in love with the first person or animal she sees, a joke that will teach her a lesson. Shakespeare shows what happens to females if they try to take matters into their own hands.

I talked about how I knew I had to include specific examples from the play, such as when Hermia is not allowed to marry Lysander, the man of her dreams. Her father gives her an ultimatum, so she flees, thinking it may be her only recourse. But I knew that one example would not be enough to make my point about how Shakespeare develops the theme of female power. I added the conflict between Oberon and Titania, conveying the idea of Titania's powerlessness when Oberon does not get what he wants.

Finally, I added a third paragraph about the document we read together, *A Maid Hating Marriage* (Erasmus 140–48; Paster and Howard 227–31). In this paragraph, I talked about using a transition to show that I was adding another example from a different document and knew I had to include the title and the year it was written. No one really knows what Shakespeare read during the time he was writing, but I assumed he was familiar with many of the great writers of his day, including Erasmus. I asked my students what I should do after I mentioned the title and author. "You need to talk about it," said Messiah.

Another example is from the primary document *A Maid Hating Marriage* written by Erasmus in 1523, approximately seventy years before Shakespeare wrote *Midsummer*. In this play, two characters are trying to figure out a problem. Catherine wants to go into the nunnery and she is asking Eubulus for advice. She complains that her parents want her to marry instead. Her friend tells her she must obey her parents. Shakespeare may have heard about the play and understood the power struggles between fathers and daughters at that time.

"Right," I said. "What I need to do is add a few sentences about that play and then say why I believe it's important."

These students did not see an entire essay, but they did see me work through the first draft of a few sections, similar to their writing on their assessment. Next, we talked about today's question: "How does Shakespeare develop the theme of conflict and resolution, using two primary documents, including *A Midsummer Night's Dream*, as evidence?"

"Let's define our terms first," I said. What is *conflict*?" They were able to tell me that a conflict is a problem, and the resolution is how it is solved. We made a list: Egeus wants his daughter to marry Demetrius, Hermia wants to marry Lysander, Oberon is mad at Titania about the changeling boy, Puck puts the flower drops in the wrong person's eyes. They realized they had evidence from the play. We reviewed the visual documents they had seen so far: the Amazons, Pyramus and Thisbe, *Robin Good-Fellow*, and the scold's bridle. We talked about how to analyze a visual text and reviewed *Of Domesticall Dvties* (Gouge). We scanned the documents from act 2, *The Gossips Braule* and *A Maid Hating Marriage*. I also projected the frontispiece of the 1619 edition of Samuel Rowlands's *Well Met Gossip: OR, Tis Merrie When Gossips Meete* (Figure 4.11)—a dialogue between a widow, a maid, and a wife, considered to be the three female stations of life beyond childhood.

During a time when "good" women were chastised unless they were silent, virginal, and obedient, Rowlands's dialogue of three women enjoying time together without men may have seemed outlandish. As we walked through the highlighted portions of the play *A Maid Hating Marriage* (Erasmus 140–48; Paster and Howard 227–31), we talked about the two main characters, Eubulus and Catherine. They are best friends and saddened because Catherine may not be able to go into the nunnery. Her parents want her to wed and tell her to wait until she is seventeen—she complies, but then they change their minds. Eubulus tells her to obey her parents. This shows a big conflict. Projecting the sample introduction on the screen, I gave the students the last fifteen minutes of the class to write. They wrote. Just before the bell rang, I asked them to raise their hands if they were not finished. Most of the class raised their hands. I cheered! "That means you had more to say. Congratulations!" Some days are like that. Just plain good.

Before moving on, I thought it was time to formatively check their understanding of the play. We did a 3–2–1 activity (see Appendix B).[25] Responses informed my thinking and changed the next day's teaching strategy. Students were confident about what they knew. They seemed to have the plot line in place sequentially and understood the three worlds and the conflicts that arose as character groups intersected, such as when the royals went to the green world or when the fairies interacted with the rustics.

FIGURE 4.11. Frontispiece of *Well Met Gossip: OR, Tis Merrie When Gossips Meete* (Rowlands), an early modern primary document.

Student Questions after Act 2

- Why has Puck not done more jokes?
- Who will marry Hermia and Helena?
- What does the set look like?
- Why is Helena so annoying?
- Why are the rude mechanicals part of the story?
- Why does Puck not talk much?
- What is Puck?
- When was this play created?
- Why doesn't Demetrius love Helena?
- Why can't they choose who to marry?
- Why can a girl be queen but others have no power?
- Why are there so many people in the play?
- What will happen with Hermia and Lysander?

What seemed most confusing were characters' names, early modern language, and misunderstandings when the fairies complicated human dilemmas. Most of these confusions could be cleared up with additional review and a large-group discussion. I was most impressed with their questions and desire to understand characters' behaviors as well as to predict future events.

Assigning Roles

I assigned roles for students to play throughout the unit, making sure they had a voice in who to play. Each student requested three characters they wanted to play, or which "world"—royal, rustic, or green—they preferred. Another idea is to have students play several roles but to follow one character throughout the play, noting development or place in the conflict.

Caden's question, "What is Puck?," interested me. Caden plays the role of Puck when we read aloud, so he is admitting that he doesn't know how to play the role. Our past discussions about and the visual text of Robin Goodfellow confused him. Caden was really asking, "Am I a good guy or a bad guy?"

My answer, "What has Puck done so far in the play that might help you define his character?" actually spurred significant discussion, which would be helpful as we approached the next set of documents on magic and the supernatural. Another reason to pause and reflect is that it allows students insight into the class mindset. None of us had all the answers. They knew they were working with difficult text that required a combination of reading, viewing, listening, and moving to create meaning. Even if they were not embracing confusion, they were at least in a state of toleration. My goal was to move into two short documents, one primary and one secondary, that focused on fairies (Table 4.1)—a topic most middle school students enjoyed, based on their love of fantasy.

The first document contained excerpts from *The Anatomy of Melancholy* and *The Discovery of Witchcraft*, both discourses on fairy behavior and interaction with humans. The secondary document, an excerpted chapter from *The Elizabethan Fairies: The Fairies of Folklore and the Fairies of Shakespeare*, compares Shakespeare's vision with his pop culture lore. Each student pair received both documents, each student reading one or the other. While reading, they annotated, jotting margin notes that commented on the text, such as Burton's description of Robin Goodfellow as "a bigger kinde" of hobgoblin that would "grinde corne for a messe of milk." One student wrote, "seems like human size" and "does jobs for food." Students then convened in two large groups. Standing with those who

TABLE 4.1. Fairies and the supernatural: Primary and secondary documents.

Text comparisons	Robert Burton, *The Anatomy of Melancholy*, 1621, and Reginald Scot, *The Discoverie of Witchcraft*, 1584
Pamphlet	*Robin Good-Fellow, His Mad Prankes, and Merry Iests*, 1639
Poem	Richard Corbett, "A Proper New Ballad Entitled The Fairies' Farewell: or God-A-Mercy Will," 1620
Lore	John Aubrey, "Fairies and Robin Goodfellow," *The Remains of Gentilism and Judaism*, 1688
Frontispiece	John Parkinson, *Paradisi in Sole*, 1629
Poem	Robert Herrick, "Oberon's Feast," 1648
Scholarly article	Marjorie Swann, "The Politics of Fairylore in Early Modern English Literature," *Renaissance Quarterly*, 2000
Paintings	Joseph Noel Paton, Amelia Jane Murray, Edward Robert Hughes, *Oberon and Titania, Fairies Floating Downstream, Midsummer Eve*
Scholarly chapter	Minor White Latham, "Shakespeare's Fairies," *The Elizabethan Fairies: The Fairies of Folklore and the Fairies of Shakespeare*, 1972 [originally published 1930], pp. 176–218

Note: Students can easily access the documents suggested here and elsewhere in this book through the *Teaching Shakespeare* website (shakespearedocuments.info).

read the same document, they shared their annotations, questions, and speculations. Back at their partner tables, they each made T-square notes where they reviewed the content of their documents, then boiled down big ideas into bulleted points (Figure 4.12).

I roamed the room, looking and listening for ideas from each group I could put on the whiteboard. When students noticed I was taking notes on their thinking to transfer to the board, they began to work more earnestly to see their own ideas transcribed. Eventually, I had transferred many of their ideas about the two articles to the board. This was the first time these eighth-grade students had read and discussed documents independently, creating their own meaning and comparing authors' ideas. It was loud in the room—and focused—a sure sign of engagement.

English Language Arts Team Meetings

Our team checked in with each other often throughout the day, but we needed time to discuss how our classes were faring with the play and other early modern documents. Collaborative conversations with experienced middle school teachers about classroom management and strategies helped me gain

Fairies of Shakespeare	*Digression and Discourse*
Not demonic Not sneaky Loveable Very nice Not harmful Travel for peace Cuter Refuse to discomfort people Don't demand money for service	Fairies steal stuff Capture humans Disturb children/humans Not kind Mean Tricksters (mean) Wear green Live in mountains and taverns Dangerous to refuse their fairy gifts

FIGURE 4.12. Student T-chart notes comparing fairies in two different primary documents.

confidence and skill. Did they feel the same rollercoaster effect of intermittent success and failure, independence and dependence, engagement and passivity? A meeting after school brought the rest of the team together where we could report success and vent frustration.

"It's going fine," said Kristin, looking across the table at her student teacher. "Meg is doing a great job. She did a character chart on the wall where she put up character names as they appear in the play." (See Figure 4.13.)

"We revisit that every day. These students simply cannot remember who is who." I looked at the wall and saw the names of the main characters with arrows pointing to their love interest. It was a great way to manipulate the names to show how relationships changed throughout the play.

"Most of the time, I feel like I don't know what I'm doing," admitted Meg with a sad smile. "Each day, I have to review the plot. I'm getting more and more behind!"

"Do we have a time limit set in stone?" I asked. "I'm also behind the original schedule, but, if it doesn't matter, then we're okay."

Luke nodded. "We don't have to rush," he said. "Let's just do this and not worry about it. This has been fun!"

I turned to Laura, our special education push-in teacher. "How do you think your students are doing?" I was thinking of the four I had who were struggling readers and often had trouble staying focused and centered.

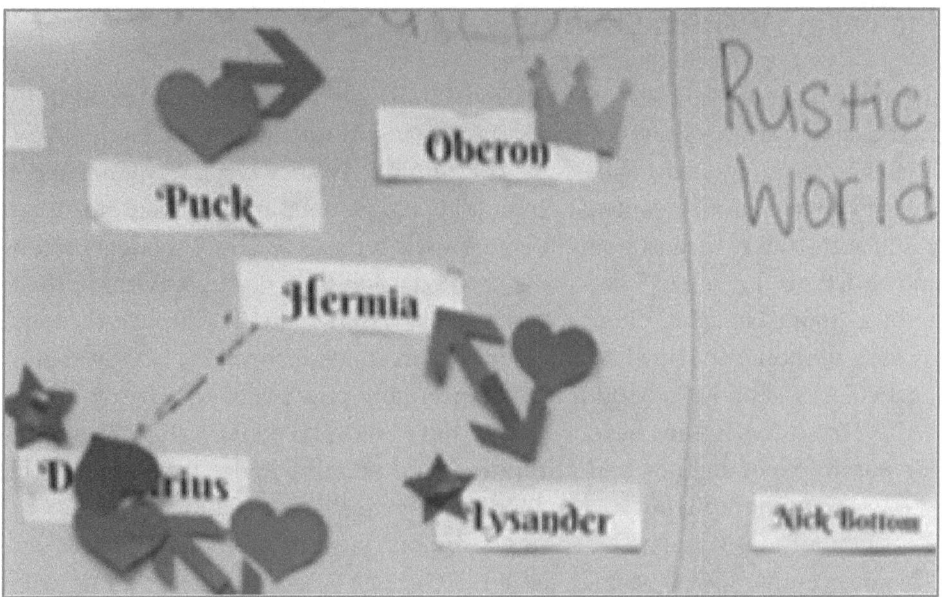

FIGURE 4.13. Student teacher's character chart, which helps students visualize characters' relationships.

"So far, so good," she said. "I often have to check in with them while they are working in small groups or independently, but we haven't had anything unusual. In one of my other classes," she added, "we had a parent call to say his daughter may not read *Midsummer* during this unit. Evidently, the play is about fairies, and that is against their religion. So, we will have to find another play for her. He wanted to use *A Comedy of Errors.* What do you think?"

"It's a great choice!" I said, knowing any team needs to be flexible and open with students and parents.

All of us had varying background and expertise with Shakespeare's plays, but some, who may have had a Shakespeare class in college, had not taught his work in middle school. This was a new experience for all of us. We reviewed the assessment and agreed we needed to make some changes from the original assessment. Laura and Kristin suggested we use the same question, but include some documents the students had already seen and some new documents, including both visual and digital. We had some students who required more time and some who needed to use a computer. Laura suggested we use a writing template, similar to the one we used in class, already filled in before they wrote, and some would make use of their previous writing. We had students with diverse needs, and we would provide support to all students.

Increasing Writing Stamina

To move toward the assessment incrementally, students practiced writing the first part of the assessment essay by developing ideas about how magic permeates the play. They had increased writing time to twenty minutes by the end of the third week, and I wanted to maintain engagement and momentum. When I told my students I was going to share their writing to show models of good introductions, I realized I had just stumbled upon the one strategy that proved to be a "game changer." Suddenly, students' writing stamina improved as well as their vocabulary. They had more interest in spelling correctly. One student in particular, Vassar, is a young man who normally puts his head down while we write. He always has his head in a book, but I knew, if I could just get him to put his pen to paper, I could find out more about what he knew. I was correct. He wrote one paragraph, but it was definitely worth sharing (Figure 4.14).

I pointed out some of Vassar's vocabulary, such as "remotely dabble" and "magical entity." As I walked the class through Vassar's introduction, some of the students commented: "I can't write like that" or "Dang, that's boss." I could see Vassar was somewhat embarrassed, but his smiling eyes told me I had shown the others something amazing. One of his talents was writing. From that day forward, when the class wrote, Vassar wrote. When I projected student writing, I could see they were looking for their own pieces, so I made sure that all of them had their writing up at least once.

The final practice we had was focused on the theme of how rank affects work and the role of the rude mechanicals in *Midsummer* (Table 4.2).

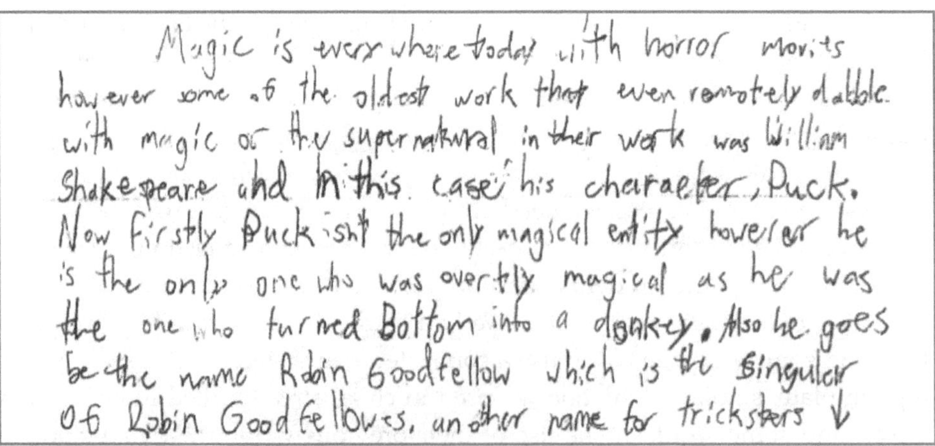

Magic is everywhere today with horror movies however some of the oldest work that even remotely dabble with magic or the supernatural in their work was William Shakepeare and in this case his character, Puck. Now firstly Puck isn't the only magical entity however he is the only one who was overtly magical as he was the one who turned Bottom into a donkey. Also he goes be the name Robin Goodfellow which is the singuler of Robin Goodfellows, another name for tricksters ↓

FIGURE 4.14. Vassar's introductory paragraph.

TABLE 4.2. Documents about work and rank.

The Noble Art of Venery, or Hunting	George Turberville, 1560
The Schoolmaster	Roger Ascham, 1570
Richard II, 3.4.30–58	William Shakespeare, 1597
Paradise Lost, Book 4	John Milton, 1660
The Statute of Artificers 1562	House of Commons, 1563
The Description of England	William Harrison, 1587
Portrait of Melancholy Young Man	Isaac Oliver, 1590
"The Mechanicals and Their Crafts," *Springboard Shakespeare: A Midsummer Night's Dream*, pp. 9–10	Ben Crystal, 2013
The Role of the Rude Mechanicals in *"A Midsummer Night's Dream"*	S.A. Markham, 2012

I chose one excerpt from the Statute of Artificers (Paster and Howard 182–85), because of its publication date, thirty years before *Midsummer* was written, and an accompanying visual[26] that I knew would be of interest to middle-school students. The statute was passed to banish idleness. In other words, laborers *had to go to work*. The interesting part of this statute was that only those adolescents whose parents earned three pounds per year could work, meaning that the statute actually prevented poor people from improving their lot. Using a shared reading strategy, I gave each student a copy of the excerpted statute, and we read through the five short sections, followed by an analysis of the sixteenth-century woodcut of a beggar whipped and dragged to the gallows to be hung (Figure 4.15) (P Thomas 152).

Students were aghast at the visual representation of a poor person who would be hung for begging in the streets. Compared to the freedom in our own country, and the countless people on the streets they have witnessed sitting or standing on corners with signs or openly approaching shoppers in parking lots, this treatment of the poor and downtrodden may have seemed foreign yet familiar.

In a discussion that vacillated between the past and the present, students voiced dismay about hostility toward the poor and recent attitudes toward immigrants. They were equally surprised about early modern workers who knew, by law, that they had to work. Truthfully, I had trouble with this document. I know I could have done a better job of breaking it down, wondering if only incorporating the visual text would have been a better choice. As always, my students surprised me with their insights. Several students focused on the text. One student said, "I want to write about work on the final assessment."

FIGURE 4.15. Woodcut depicting a beggar being whipped through a town, on his way to the gallows as punishment for loitering (plate 17; see also P Thomas 152).

"Why?" I asked.

"Because there's so much to say about the play and about my own life. I'm trying to imagine what it would be like to live in a place where you could only get a job when your parents owned land and had money." Other students added to the discussion.

"It says in Section VI there's a 'penalty for [unduly] dismissing servants.'"

"Yeah, that means servants can't be fired."

"But the servants can't leave either."

"So, what do you make of that?" I asked.

"They seem like prisoners, in a way."

"Well, let's read the next line," I suggested. "Ryann, will you read?"

"'In all, the statute consisted of forty sections seeking to limit the mobility of workers, to prevent unemployment and vagabondage, to control the hours and conditions of work, to adjust wages.'" Ryann looked up, clearly puzzled.

"Let's take this slowly," I offered. "If Parliament would like to 'limit mobility,' they may not want workers moving around a lot. It says they don't want unemployment or vagabonds, which are people who don't live anywhere in particular. They roam about, looking for food and shelter. So, what do you think? Does this statute seem like a good thing?"

Document Discussions

Documents deepen discussion about the rude mechanicals, moving beyond the comic and shedding light on the plight of the working class.

"I guess," said Ryann. "They just don't want people out of work, probably so they won't beg and try to get something for nothing. Can I write about this one on my essay?"

"You sure can!" I was beginning to think carefully about the final assessment. These students knew the play and they had discussed a wealth of documents to give them an idea of the sociocultural context of Shakespeare's world when he was writing. Their ideas and possible stereotypes of the rude mechanicals were shifting. When we first met the rustics, weeks earlier, in act 1, I had asked them to describe these six characters. Messiah had shouted out, "Poor people!" Now their idea of poverty, and the idea of how the poor were treated, was changing. It was less based on one Shakespeare play and more on the synthesis of many documents. Similar to the high school students who concluded the ghost of Hamlet's father was "an early modern ghost," these eighth-grade students were beginning to understand class structure through different lenses.

> Reading literature without a view to historical trends and the shape of the world as we know it in the present can lead us to underestimate the capability of literary artists and to trivialize the act of literary interpretation. (Carey-Webb par. 8)

As predicted, middle school students, who were growing their own adroit armor, demonstrated the seeds of intellectual savvy. I was proud of their growth and honesty as they discussed how early modern themes continued to resonate in their own lives.

On the day of the assessment, many entered with some nervousness, but most felt confident about what they had learned about the play, the documents, and the assessment. They knew they could choose any theme on which to write but had to choose from the documents provided in the assessment. When they opened the booklet,[27] they smiled. They had seen most of the documents: *Of Domesticall Dvties*, *The Scold's Bridle*, the engraving of the Amazon warriors, the painting of Pyramus and Thisbe, the picture of Robin Goodfellow, and, of course, the Statute of Artificers. What they had not seen before was an excerpt from act 3 of *Romeo and Juliet*, where Juliet beseeches her father to listen to her. An accompanying contemporary picture from the 2007 movie version shows a belligerent Capulet screaming at his daughter: "Hang thee, young baggage,

FIGURE 4.16. Ryann and Rebecca writing assessment essays.

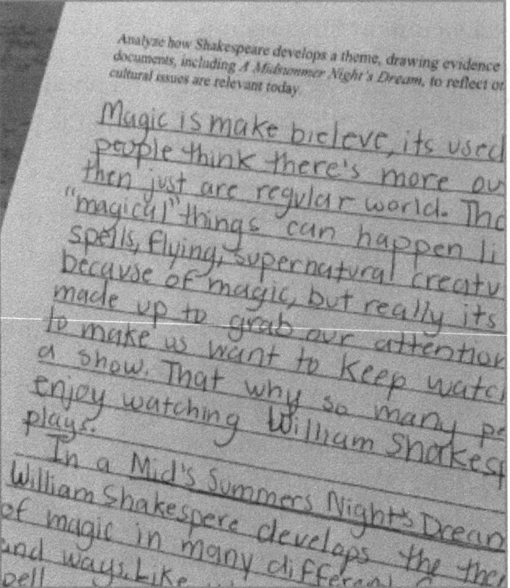

FIGURE 4.17. Ryann's essay.

disobedient wretch!" (3.5.158). They recognized the play as well as the discord between father and daughter, similar to Hermia and Egeus in *Midsummer*. They wrote for an entire hour (Figures 4.16 and 4.17).

The next day, I shared many essays as proof we had *all* succeeded. What was most important, however, was how the students felt about the experience with Shakespeare using primary documents. Brianna wrote, "I think I was well prepared for the assessment. I thought I had lots of practice. I am very proud of my writing."

Should All Middle School Students Read Shakespeare?

The teachers' feelings about incorporating primary documents into the curriculum varied, depending on their personal comfort and experience levels with Shakespeare. They admitted to feelings of trepidation about walking into unknown territory, and, for this reason, I decided to survey them intermittently to see if their feelings changed over time: immediately after teaching, six weeks after teaching, and then, finally, three months after teaching *A Midsummer Night's Dream*. Immediately after the unit's completion, all five teachers reported that the documents "helped students understand Shakespeare's world." Two teachers added further that students better understood themes in the play, and, surprisingly, they felt they were better teachers as a result. All but one would incorporate documents the next time they taught. One wrote, "I'm not sure," and then followed up with "I would not use them as the primary focus. To me, the main objective is an understanding of the play. When the documents can aid this without taking away time from learning the play itself, I will use them as supplements to increase student understanding." Although opting to use them again, the other teachers qualified their responses. One said, "I would use fewer documents, only choosing a few important ones to help them understand the time period." Another added, "Allow more time in class to read and interpret the documents and connect the documents to scenes in the play."

When asked what they learned from the primary documents, teachers conveyed an interest in learning about the time period through this unique approach. One teacher stated she gained "a more accurate picture of how Shakespeare's plays would have been understood in his time." All teachers who used primary documents described their own learning as "valuable," "interesting," and "accurate," admitting that students made connections to themes on a deeper level through close reading of primary documents other than *Midsummer*. The entire unit was described as a process in which students gained confidence as they learned to discern the relevance of the themes to their own lives.

Meg, the student teacher who was working with a veteran middle school teacher, changed her thinking about student learning after six weeks of reflection. She was ready to think about how to adapt both the material and the process.

> When I was in it, it wasn't going as well as I thought it did. Now I feel differently. They did better than I thought when I was teaching it. They looked at more complex text and language and, overall, it helped strengthen their regular reading and writing. It doesn't seem as hard to them now. I thought they did well on the assessment. The kids who are already strong did well. The others, those who have [Individualized Education Programs]—it was harder for them. Really, though, they all can do it, and it should be continued.

Three months later, the middle school team met to consider whether or not to teach *Midsummer* again the following year. The consensus was that all students would experience Shakespeare's comedy again next year using primary documents. Kathy, the veteran teacher who also teaches one eighth-grade honors class, said, "What I liked the best was that it was a good way to integrate primary sources. None of our other units require that kind of reading and synthesis, so this was their first time. The struggle didn't surprise me."

Kathy felt students seemed to take this unit of study more seriously. "They wrote and wrote and wrote," she said. "It was pretty awesome."

Students also supported the use of primary documents while reading *Midsummer*. Ninety-two percent reported on the final survey that the documents they read were either "somewhat" or "very important" to the study of Shakespeare, but their written comments were as diverse as the classroom population. For every positive comment, such as, "I thought it was cool learning about some of the history behind it all," blatantly honest students wondered if they would ever "use" Shakespeare again.

Teaching *A Midsummer Night's Dream* to middle school students was challenging yet magical. Intuitively, these students connected with Hermia's dilemma, laughed at Bottom's antics, and wondered about love-in-idleness. But it was thirteen-year-old Hannah's comment that cemented my belief in middle school English/language arts curricula that embrace the Bard. She said, "It's important to learn about Shakespeare, so you can start believing."

I'm a believer.

5

Discovering Shakespeare's Sonnets

At the end of the school year, many high school English teachers reflect on what they taught, how students progressed, and where gaps appeared. Did we teach enough grammar? Is the curriculum aligned? Is my teammate progressing? Very rarely do we wonder if we taught enough of Shakespeare's sonnets. In fact, if we teach one sonnet, we may feel gratified. Yet, most teachers will admit that the sonnet structure, a tightly bound argument, is meaningful and worthwhile. Then why not? Why do teachers shy away from teaching the poetry that Shakespeare turned to after the theaters closed, poetry often noted as titillating, provocative, and lustrous? In many cases, high school teachers simply do not have time. Some feel tied to the poets and poetry anthologized in textbooks provided by our school districts. Some are drawn to the contemporary forms, such as spoken word, that initially seem more accessible and relevant to our students. Some may feel most comfortable teaching other types of imaginative literature, shying away from the genre that requires close, *close* reading.

> Studying the sonnet structure is an academic pursuit of the reader as writer. (Henning)

So, why the sonnets? And, specifically, why more than one Shakespeare sonnet? According to Helen Vendler, Shakespeare structures the sonnet predictably, incorporating three quatrains, followed by a couplet, and using a systematic *ababcdcdefefgg* rhyme scheme. Students may find more than a few predictable fourteen-line poems "enough." Even so, Shakespeare does not unfold the speaker's emotional perceptions through a prescribed, sequential strategy. It may be that, for each sonnet, Shakespeare hands us his magic reins to steer our course through his thought nuggets. And that is what the sonnets do: provide us with one man's imaginings—his doubts, his fears, his dreams, and his joys—all in fourteen-line imaginings.

This book has been wound around early modern historical and cultural themes, those big ideas that weave their way into and thus construe the making of a man. It may be true that Shakespeare turned to sonnet writing when the theaters closed. It may be that a Renaissance sonneteer could survive on words alone if aligned with an affluent patron. This chapter, however, is not solely about how to teach a sonnet. It is not about looking for developing themes. It is not about aesthetic richness or sensual images or dramatic insight. How Shakespeare constructed his sonnets is indeed interesting, but this chapter is what I would call an experiment in teaching. It is about freedom within the classroom, handing enough rope to each student to lasso ideas but not too much to do damage. It is less about failure and more about the process. It is seeing where a student will go if given the opportunity to create and search simultaneously, to turn on a dime when the road just isn't right but the alternatives aren't clear. It is, if I had to name it, Sonnet Moments.

I know what you're thinking. "This sounds a bit too free" or, "I could never do this" or, "What is the point?" Those were my exact questions as I wandered off the beaten path of teaching Shakespeare's plays, all poetic, dramatic, iambic narratives, and wondered what would happen if students read his sonnets with no prescribed end goal. What if students simply read them and wrote about the ones that had speaking power, the ones that made their hands clammy and their tongues dry and their hearts hurt? What would happen? It occurred to me that with the freedom to turn—either facing back at the past or to the side at today or forward to the future—students might instinctively reach for more information in the form of primary documents. Would they want to know if the speaker was Shakespeare himself or if the love interest was certain or if the rival poet's effect was downright debilitating? I wondered what my students would wonder.

Having taken Shakespeare courses and read the scholarship, I have a few ideas of my own about what it might have been like to live in the sixteenth century or what possessed a young, imaginative, hungry playwright to sit, quill in hand, and write for bread and butter. Were I him, my business sense would have joined hands with my fictive self, and I would have written what I knew my readers desired. But what seems most important is whether Shakespeare's sonnets are worth the time. Are they for everyone? If Vendler is correct in stating that a poet's duty is to "create aesthetically convincing representations of feelings felt and thoughts thought" (16), I believe that, if given time, high school students could and would lose and find themselves in sonnet moments of arousal and self-loathing. They would hear Shakespeare's voice not as a single man's but as one string in a symphony of vocals.

My hope was that William Shakespeare's sonnets would seem "real" to today's teenagers. What I mean is that their believability would be based on reading his words within a twenty-first-century cultural mindset, understanding that we are all part of something bigger. Certainly, all one hundred fifty-four sonnets emanated from one mind, but they are also evidence of lasting art that follows an infinite trajectory and one that undoubtedly originated long before his birth. As readers, we gaze up as thoughts ebb and flow, identifying with those that cement our stances in literary imagination. But, as writers, we do more than gaze—we latch. Our words become part of the locomotive force of thought. Once written, then immortal. Would my students appreciate Shakespeare's sonnets as moving, forceful moments in their lives? I needed to find out.

The Sonnet Project Goals

- To explore Shakespeare's sonnets through early modern primary documents
- To find relevance in Shakespeare's sonnets by exploring pop culture today

When I suggested a new open-ended sonnet project to my juniors, I decided to follow four students' journeys of their own making. I realized students in our English department had a great deal of choice during independent reading. I also realized that some choices had been "teacher guided." Certainly, I couldn't imagine simply handing students a play to read without some direction. But I wanted to see how students would steer their own courses if given ample freedom and a book of Shakespeare sonnets, a journal, and loose parameters.

The Sonnet Project Survival Kit

- project handout: guidelines and sonnet groupings
- Shakespeare's complete sonnets (digital or electronic)
- journal: spiral notebook or composition book
- pen
- calendar (for deadlines, group meetings, and presentations)
- sticky notes
- 4 × 5 note cards

I provided a handout[28] to each student, outlining two general goals: to explore Shakespeare's sonnets, as well as other early modern primary documents, and to find relevance in Shakespeare's sonnets by exploring pop culture today. The general requirements, such as daily journaling about sonnets, research, and process, became learning targets, which would encourage students to think about the *how* as much as the *what* during this three-week study. I purchased different sonnet books, some with only the sonnets and some Folger editions that provided more assistance in word definitions and explanations. Students chose the type they preferred as well as a journal for their writing and knew this was an "experiment" of sorts, a project that would be student driven and project based, although the final "project" could be nothing more than sharing their learning process. The struggles with understanding the sonnets and researching the time period would be as informative and important as how it was shared with others.

Managing Independent Reading

I should mention that I was worried. I had faith in my students, but I wasn't sure if I had faith in my process. Normally, students are teacher monitored, teacher facilitated, teacher bound. Normally, teachers are success monitored, assessment facilitated, curriculum bound. Would students adapt to a self-driven learning experience? Although all of my students had read at least one Shakespeare play, they unanimously voiced concern about "not knowing anything about Shakespeare's sonnets." Still, they wanted to learn.

Meet the Explorers

Sam described himself as a diligent student who does what he can "to make a good future for myself." He believed a study of the sonnets could be something fun and admitted, "I wouldn't usually do something with poetry."

The Sonnet Project Guided Steps

1. Reading sonnets and journaling about how Shakespeare's language created profound moments in thinking
2. Researching early modern and contemporary documents that illuminate meaning, relevance, and connection to today's world
3. Exploring options for sharing findings
4. Reflecting on how experience broadened learning and prompted more questions

I have always loved history and looking past the original plays and seeing what was going on." Sam's background in Shakespeare included reading *A Midsummer Night's Dream* in eighth grade, *Romeo and Juliet* in ninth, *Macbeth* in AP Literature, and *Othello* on his own. "Before this year," he said, "we never really read Shakespeare for understanding, just for the plot. I knew the themes—like *Romeo and Juliet*—the themes of love. I was always told what it was about, what the teachers wanted me to know. Now it's more open ended. I want to see what other themes are prevalent."

Jill described herself as very focused, especially during a big project. "Sometimes I think I push myself too hard," she admitted, "but I'm trying to find better balance. Sometimes I let school run my life." Jill wanted to read the sonnets because she loved Shakespeare and had never done anything like this before. "I thought this would be a neat way to find out more about him in a different way." Jill had read several of Shakespeare's plays and saw one stage production in Chicago. Despite not understanding all of what was happening as a younger student, Jill saw Shakespeare as a challenge once she entered high school and tried to figure out the early modern language. "We did a packet or watched on the screen, and we'd have half the original and half rewritten, but, personally, I like trying to figure it out by myself." Jill said she has never read any sonnets other than "Shall I Compare Thee to a Summer's Day" as part of a Shakespeare unit in ninth-grade English, after which they had to write a sonnet.

Hannah had always been interested in the sonnets and recounted her ninth-grade experience with reading only one. Like many other high school students, Hannah read *Romeo and Juliet*, but it was confusing. "I couldn't understand why these teenagers did what they did. I thought it would be interesting to study Shakespeare. I knew he was a playboy—a little bit of a player—but I didn't even know he was married. Apparently, he had kids. One of my teachers said he liked to be different, and I think it's good to go against the grain like that."

David was a self-proclaimed boundary crosser, but only if he learned something from that experience. "Time is precious," he said, "so I like to have a reason for learning." He explained his fascination with pre-nineteenth-century texts as "related to the time period," knowing Shakespeare was the best during the sixteenth century. David admitted he was not necessarily into poetry, but the sonnets seemed like a story on one page. "I know nothing about the sonnets, really. But I am interested in his style and what he has contributed, like the screenwriters of today."

Diving In

I knew my students would have a more enriched experience if they had some prior knowledge about sonnet groupings, so I provided some information about the number of sonnets, which ones were written for a "young man" and which ones for the "dark lady." Within these two groupings, I also provided subgroupings, such as procreation, the rival poet, love triangle, and aging. But, then, I had a bit of a "What now?" moment. I wondered if these students could maintain momentum through the project. Would they wonder what to do after reading Shakespeare's work? To ease my own mind, I established, organized, and maintained a framework for myself.

Loose–Tight Framework

- daily reading and journaling
- bi-weekly check-ins
- weekly collaborations
- reflective writing
- questioning
- probing
- researching

These four students had full range of motion throughout the project, but I had resources in place for all of us. I checked in with them daily, and they felt free to come to me throughout the three weeks with thoughts, questions, and concerns. How each approached the sonnets and the cultural/historical backdrop of early seventeenth-century Europe was based on how the sonnet language and the themes stirred their thinking.

I asked David how he read the sonnets: "What is your process?"

"I used the left side of the page to help me figure it out. First, I read the sonnet three times and then read the left side. It gave a summary and the definitions—this was the Folger part. That way I could see if I had gotten it on my own, but I could double-check my thinking."

"How have you previously studied Shakespeare?" I asked.

"Normally we listened to the teacher read parts of a play alone, and parts of it we read along. We were silent, though. We didn't really analyze. Sometimes we would act it out, but I don't *think* when I read that way. People were memorizing their parts and not even thinking about what it meant. I didn't like that."

"What do you like?"

"Well, in eighth grade, we read *Midsummer* and analyzed it as a piece of literature. We did a lot of writing and looked at Shakespeare's life. I liked that. I would like to read a few plays—maybe read just the beginnings—and say to myself, 'Where are these plays going? What are the common grounds?' I'm just not sure about the sonnets yet."

Reading and Journaling

Daily journaling about the sonnets was crucial (Figure 5.1). I knew that reflecting on Shakespeare's language would allow students ample time to turn inward. Some lines would tug at their hearts while others would not connect. After initial reading and writing, students noted how grouping the sonnets led them to create their own narratives about Shakespeare's imagination and possibly his life. "If you put them side by side, you can see how they weave together," Sam said. "Shakespeare wrote a lot about time and love. He saw time as the inevitable passage of life. It also dealt with love too, like the one where he wrote about devouring time." When asked which sonnets *spoke* to him, Sam knew right away. "I really like number 19. It was so deep. Nothing can stop time's passage. But, with love, it makes it easier. With literature, one can stay forever young."

Hannah also shared the meta-narratives she created by reading the sonnets in groups. "I haven't gotten through all of the sonnets yet," she said, "but the ones written to the young man are really pretty, especially the first ones where he says to have children. These sonnets are like the back door into his life."

Students knew that much of Shakespeare's life is a mystery and that his plays and poetry provide most of the entryways into his life. Creating meaning within the sonnets often led to self-created dialogue that created a bridge between his world and theirs. It was this connection, however tenuous, that engaged and engulfed them. They wanted more.

Creating Sonnet Moments

Throughout the first week, Sam, Jill, Hannah, and David wrote about what the sonnets were *doing*. Sam began his journey by writing questions he wanted answered as he read. Initially, his questions were centered on whether Shakespeare's experiences were driving his writing. His final question, however, focused his direction: "How does Shakespeare's work translate into modern pop culture?" Sam was not only finding connections among the themes, but also noting similarities between the sixteenth and the twenty-first centuries.

FIGURE 5.1. Student sonnet journals.

He noticed the human obsession with time and its "omnipotent nature." In Sam's earlier writing, he saw how love, Shakespeare's antidote, "has the power to combat the haunting progress of time." I looked forward to reading Sam's writing at the end of each day. His prose, descriptive and thoughtful, provoked my own thinking. He described the symbiotic relationship of time and love in sonnet 12: "But wherefore do not you a mightier way / Make war upon this bloody tyrant time?" According to Sam, time is a powerful being whose "clutches have everyone." In his journal, he asked, "What happens when an unstoppable force meets an immovable object?" From this moment, the idea of how art represents love and time became the connecting bridge between these two foes.

Jill and Hannah decided on a process together. They read the sonnets silently without supplementary help and wrote a short summary and reaction. Next, they searched the Folger edition to check understanding. In Jill's notebook, with the marginal headings "My Thoughts" and "Folger's" for each sonnet, she also included her comfort level with the poem. She evaluated sonnet 3 as "harder to understand" and, after reading the Folger explanation, realized that the speaker was not addressing himself, but, rather, the reader. Her writing, organized and methodical, revealed some frustration, especially with sonnet 7, which caused "the most confusion so far." Deciding this sonnet to be "a little sexist, if you ask me," she wrote about how fading beauty can be forgotten through procreation if only a son, mirroring his father's image, is born. After exploring the sonnets for four days, Jill decided to research fashion to see where it led. She wrote, "I don't know much about fashion, so this could be interesting." In her writing, she explored some ideas about fashion during Shakespeare's time as well as costumes from his plays.

Hannah chose to read the introductory material in the sonnet books to learn about Anne Hathaway and their children, one category proposed by the editor. Her notes included themes, such as "jealousy, obsession, self-loathing, delight, and lust, as found in the introduction." At the end of day one, Hannah posed some exploratory questions:

- "Who is W.H.?"
- "Was Shakespeare in a homosexual relationship or was he writing about a friend's experience?"
- "Was he having affairs?"
- "Did he marry Anne because she was pregnant?"

Working together gave both girls autonomy and collaboration. Each read the sonnets silently and took personalized notes. Unlike Jill, whose writing was divided into two categories, Hannah's notes were divided visually by sonnet. By day five, her thinking and writing had changed; she was now more reflective. She wrote, "I definitely see a lot of stuff about beauty and living on and leaving heirs. But I also see happiness in them too." Later, her ideas changed again and she remarked:

> I'm kind of looking at maybe delving into looking at how events going on around him impacted his writing . . . another thing that seemed interesting was looking into who exactly commissioned the sonnets and what they paid for them and could you making a living off of writing them . . . also looking into what made him start to write about rival poets could be super fascinating.

Hannah had many paths she could take but decided to begin researching as many as possible to find the one less traveled.

Inquiry-Based Research

Students understood that this project would be self-driven. They understood that the sonnets would speak, move, and lead them. None of us knew exactly how this would happen. I didn't say, "Today we will begin our research." I didn't ask, "How many pages did you write today?"

I did say, "Tell me about one of the sonnets you wrote about yesterday." I did ask, "How does that particular line speak to you?" Students did not read the same number of sonnets, and some spent more time researching early modern and contemporary documents before, during, and after our conversations. Sometimes we talked for a few minutes at the beginning of class, and sometimes we spent half the hour researching documents together. Hannah told me that she thought Shakespeare "was an interesting dude," but that people don't really know much about him. One of the reasons Hannah was interested in the sonnet project is because of her interest in research. "The original is where you need to be."

During the first week, most seemed busy reading and writing, with the exception of David, whose schedule and involvement with an AP biology project precluded consistent work within the classroom. His writings, sandwiched into his free time, illuminated some interesting questions. Focused on the publication of the sonnets in 1609, David's concern was centered on the purpose, more than the themes, for Shakespeare's writing. He wondered if Shakespeare's sonnets were simply musings, exercises in sonnet writing, and nothing more complicated than "a laundry-list of reasons for himself to be with someone . . . one hundred fifty-four reasons for himself to find a mate." It occurred to David that Shakespeare's plays contain love, heartbreak, and loyalty. Could it be possible that the sonnets were a break from the dramatic genre and not, in fact, for publication at all?

After spending time reading the sonnets, Sam talked about how he loved the freedom of the project and the opportunity to decide for himself how to use primary documents to explore Renaissance art that might also connect with the themes of Shakespeare's sonnets. "I've never read any of Shakespeare's sonnets before, so focusing on the ones that spoke to me—and reading those over and over—helped me feel more confident," he said.

"Which ones were you drawn to?" I asked.

"I was super into the love relationships, so I started researching paintings because I love art." Sam's process was searching the internet for famous paintings from the early modern period that fit the theme of love. "I don't confine myself to one research method," he said. "I wouldn't have found *Everyman* if I hadn't done it this way. I let the research take me where I wanted to go."

When asked what she had learned so far in her early research on the sonnets, Jill saw a contrast between the themes she saw in the poetry and what she had found out about in her research on his personal life. "One thing that sticks out to me is that he talks about what love should be and yet in his own life he was writing to a mistress." Jill was drawn to the "dark lady" sonnets and wanted to find out who he was writing to and why.

Finding a Niche

By week two, I met with students individually to answer questions and to listen to each student's ideas about the sonnets and what types of primary documents would support and guide their research.

> **Document Discussions**
>
> Not all students may have common research skills, which will require either mini-lessons or written instructions on how to navigate websites to find early modern documents.

Our individual conferences reminded me of how diverse these four students were in their processes. Jill had copious notes on each sonnet but seemed somewhat unsure of how she would go about researching fashion. She seemed slightly resigned to, rather than excited about, her topic. We discussed how some scholars divided the sonnets into two groups, the first one hundred twenty-six written from the speaker's point of view to another man and numbers 127 to 154 written to a "dark lady." Jill's eyes lit up as she said, "I want to look into the mystery of the *dark lady*. He references her but never gives an explanation about who she is. I want to research this mystery." After our meeting, she posed questions in her journal:

- "Who was the Dark Lady?"
- "How is she connected to Shakespeare's life?"
- "Did she represent anyone/anything?"
- "Was she a living person?"

Jill's list, "Things to Look For," reminded her to focus on visual descriptions as she reread and to research repeated words and changes in tone throughout the sonnets. "I'm just absolutely fascinated by whoever this person was and why there's a ton of sonnets about her." Invigorated, Jill excitedly went to work and jotted words in her notes about themes. She found repeated words, such as *black*, *beauty*, and *mourning*, and thought about unconventional beauty as an emerging theme. By day nine, she noted that she was neither focusing on one sonnet nor one theory. Rather, "I'm focusing on the mythology/conspiracy of the Dark Lady and the prime suspects: Lady Penelope Rich, Mary Fitton, Jane Devenant [*sic*], Lucy (an African prostitute), and Queen Elizabeth." Both Hannah and Jill collaborated on the research, settling on Mary Fitton. Jill's notes were filled with possibilities, including "the *real* W.H." She believed it would have to be to William Herbert, as if to say, "I know your secret" or "Look who I'm with, too." Hannah seemed as interested in the object of the speaker's love interests, having found two websites she was scouring: *The Monument*, written by Hank Whittemore, and *Shakespeare's Sonnets*, written by Michael Delahoyde of Washington State University. Both websites provided information as Jill and Hannah debated the age-old question, "Who were the objects of the speaker's love, fear, and jealousy?"

Each day, Sam focused on artistic representations of love to compare how love was expressed in paintings during the Renaissance period. Were early modern ideas of love different or the same as today? After great difficulty in finding a piece of artwork, he chose Jan van Eyck's *Arnolfini Portrait* (Figure 5.2), analyzing how the couple's relationship is depicted.

What Sam found most interesting about the painting is the lack of obvious emotion conveyed by both the husband and wife. "They seem to be expressionless," he said, "but I think it was more quiet between a husband and wife because it was sacred. At first, I thought it would be futile to try and use the two for a theme of timeless love, but, as I inspected the work more, the love became more apparent." Sam picked up on subtle clues in the painting, such as the placement of the figures, the woman close to the bed in a traditional motherhood role and the husband toward the window with the light of the patriarchal world shining through the window and on his face. "The green dress," Sam noted, "is seen as symbolism for new growth," in addition to the dog between the two but closer to the woman as a signifier of loyalty.

To tie the two themes of love and time together, Sam chose a modern painting: *Town of Time* by Sergey Tyukanov (https://artshareon.com/2013/03/town-of-time-1/). Despite the dead disrupting the living in the painting, Sam realized that time was something that cannot be erased as shown by the hourglass-shaped buildings. "The artist provides an insightful view on time, showing it both as civilized and destructive," he wrote. Sam's attention to detail focused on the couple sitting atop the tallest clock tower, seemingly oblivious to the rampant destruction below. "The lovers are left in a world of their own," he mused, "demonstrating the nullifying power love has over time." Sam chose sonnets 18 and 19 that personify time as an unstoppable force as well as a foe. In number 19, the speaker understands the power of words. Unlike time, where the present is quickly swept into the past, writing can be savored, kept, cherished.

FIGURE 5.2. *The Arnolfini Portrait* (van Eyck).

In this sense, the speaker's love poetry can be timeless and more than simply a measurement of age. Sam cited the final line, "My love shall in my verse ever live young," as the part of the poem that "says it all."

Sam's exploration of Shakespeare sonnets that speak to the symbiotic relationship of time and love eventually brought him to some new thinking. He described his reaction to the first line of sonnet 12, "When I do count the clock that tells the time" as rather transcendent. Now he thought about the speaker's feelings about death. "It seemed as if Shakespeare reviled death," he wrote. "By using words such as 'hideous,' a tone is established. It seems like Shakespeare was mad at time, rather than frightened by it. However, he knew its power and saw there was little one could do to stop it."

Time is also the enemy in Marvin Bell's 2000 poem "To Dorothy," a love poem Sam researched to make a statement on eternal love. The goal, finding relevance in Shakespeare's work, prompted a search for more contemporary poetry that mirrored the sonnets' sentiments. "In Marvin Bell's poem, time is the enemy," Sam said. He quoted a few lines, "'If I lost you, / the air wouldn't move, nor the tree grow.' Love is extremely powerful," he said. "So powerful, in fact, some would rather cease to exist than live a life without it." And it looks like time just stands still without it. Nothing grows. Nothing moves. "Both Bell and Shakespeare are saying the same thing," he concluded.

The Power of Collaboration

In addition to working independently, students needed time together to discuss their findings. I was excited about the opportunity to listen to their discussion, following the twists and turns I hoped it would take. I had no idea if they would simply summarize their research or if their discussion would lead them off the beaten path into uncharted territory. Initially, students began by sharing their work. Sam gave some background on his process, walking the girls through his PowerPoint presentation. Jill shared her ideas about the dark lady, as well as her list of possible "suspects" (Figure 5.3).

Ruling out Mary Fitton because her life didn't seem to coincide with Shakespeare's, Jill said, "Jane Devenant [*sic*] is popping out to me. When I was researching, I found she was the wife of an innkeeper in Oxford. In 1606, Jane had a son who later revealed, 'I am the son of Shakespeare.'" Jill summarized

FIGURE 5.3. Jill, Hannah, and Sam sharing sonnet ideas.

her feelings about sonnet 127: "He uses the word 'dark,' referencing eyes, skin, and hair. His language relates to one of his earlier plays from *Love's Labour's Lost*, and I found a theory that his sonnets and the play were written for a certain person, the 'dark' lady."

"Was the dark lady African?" asked Sam. "I feel like Shakespeare wrote about women in a progressive way. Othello was a Moor, and Shakespeare didn't stereotype him in any way. Segregation in Britain may not have been as bad as it was in America. Shakespeare seemed to be ahead of his time."

"I wonder if he's defending his mistress at the same time he was writing his sonnets," Jill said.

"Maybe he fell in love with someone else but couldn't show it. I wonder if he couldn't marry a Black woman. I don't have the feeling he ever loved Anne Hathaway. He abandoned her when he went to London. This idea of 'forbidden love' in *Romeo and Juliet* is kind of like this idea of not being able to marry who you want."

"In Othello, he marries Desdemona, who is white," answered Sam. "You never really hear about what was happening in that part of the world. Were Black people discriminated against? I know nothing about that. I feel like they didn't depend on slavery like Americans did. I'd like to read the laws about slaves at that time. Slave masters too. Or firsthand accounts of Black people at the time."

"Look on Folger's *LUNA* and put in *slavery* to see if Black people were discriminated against," said Hannah, who was typing furiously on her laptop. "I found ten items on slavery and an image during when Cromwell was in power" (Figure 5.4).

FIGURE 5.4. Hannah researching primary documents about the British slave trade.

Hannah spent time looking up documents while the others looked on. "It talks about the Turks taking slaves," she said. "*The History of the Royal Slave* was written in 1688, not that long after Shakespeare's writing. I wonder if Shakespeare had the personal experience of the things he talked about."

"Did he do this for the money, or was he truly in love with someone else?" asked Jill.

"I have no idea," answered Sam. But Hannah, the group's research expert, was already into *The National Archives*, the official archive of the UK government: www.nationalarchives.gov.uk.

"It says here slave trade routes were not open until 1698, well after Shakespeare passed away, but that, in 1640, the slave trade was booming."

"Are you familiar with Joseph Turner's painting [Figure 5.5]?" I asked. It was becoming increasingly difficult for me to absent myself from the group's conversation, and I noticed we were getting close to the end of our hour together.

"See if you can pull up the painting, Hannah. The painting was done in 1840, but depicts what was happening in in the late 1700s. Slave trade was very real at that time. Men, women, and children were thrown overboard because they were sick and wouldn't bring in any money if delivered in that condition."

FIGURE 5.5. *Slave Ship* (Turner).

"What's that sticking up out of the water there?" asked Hannah.

"A foot," said Sam. Everyone was silent. And then the bell rang.

"Oh, no!"

"Hannah hasn't even talked about her research!" said Jill.

"We definitely need more time," said Sam.

I loved the fact that these students were so excited about sharing their findings yet did not simply stop at that point in their process. They were raising and developing important questions that called for further exploration. I wanted to position myself as interested in their inquiry and eager to learn more along with them. At this point, the best way I could facilitate our group's community was to read their writing.

The next day, the students journaled about their collaborative discussion and how it informed their thinking. Sam wrote about how the conversation suddenly shifted when he asked Jill if she believed the dark lady to be African. He said, "Suddenly we were all enthralled. Never before had I thought about who the *dark lady* really was. So, I asked the question, 'What was life like for Black people in England during Shakespeare's time?' All three of us begin to formulate ideas; however, none of us have a clue. Never before had we been presented on black lives in England in Shakespearean times. We knew a lot of the African American fight in America."

Hannah's writing was equally passionate about her learning that day. She referred to the topic of slavery in Britain as a "rabbit hole that we decided to explore." Hannah's love of research led her to pictures of African children during that time period. "In those pictures, their clothes look to be very well made. They aren't what many would—at least in the US—expect a slave to wear. One of the children even had lace on her bonnet and frock. From there, we looked up some of the laws pertaining to slavery and found that there was more trade of non-living goods than anything else. Also they were more indentured servants than they were slaves. So, we were thinking that it could have been possible for the *dark lady* to have been of African descent." Despite the focus on Jill's project on the dark lady, all three found connections to their own projects, realizing in short order how primary documents, both visual and digital, could fill in the gaps, answering questions that they were posing during their time together. None of these students seemed concerned about the final product as much as they were interested in deepening their knowledge about Shakespeare's world when he was writing. Using *LUNA* through the Folger Library, Jill found documents about slavery as well as about trading goods. Finally, she turned her attention to Amelia (also *Aemilia* or *Emilia*) Lanyer as another possible "suspect" in her search for the dark lady.

Simon Forman, an astrologer, wrote about those who came to see him regarding their future. Jill found his journal and noted that Lanyer had visited him several times during 1597, which was just before Shakespeare turned to sonnet writing. Forman's notes indicated Lanyer was concerned about her husband pursuing knighthood, her miscarriages, and how she missed her days in the Queen's court. According to Jill's notes, "Forman was interested in having sexual relations with her." By the time of the presentation, Jill identified both Davenant and Lanyer as possible subjects for many of Shakespeare's sonnets. "The true identity of the Dark Lady will probably continue to elude us for years to come."

What I found most interesting about Jill's process is that she began the project with an interest in fashion.

Document Discussions

When students research primary documents to find answers to their own questions, they need time to collaborate to discuss what they have found and to gather ideas for more research. Small-group members will often find connections to their own research threads.

It took her approximately two weeks of daily reading, writing, researching, and discussing to arrive at an impassioned project topic. The road she took was as important, if not more, as her end goal, to share what she had learned. Finding Forman's journal was the gem she uncovered in the process and her most treasured find. I could have provided Jill with articles or with information I have collected, but Jill's excitement about her research grew with *her* discoveries. Her personal *sonnet moments* became the impetus for growth.

Sharing the Wealth of Shakespeare's Jewels

On presentation day, students in the Sonnet Project shared their findings in a variety of ways (Figure 5.6). Sam preferred to project a PowerPoint for students to see the art and poetry he researched from both the sixteenth and the twentieth centuries.

It was important to him to use this mode as a tracking system, to remember the detail sequence as he summarized how Shakespeare's themes of time and love intersect and cohabitate space. Sam ended his presentation with a final thought about the project: "Never before have I looked at Shakespeare's work as I do now. I had never really had any background in reading Shakespeare's

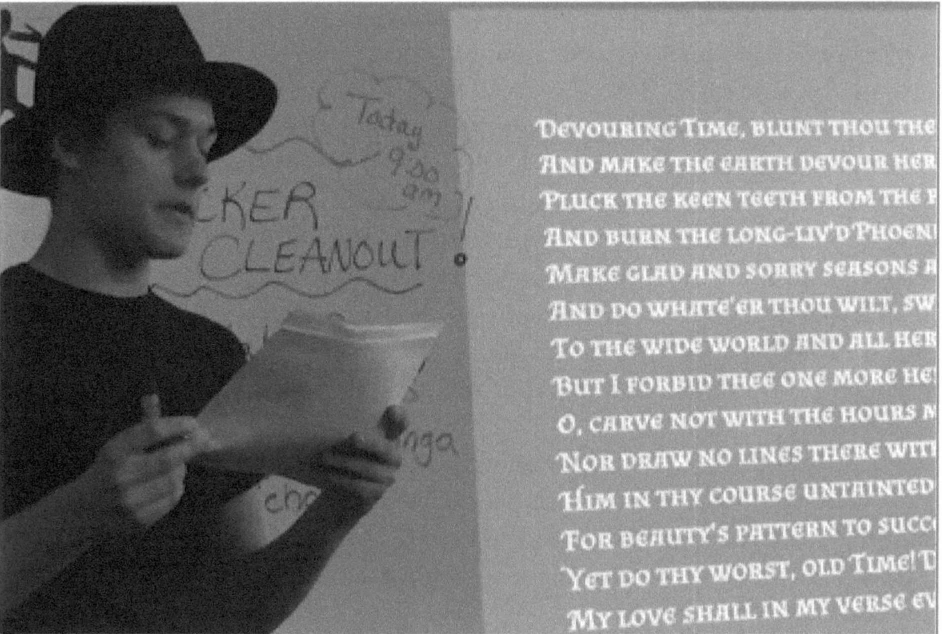

FIGURE 5.6. A student presenting sonnet research findings.

sonnets, even though they were easier to read than most of his plays." In his journal, Sam admitted that, after the project's completion, he felt much more confident in himself. The work was difficult, he explained, but taking the time to dig was worth the effort. "The reason his sonnets are so important is because they allow for the exchange of ideas through time itself," he wrote. He felt the process booted creativity and challenged him to read between the lines. "So why don't schools focus more on his sonnets?" he asked. "Plays are equally important, but, with his sonnets, there is a free range of themes and ideas one can take from just one piece." Sam's conclusion was that students need to think deeper.

Both Jill and Hannah presented their research at the same time, and both simply stood up in front of their peers and explained their research process and their findings. Jill acknowledged that they took different approaches to their work, even though both of them were trying to solve a dilemma. "I wanted to figure out who the dark lady was and came up with the top four suspects," she said. After explaining her reasoning for ruling out two, she named Queen Elizabeth I as a possibility. "I don't think it's her, though, because you don't really expect the Queen to have an affair with Shakespeare. Also, there weren't many times in history when they met." Jill believed Amelia Lanyer is the most likely candidate, because Simon Forman wrote about her in his journal. "His notes reveal it could be Shakespeare."

Hannah identified the second mystery: "Who was the *fair youth* who was the subject of Shakespeare's first one hundred twenty-six sonnets? All of his sonnets seem to be written for *WH* who could be one of his patrons." A lot of sonnets were commissioned. The first twenty-six were to a "fair youth," who could be William Herbert, 3rd Earl of Pembroke, or Henry Wriothesley, 2nd Earl of Southampton. "I've done a lot of research on the matter, and I don't really know who the fair youth could be," she admitted. "But another interesting tidbit is that some people think Shakespeare didn't write the sonnets. I know personally that, if someone else was writing sonnets and had my name on it, I'd throw a bit of a stink about it. I don't see a lot of people who would do that. Shakespeare is so big—why don't we know this stuff about his life? We really don't know much about him."

"You both read most of the sonnets," I said. "Most teachers tend to teach the most famous, such as 'Shall I Compare Thee to a Summer's Day?' (18), 'Let Me Not to the Marriage of True Minds' (116), or 'My Mistress' Eyes Are Nothing Like the Sun' (130). What do you think about the sonnets you read compared to the ones most often taught?"

"Don't just do the famous ones," said Hannah immediately. "Those aren't the ones that are interesting. It's the others that really tell stories we want to know."

Conclusions

Teachers may wonder if an independent Sonnet Project could ever work with general English classes. I can hear you say, "Okay, this may work for honors, but it would never work with my students. My students are struggling readers. It just won't work." Perhaps not in this way. But I do believe that Shakespeare's sonnets can create opportunities for learning and growth for all students. Having taught Shakespeare using primary documents at both middle and high school levels, including struggling readers and disengaged learners, I know students are interested in gender, stories, love triangles, jealousy, and inequality. And, according to all of the students who were involved in this project, they all love a good mystery and the chance to solve it. The most important teacher tool for teaching the sonnets to all students is the Gradual Release model where collaboration and independent practice are the hallmarks of practice. The following ideas may help as you gather ideas for helping your students find their own *sonnet moments*.

Background Information

Providing background will help students gain confidence and independence. For this reason, I developed a handout that outlines the sonnet structure, and some basic background information on Shakespeare's body of work as a whole, such as how many he wrote, scholars' ideas about subject matter, possible chronology, patterns, the dark lady, and the rival poet. The goals, process, and parameters of the project can be adjusted to suit any timeframe and age group.

More Time for Collaboration

Students need more time to share ideas and work together. Conversations may take unexpected twists and turns that lead them on exciting adventures. I recommend beginning with small increments of time where students have only five minutes to discuss a topic and are held responsible for sharing their findings. Eventually, add more time as students demonstrate focused conversations.

Socratic Seminars

Students benefit greatly from large-group discussions, especially those based on shared reading. Allowing students to read a sonnet and discuss what it means in a large group helps students clarify thinking and add ideas. To scaffold this experience, allow students time to read and annotate the sonnet, followed by *partner-talk* with the person sitting next to them. Project a global question, such as "How does the speaker define beauty?," on a screen or write it on the board after reading sonnet 130. Students should be encouraged to take notes during the discussion to help them craft their writing on the same question the next day. (See also Appendix B.)

Student-Generated Rubrics

Allow students to create the rubric for a Sonnet Project. After reading many of Shakespeare's sonnets and discussing some of the narrative possibilities, provide a rubric template that is broad enough to include diverse exploratory projects. Allow students to work on rubrics in groups, which will also provide opportunities to discuss interest areas.

Focus on Primary Documents

Students need help with how to access primary documents. Some may wish to concentrate on visual text while others may wish to research journals, letters, recipes, sermons, or catalogues. Primary documents provide inroads to Shakespeare's culture, which depicts his own popular culture. Most students who study either his plays or poetry are immediately drawn to how his life differs from their own twenty-first-century lens.

Journaling

The value of writing every day in middle and high school language arts cannot be overlooked, and creates a platform for discussion in small and large groups. Daily topics that include student learning—whether they hit a dead end or a jackpot—provide students with clarification of what they are seeking as well as what they are finding. For teachers who regularly confer with students during independent reading time, journal entries can be the focus of discussion and a time for individualized help. *Silent reading discussions*, when students read others' journal entries and provide written, rather than verbal, feedback, is a time when students find out more about their peers' inquiries in a non-judgmental environment. Journaling can also provide the seed for further research, such as when a student writes about Shakespeare's sonnets on nature and later delves into John Gerard's *Herball* (1597).

Focus on Process Rather Than Product

Part of the beauty of the Sonnet Project was the freedom to decide how to share findings.

> **Document Discussions**
>
> Sonnet Projects can be a whole-class activity, a research club, or part of a larger student-selected research project. Students do best when they have the freedom to explore, research, collaborate, and share.

Sometimes students are so worried about the product that valuable research time is cut short, just when the process is becoming most exciting. It wasn't until the last week of the project that the students realized their individualized topics all had a similar thread: racism in Britain. Without time to research, write, and *collaborate*, their individual research topics would have been the pinnacle of their learning. Research and writing each day can become tedious without an end goal, and, based on the class make-up and dynamics, sharing can become part of the process without becoming overwhelming.[29]

Looking Ahead

The final step in the project allows inquiry to continue long after the project's end. Similar to a toboggan run where initially we slide quickly down a chute—or a "rabbit hole," as Hannah described—doggedly and single-mindedly searching for answers to personal questions, we finally shoot out of the chute, destination unknown. As learners, we know that our process never simply stops. We continue to travel at breakneck speed, veering left or right, tumbling over, or simply slowing to a stop. It is indeed during this end run that we consider and reflect: "Where should my research go next?" I do know, from student discussions during the Sonnet Project, that they became extremely interested in Britain's history of slave trade in comparison to that of the United States. They also considered *othered* groups during the seventeenth century, based on how Shakespeare portrayed Africans, Jews, and women in his plays and sonnets. Often, Sam mentioned how progressive Shakespeare's writing must have been and wondered if he faced personal tribulation as a result. Finally, Shakespeare's personal life—his wife, his children, his alleged mistresses—all seemed both intriguing and conflicting. Students wanted to know more, but we simply ran out of time. Essentially, the project ended, but the thinking continued.

Should We Teach Shakespeare's Sonnets?

The short answer is "yes," but the long answer involves prioritizing. Many school districts are working to prioritize standards, aligning their curriculum both horizontally by grade-level course teams and vertically from kindergarten through twelfth grade. Assessment rubrics need to be specific enough to determine whether students have successfully learned the material yet open-ended enough to allow teacher flexibility in how they meet the standards. It's challenging work. Can teachers, for example, substitute a sonnet string for a Shakespeare play? What is the defining goal? To read a play or to have experience with his poetic language? In one of the eleventh- and twelfth-grade-specific Common Core reading standards, the language specifies that students "determine the meaning of words and phrases as they are used in the text, including figurative and connotative meanings; analyze the impact of specific word choices on meaning and tone, including words with multiple meanings or language that is particularly fresh, engaging, or beautiful." Shakespeare, as well as other authors, are specified in the language. As we teachers grapple with the standards, choosing which authors have high priority in the curriculum, we will also need to consider student choice. That may mean total choice during independent reading time. It may mean some choice as they form literature circles. It may mean very little choice in shared reading opportunities or during the study of a whole-class novel. We do know students should have ongoing, diverse opportunities for reading, writing, speaking, listening, and research, all during their sacred time in language arts. A study of Shakespeare's sonnets could satisfy standards from each strand. Moreover, standards aside, what students learn from reading different kinds of documents, exploring controversial ideas and materials, and making comparisons and connections across documents, period, and ideas is invaluable. Specifically, what I noticed about these students' diverse interests is their growing skill with inquiry. I had not realized how much skill in questioning relies on practice. Initially, students read the sonnets independently and collaboratively, looking for meaning based on their ability to scrutinize language. Close reading is a skill they knew; none of these four students had experienced any other way of diving into early modern poetry. It wasn't until they began to search the perimeters of the poetry through historical visual and digital documents that they began the real search for meaning. The more they discussed, the more they questioned. Inquiry skills improved with practice.

It may be that teachers who feel most personally comfortable with Shakespeare's language are the ones who are most likely to include the sonnets, either in addition to or as a replacement for one of his plays. Those who have studied Shakespeare as undergraduates, specialized in graduate early modern studies, or trained in workshops at state or national conferences may feel more "qualified" to expand curricular time on Shakespeare's sonnets. The truth is we all continue learning, and sometimes we learn from our students' insights in ways that intrigue and delight us.

Scholarship is the backbone of what we do in the classroom, the very fiber of which angle we take or how we structure the content of lessons. Experience provides the confidence we have in predicting how content will be received and in knowing where the stumbling blocks will be encountered. Discussion and feedback provide growth to the entire learning community—teachers and students. How classes push forward, both as a dynamic group and as a safe harbor, depends on the inner workings of each student and the inter-workings among students and groups. To be clear, Shakespeare's work is dense and powerful, yet sometimes fraught with anxiety and confusion. As teachers, we may sometimes feel insecure when we let go of controlling reins and see just what happens when we allow students to move forward independently. Despite all odds and self-doubt, Shakespeare's words direct us: "Shall you pace forth, your praise shall still find room, / Even in the eyes of all posterity" ("Not Marble" lines 10–11) So, yes, teach the sonnets. Explore human nature. Seek answers. Enjoy the journey.

6

Shakespeare Book Clubs

Teaching Shakespeare can be difficult, but teaching four plays at the same time? In the same classroom? During all the years I have taught Shakespeare, the close reading of one play has been my standard, sole approach until I discovered how primary sources enrich any pedagogy. Now, more than ever, I am challenged with finding methods that will satisfy my students' hunger for meaningful conversations, reading, and writing. The 2020 global pandemic and our nation's struggles with racial equality and equity have opened dialogue among English teachers on Facebook, Twitter, and Instagram. Many wonder if Shakespeare could or should be taught using virtual or hybrid platforms, and I often feel a nervous undercurrent permeating our best and brightest teachers. Two books, written by notable Shakespeare scholars Emma Smith and James Shapiro, allow new thinking to surface: first, Smith's ideas about Shakespeare's "gappiness," the gray area where new thinking lives, and, second, Shapiro's argument that America's ongoing challenges have continually been addressed in Shakespeare's plays (see Table 6.1).

Shakespeare's problem plays, those that push genre boundaries and explode gray areas, began to take center stage in my own mind. I wondered if Shakespeare could puncture the doubt, anxiety, and fears students face today, especially those who feel isolated. Students working from home, however, might find Shakespeare's language too difficult to handle on their own—too remote for remote learning. Yet, one question continued to nag me: "How can twenty-first-century students connect with Shakespeare's work?"

TABLE 6.1. Notable scholarly texts.

Of Human Kindness: What Shakespeare Teaches Us about Empathy	Cohen, 2021
Shakespeare and Trump	Wilson, 2020
Shakespeare in a Divided America	Shapiro, 2020
This Is Shakespeare	Smith, 2020
Tyrant: Shakespeare on Politics	Greenblatt, 2018

Teachers struggle to stay afloat as we facilitate multiple learning platforms and manage myriad emotional crises. Many ask questions. Few have answers. Students are often confused, overwhelmed, and angry as they try to make sense of the pandemic, protests, and promises. Shakespeare's problem plays, those that explore cultural and societal attitudes about gender, race, alienation, and abuse, answered the call for relevance. These narratives push us to think about what it means to be human because their characters face moral decisions with difficult odds. Some are blocked from loved ones. Some are manipulated by heartless villains. Some are powerless against abusive authority. As readers, we relate with not only the problems but also the lack of solutions. We realize endings rarely have clean edges. In essence, it's a lot like real life.

Shakespeare's problem plays, some rarely taught in American high schools, reveal challenges that many of us understand and experience. In fact, the congruities are profound.

Document Discussions

Shakespeare's problem plays open pathways to make connections to the past:

- Why do we reject outsiders?
- What does it mean to be humane?
- How do we show mercy?

The recent #MeToo movement has striking similarities to Isabel's horrendous experiences with Angelo in *Measure for Measure* (1604); the hate crimes in *The Merchant of Venice* (1596) bear witness to twenty-first-century world events where pleas for tolerance go unheeded; racial slurs in *Othello* speak volumes as we watch our fellow Americans beg for equality and equity through protests, riots, and violence; domestic violence severing family units and violating human rights takes hold in *The Winter's Tale*. These plays speak volumes to twenty-first-century students, and I am convinced nothing is more important than grappling with difficult issues in English language arts classes. Thus, the Shakespeare Book Club approach was born.

Virtual and Hybrid Book Clubs

One advantage of reading Shakespeare in book clubs is student choice, but my initial concerns focused on how to manage four groups in hybrid and virtual settings. Most teachers are on the hunt for engaging and accessible ideas for teaching Shakespeare, but even partial online teaching has limitations. Some of my students now have full-time jobs; some take on daycare responsibilities; some are working through anxiety. Despite myriad obstacles, I knew I had to make Shakespeare's plays accessible and engaging. To begin, I relied on essential literacy practices to guide planning and orchestrate goals (e.g., MAISA Disciplinary Literacy Task Force, Michigan Department of Education). Scaffolding steps toward comprehension was key because I knew struggling readers would need support. Prereading experiences, those strategies and activities that build background knowledge and provide contextual understanding, were necessary components. If students had prior experience with early modern language, the basic plotline, and the moral issues each play presented, the reading process would be manageable in both online and face-to-face settings.

Why Should Students Read Shakespeare in Book Clubs?

- To provide context for both early modern and contemporary writers
- To provide opportunities for inquiry and discussion about the relevance of Shakespeare's writing
- To provide student choice in personal expression

My first question—whether Shakespeare's problem plays would speak to my students in important ways—led to how I could make it work, regardless of the modality.

Virtual students reading in groups without my physical presence needed familiarity with key characters, their motivations, and their struggles. The PBS *Shakespeare Uncovered* documentary series on Shakespeare's plays are exceptional resources for preparing students to read. Leading actors share their insights on the plays, such as David Harewood's experience as the first Black man to play Othello, the statue that may have inspired Shakespeare to use the name *Isabella*, the reason for Shylock's alienation in Venice, and the challenges embedded in playing a monarch-turned-tyrant who falls prey to unorthodox paranoia. Spending considerable time viewing, discussing, and writing about the plays before diving into the text improves the reading process, because it provides practice with the language, tone, and sequencing through a multimodal approach. The documentaries provide clips from movies and plays, but they also include interpretations of a perpetrator's motivation as well as the victim's response. Iago's psychopathic behavior, evil for the sake of evil, might be one book club topic of conversation before reading aloud together. The more frontloading students do, the more invested in the play's narrative they become. Prereading activities must engage *and* propel students into active reading (see Figure 6.1).

In addition to prereading strategies, active reading requires sustained engagement with the text, which can dwindle easily without purpose, discussion, and reflection. Reading aloud in book clubs allows students dynamic opportunities to experience Shakespeare's language and helps them *stay* engaged. Successfully facilitating book clubs in one class or managing breakout rooms on Zoom depends on some organized chaos if students take time to make decisions. First, students must decide *how* to read. Will they take parts or read in a round-robin style? Will they stop often or barrel through? What steps will they take if comprehension breaks down? Second, students need purpose for reading.

PRE-READING	ACTIVE READING	POST-READING
Shakespeare Uncovered (PBS)	Select parts and read aloud in book clubs, tabbing important speeches	Brainstorm ideas for remix project
Notes on plot, key characters and societal issues found in specific problem plays	Teacher mini-lessons on structural devices, followed by formative checks through discussion and writing	Research 16th and 21st century primary sources on issues raised in play
One-pager designed by entire group	Collaborative groups	Creatively synthesize sources in remix project
Flipgrid commentaries: students discuss problem play and ask for specific support	Multiple and diverse groupings to learn about other plays	Provide feedback for other groups
Primary source search of early-modern artifacts surrounding issues found in plays	Reflective writing	Present to real audiences

FIGURE 6.1. Pre-reading, active reading, and post-reading.

Active Reading Ideas

- stop and jot
- sticky notes
- annotations
- one-line summaries
- one-minute discussions
- scene summaries
- scene titles
- sketches

Searching for powerful moments in the plays that they learned about during the prereading activities is a viable activity because students use what they know as jumping-off points. Sticky notes, tabs, or highlighters provide ways to mark anticipated lines or scenes they wish to revisit. Specific speeches, such as Isabella's pleas for "justice, justice, justice, justice" (*MM* 5.1.27), Shylock's rhetorical "Do we not / bleed?" (*MV* 3.1.63–64), Leontes's guilty admission of his "ill suspicion" (*WT* 5.3.186), and Iago's uncompromising "What you know, you know" (*Oth.* 5.3.355) are lines they have heard and understand and now anticipate. Marking text while reading aloud is a type of *meaning making*. Students look for moments that speak to them personally and share those moments with each other as evidence for connections they have made to their own world. Finding the golden thread that spans four hundred years from Shakespeare's world to their own begins with understanding how the play was situated in early modern society through their own twenty-first-century teenage lenses. Connection does more than build meaning. Connection *is* meaning.

The most important part of reading Shakespeare in book clubs allows students to take the reins in their learning.

The most important part of reading Shakespeare in book clubs allows students to take the reins in their learning.

If students are learning in multiple platforms, time spent at home on their own must be valued and rewarded, but it must also be reasonable and accessible. Teachers must create space for students to wonder and provide activities for groups to discuss and question. I realize now that student questions are not always quelled by simple answers. Learning the value of gradually releasing and trusting student autonomy has taught me more than simply how to use technology in virtual settings. Student discussions outside of class or in groups out of earshot are rich with inquiry and supposition.

I also trust my students will tell me what they need, how much to lead, and how much they are learning. The final assessment, the Multimedia Remix Project, allows students to illuminate and demonstrate their connections between Shakespeare's world and ours in dynamic ways. During both pre-reading and reading, they gather pop culture artifacts from the sixteenth and twenty-first centuries to create meaning that situate text within cultural norms. The Multimedia Remix Project provides opportunities to place their personal stamps on learning by tamping down doubt and revving up confidence about how they feel about the troubling issues the plays present. It is possible students will use their voices to inform. It is possible they will use their voices as social justice platforms. But it is also possible students will use their voices to calm their own souls—sometimes it is therapeutic to write, listen, or talk into fears. The gray areas in the play may be where the questions live, but it may also be where the meaning rests.

Virtual Teaching

I was ready to kick off the unit, but I wanted evidence of how students fared in different settings with both novice and experienced English language arts teachers. My student teacher Ali had never taught Shakespeare before and became a new set of eyes and ears throughout this journey. Mindi, a twelve-year veteran in California, was eager to embark on a virtual excursion into Shakespeare's problem plays, using online versions of the plays. Together, we spanned almost fifty years of experience with one hundred twenty-five high school students of varying levels of interest and ability. Generous DonorsChoose contributors supplied the plays for the Michigan students, but the California students read Shakespeare's works using online scripts. The hybrid and virtual students needed organizational strategies for scheduling meetings, researching artifacts, making notes, and contacting groups. The Michigan cohort, divided into four quarters or nine-week blocks, had three classes. The California cohort, one class, worked in a hybrid format under Mindi's supervision. Both groups experienced virtual learning, prompting me to create daily lessons on Loom. These videos, available to all students, include book talks, mini-lessons, and assignment descriptions.

Prereading

We began with a *KWL* activity to find out what students *knew* (*K*) about Shakespeare, what they *wanted* (*W*) to know, and what they previously *learned* (*L*). Some had read *A Midsummer Night's Dream* at the middle school, but most had at least one Shakespeare play, *Romeo and Juliet*, under their belts.

Prereading Activities

- KWL
- Triad Talks
- Choice Reading
- Whole-Class Discussions
- Read–Pair–Share
- Warm-Up Writing
- Pocket Research
- Documentaries
- Flipgrid Recordings
- One-Pagers
- Padlets
- Answer Garden
- Hyperdocs/Hyperslides
- Jamboard
- Topic Speed Dating

Using a Google Doc, a projector, and a wireless keyboard, a student scribe recorded our discussion. At first, students were quiet, so they met in triads to talk about their experiences with *Romeo and Juliet*. Each group shared at least one idea that helped students feel more comfortable speculating about Shakespeare's writing. "Didn't he write in *Old English*?" Rob asked.

"Let's think about Shakespeare's writing as *early modern*." I said.

"Well, what's *modern*, then?" asked Sami.

"What you are speaking now," said Jenna. "But then what was *Old English*?" Students turned to me.

"Old English is difficult to understand," I said. "Most of the words don't sound like ours. *Beowulf* was written in Old English. Middle English sounds more like our spoken words. You can hear some of the same sounds as in ours."

"Well, I couldn't understand any of that Shakespeare stuff," said Jocelyn.

"What helped?" I asked.

"My teacher had to explain everything. But, when we went to Chicago to see plays, I loved that! I got the whole thing!"

Sharing what we knew built background knowledge by taking kernels of information and building bridges. If a student said plays were performed in the Globe, I could add what I knew to fill in the gaps and prompt more questions. Some of their questions morphed into debates about whether Shakespeare wrote the plays, the types of plays he wrote, the rumors that he was gay, the germ-infested crowds, the coincidence of twin pandemics, the invention of new words, the trials of religious strife, his marriage to Anne Hathaway, his strong female characters, and the male-dominated society.

Building Background Knowledge

- Discuss prior experiences with Shakespeare in triads.
- Capture thinking on chart paper or shared document.
- Read article or peruse books.
- Phone-research interesting facts about early modern London, medical practices, entertainment, customs.
- Create categories of knowledge: social issues, family structure, power and status, poets and playwrights.

Some had heard about *iambic pentameter* but had no idea what that meant. They also knew about a few movies based on his plays as well as some of the spin-offs, which was a perfect segue into *book talks*.

The book talks I included were written on the board, so students knew the books were all related to Shakespeare and especially the problem plays. I included fiction, nonfiction, memoirs, and podcasts, which I shared each day we were together and included on the online videos.

Book Talks

- *Exposure*
- *I, Iago*

- *Shakespeare in a Divided America*
- *Vinegar Girl*
- *Hagseed*
- *The Voices of #MeToo*
- *This Is Shakespeare*
- *Station 11*
- *Shakespeare Saved My Life*

Students were anxious to choose book clubs, so I used this method to explain the plays. *Book talks* are the best prereading activity for creating interest and engagement in reading. Taking students right to the part when they are on the edge of their seats asking, "And then what happened?" is one of my favorite parts of teaching English. In *Measure for Measure,* students leaned forward when I told them how Angelo tells Isabella he will free her brother if she sleeps with him. In *The Merchant of Venice*, their eyes widened when I said, "And then Antonio's ship sank, which meant he now had to give up a pound of his own flesh." I heard a few gasps when I said, "Iago's ultimate revenge would be to persuade Othello to murder Desdemona for sleeping with Cassio." *The Winter's Tale* came alive when students learned that King Leontes believes he killed his entire family after unleashing his tyrannical paranoia.

And then I did the unthinkable: I simply stepped back and let the students take over. They decided which books they wanted to read. They decided how to form the book clubs. They filled their own Book Club Kits.

Book Club Kits

- gallon-sized Ziploc bag
- Shakespeare problem play
- sticky notes
- project description and rubric
- pen or pencil

They discussed how to communicate. As they made plans, their excitement grew. Mine too.

When students were in class with me, we worked on activities that might have been more difficult when they were at home on their own as virtual learners.

It was important for them to understand what problem plays have in common and to discuss how all of the plays expose social ills, illuminate moral dilemmas, invite difficult questions, suggest uneasy solutions, and push genre boundaries. At the outset, I chose specific plays that dealt with uneasy topics. *Othello*, for example, is one of Shakespeare's greatest tragedies, yet many readers find the racial slurs troubling and the ending disconcerting. When Iago is confronted with his treachery, he states, "What you know, you know. / From this time forth I never will speak a word" (5.2.355–56). Othello's feelings of powerlessness and alienation at the hands of "honest Iago" prick our sensibilities and drain our emotions. We are undone. Similar to *Othello*, most problem plays elicit unsettling questions: Why is Isabella silent at the end? Why does Hermione forgive King Leontes for his disloyalty and outright cruelty to her and his family? Why is Shylock ousted from the community with nothing?

Why does Shakespeare leave us wondering?

At the end of the first day, students shared their reflections on reading Shakespeare in book clubs (Figure 6.2).

Some mentioned feeling anxious, but most loved the idea of trying something new, especially now during an entire year riddled with anxiety, remorse, and loss. What they wanted more than anything was direction and purpose.

I chose the play: The Winter's Tale because I found it extremely interesting how one character would so strongly begin to believe in something with no evidence, and even go as far as to have disdain for a newborn baby, and put his wife in jail. When hearing about it, it just sounded very drama filled and entertaining, so that's why I chose it.

As to regards on my schedule on how to prepare for this project, I plan to make a schedule with all of my homework and learning from my three classes, and aim to get all of my work done. For this class, I am going to also aim to stick to the day by day schedule that is posted, and if I fall off, to have the weekend to be my grind days if I can allow it. During the third week is when I start to go back to work, so before that, I am going to try and make myself fit on a personal schedule.

The main part that I am worried about would be having enough time to finish reading the play (week 2), but ~~[illegible]~~ with a schedule, I think I'll be able to do it.

FIGURE 6.2. A student's initial response to the Shakespeare Book Clubs project.

Understanding the entire project with both individual and group assignments and the assessment spelled out allowed them to organize their time away from school. Having spent an inordinate amount of time learning away from the classroom, students also appreciated having time to work collaboratively. They were hopeful that working in book clubs would provide support groups for success.

Learning about the Problem Plays

Half of our students watched the documentaries together in groups, and half watched them at home. Their notes on the key players, the troubling issues, and the connections they made provided important background to the play (Figures 6.3–6.5).

Most noted how important it was to understand the play before the reading, but simply watching the documentaries was not enough. Some of their questions about the early modern period needed answering, which is why researching primary sources from the early modern period is part of the prereading step.

Students wondered when the Jews were expelled from Britain, what happened to women if they were unfaithful to their husbands, if "hand-fasted" marriages were legal, and how Africans were treated when Shakespeare wrote *Othello*. Primary documents, such as letters, sermons, catalogues, sketches, paintings, song lyrics, or frontispieces, also narrowed their knowledge gaps about how Shakespeare's audiences would have responded to his problem plays. I knew some students would not know where to begin the search for early modern documents. To solve this problem, I created daily Loom videos for students who were either working at home or needed review. Many students had previous experience with primary sources, but few had researched four-hundred-year-old documents to find answers to their questions about early modern daily life and cultural beliefs in London.

Document Discussions

Demonstrating how to navigate internet sites where students can find original sources provides support and encouragement:

- *Shakespeare Documented*—shakespearedocumented.folger.edu
- British Library's collection items—bl.uk/collection-items
- *Teaching Shakespeare*—shakespearedocuments.info
- *Elizabethan Era*—elizabethan-era.org.uk

FIGURES 6.3–6.5. Students created one-pagers and notes to show their thinking about the problem plays during prereading.

In the videos, I shared websites and my thinking using a Think-Aloud strategy (see Appendix B) with *The Taming of a Shrew* as a mentor text. I asked my own questions about this text and searched four different websites that might provide some answers. The documentaries also steered students to primary sources and prompted questions about "what it was like back then." Krina was interested in the handkerchief that Othello gave Desdemona, so she searched for possible pictures and found it was a symbol of love and commitment (see Figure 6.6).

She wrote:

> Many times we seek validation from our partners by way of gifts, even something simple as them lending us their sweatshirt is a sign of love. But Man! A scandal it can create when someone else takes such an item.

In addition to Robert Greene's source story *Pandosto* (1588) for *The Winter's Tale*, Belma was interested in historical accounts of accusations of infidelity that resulted in banishment or death. She found the opening trial document from the trial of Anne Boleyn, King Henry VIII's second wife, who was accused of "carnal lust" that could not be contained (Figure 6.7).

FIGURE 6.6. White linen handkerchief decorated with cutwork, needle lace, and embroidery, Italian, circa 1600.

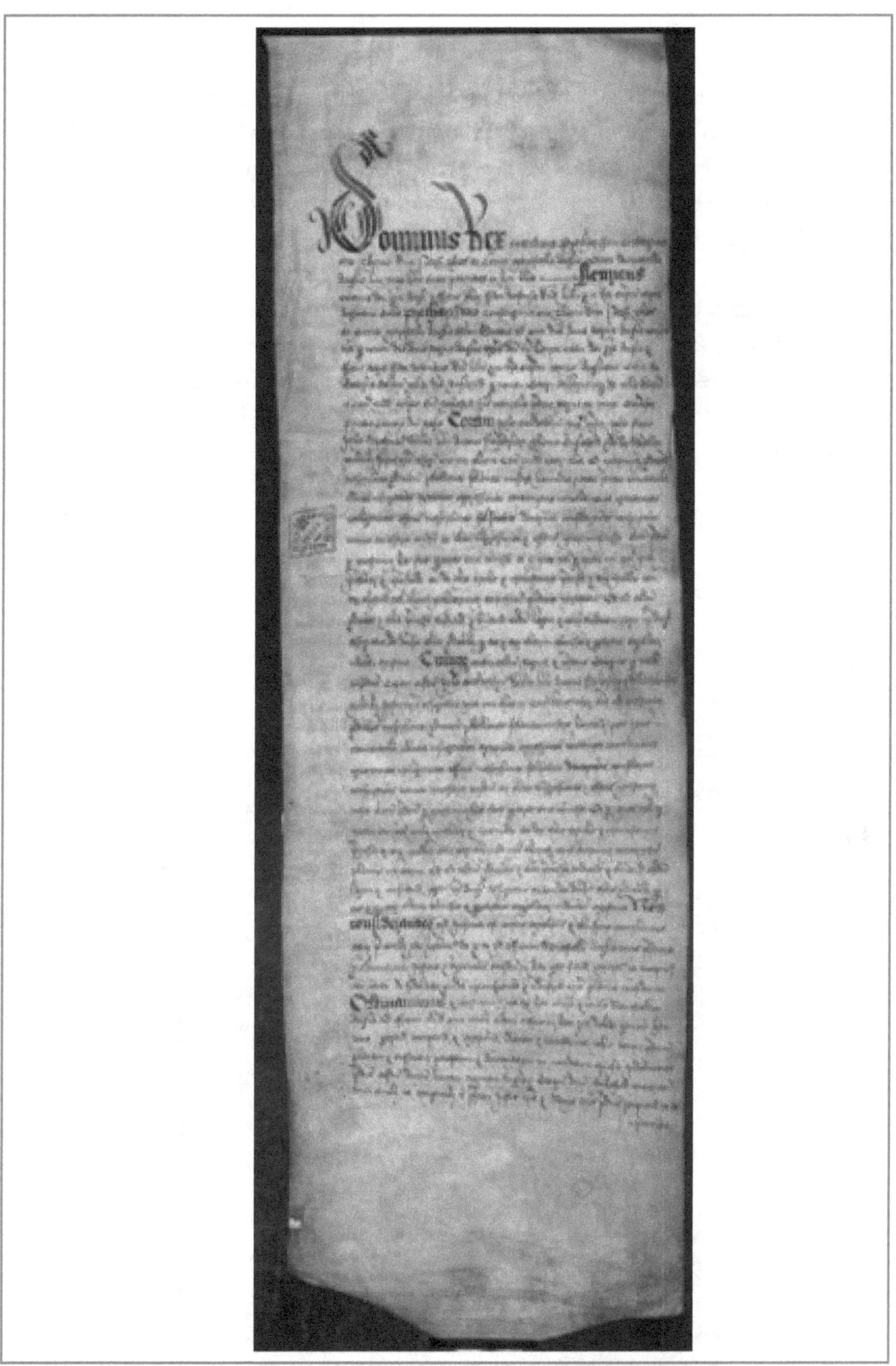

FIGURE 6.7. Example of a student-sourced document: 1536 indictment detailing Anne Boleyn's alleged offenses (as posted on *Historical Vandals*, a Tumblr blog).

Belma wrote:

> This document is the beginning of listing the charges and circumstances of the trial of Anne Boleyn. These claims did not have evidence with them, other than others claiming that the charges were correct. Anne Boleyn would then later be executed. This ties into *The Winter's Tale*, where Hermione stood trial for her "adultery" charge, which also did not have evidence.

Ailise found the frontispiece to a 1634 discourse on *panderism*, or the selling of sexual favors (see Figure 6.8).

She wondered if the document might allude to a real English proclamation of 1603, which called for the destruction of houses in the suburbs, where many brothels stood, to prevent the spread of the plague by "dissolute" people (Goodman).

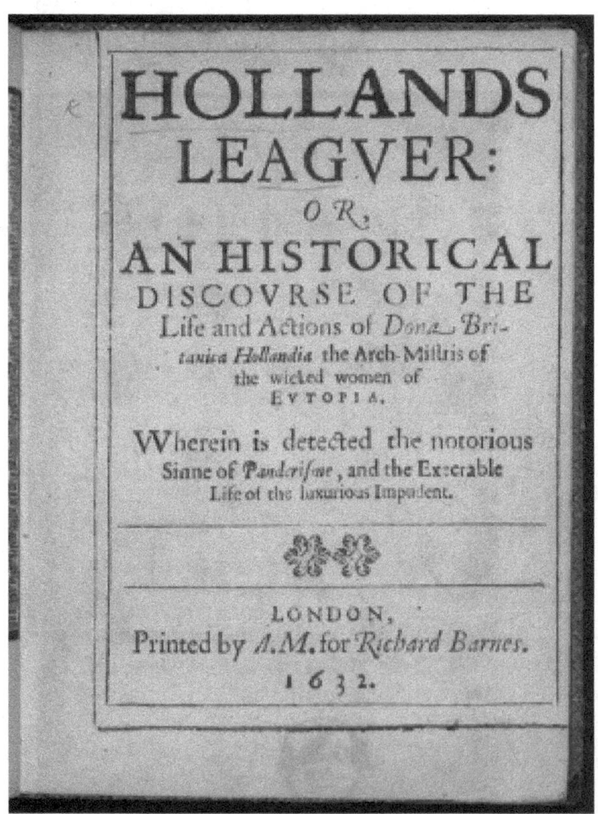

HOLLANDS
LEAGVER:
OR,
AN HISTORICAL
DISCOVRSE OF THE
Life and Actions of *Dona Britanica Hollandia* the Arch-Mistris of
the wicked women of
EVTOPIA.

Wherein is detected the notorious
Sinne of *Panderisme*, and the Execrable
Life of the luxurious Impudent.

LONDON,
Printed by *A.M.* for *Richard Barnes*.
1632.

FIGURE 6.8. *Hollands Leaguer* (Goodman).

FIGURE 6.9. Gold ducat bearing the name and image of Andrea Gritti, the Doge of Venice who issued it.

Stella was interested in the gold ducat (British Library) (Figure 6.9), and how much money, class, and race were intertwined in *The Merchant of Venice*.

Students used four websites as research starters to get them into documents and to practice their skills. Of all the work that they did to learn about the plays and the issues they present, this part was the most difficult. Some students breezed through. Others struggled with how to pose questions, how to navigate early modern spellings, and how to show what they learned. The next step in the process—and possibly the most important—was to reflect on the documents they found, what they learned, and how the research led them to more questions. Flip provided opportunities for sharing and viewing one another's findings and reflections. Some students' videos had seventy-five views, while others had only a few, but they learned from each other and realized that research, like writing, is both telling and difficult.

Document Discussions

Students can share how documents situate Shakespeare's problem plays by using Flip, voice memos, Padlet, Pear Deck interactive slides, Zoom meetings, sketch-doodles, two-page spreads, book club discussions, exit slips, 3–2–1 slips, and shared documents. (See Appendix B for more on the *3–2–1* strategy, and Appendix C for a description of the *exit slip* strategy.)

Sharing ideas pushed our thinking and opened doors to new questions. In Noelle's Flip, she shared her findings: a letter from a man to his father-in-law about eloping, a handdrawn map of Venice that included the Jewish Ghetto, secret pamphlets written by Jews about their practices, and quotes from the Torah about revenge, which surprised her because it was not supported and therefore did not support Shylock's behavior. Her questions were about the documentary's presentation of Bassanio and Antonio's relationship, which she felt might have been more than friends. She wondered whether this behavior was against the law or "what they did to prevent it." Flip provided research snapshots but also allowed individuals to articulate their learning. Asking more questions was encouraged and expected. Using research as a prereading strategy allowed students opportunities to explore early modern historical, cultural, and societal beliefs and mores that situated and influenced Shakespeare's work. Before they actually read the plays, students found connections not only between the sixteenth century and their own, but also among the different plays within one classroom.

The final prereading activity, *one-pagers*, are a creative way to reflect on the connections students made to their own world. Sketching and writing about learning was a way to move from text-to-self and text-to-text in the inquiry and research and move into the text-to-world realm. I never tire of learning from my students. They love having opportunities for creative expression, which worked for students who decided to draw in their journals and for students who preferred experimenting with online tools. Lindsey shared her thinking on *Othello* in her critical-reading journal, while Marc shared his skills and reflections using Google Slides (Figures 6.10 and 6.11).

Reading

Students enjoy reading together, and reading in small groups works well if students feel prepared. The prereading activities, created to provide background knowledge and incite interest of the problem play and the societal issues, gave students focus and purpose. As they read, they drew from what they learned from the documentaries as well as the meaning they made in their one-pagers and Flip to guide them through the play. Using sticky notes to flag powerful moments while they read aloud in groups was helpful because it prepared them for each scene's language and tone. Groups stayed on track and focused. Students told me that reading in book clubs was different because they controlled the pace and process. Some groups enjoyed taking specific parts while others simply took turns reading when a new character spoke. What students noticed

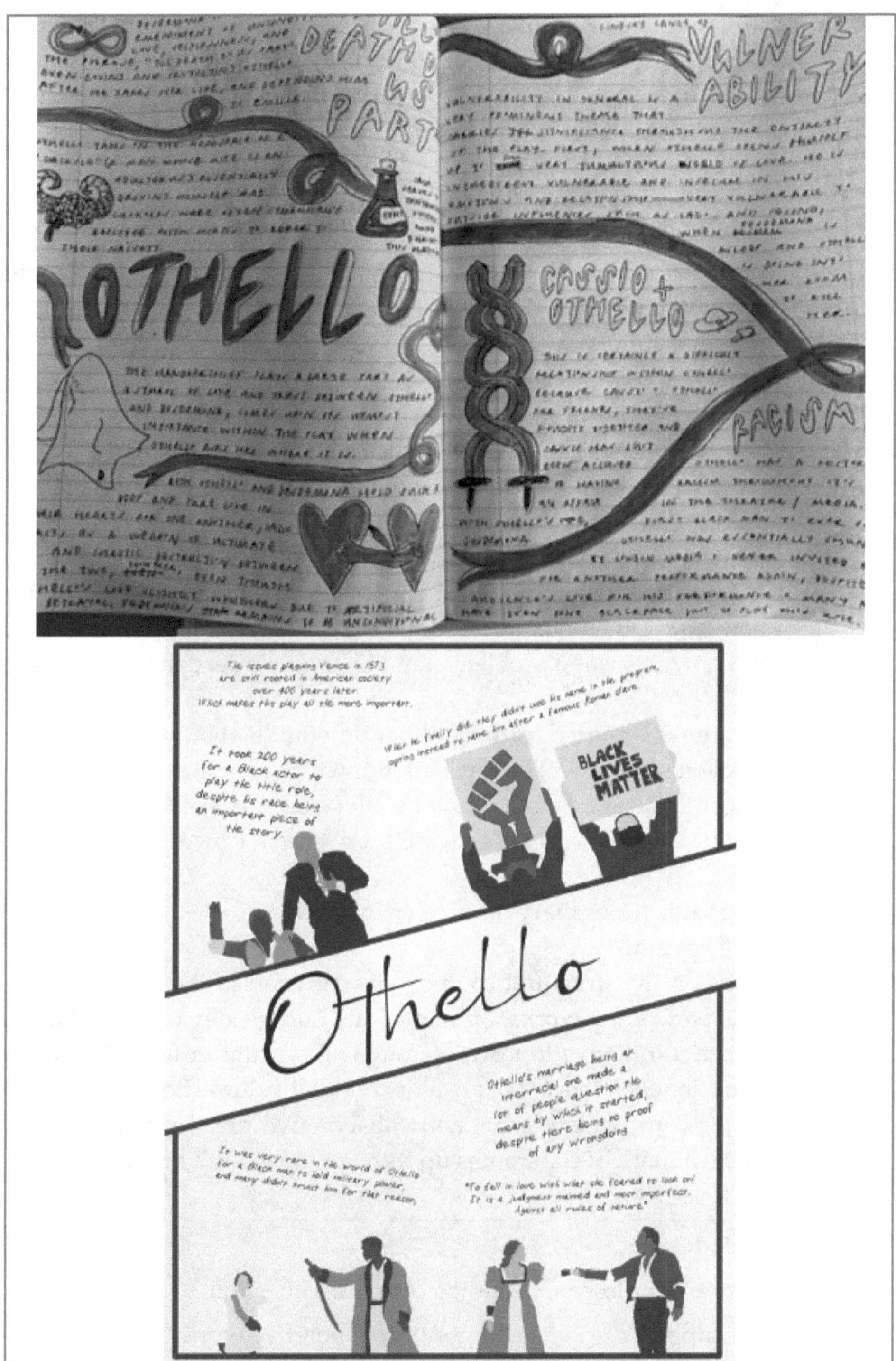

FIGURES 6.10 and 6.11. Student examples of a two-page spread and a one-pager using Google Slides.

was the control they had over their process. I roamed from group to group, but rarely interjected without requests for clarification. One group that read *Othello* asked to discuss the play's ending with me. Landen said, "I have some questions. Iago doesn't give a reason for what he does to Othello. He just says, 'What you know you know.'"

"What's your impression of that?" I asked. "What do you think his reasons might be?"

"I'm not sure," Landen said. "I mean, he's jealous of Othello, right? So maybe he doesn't think Othello deserves an answer. He probably hates him that much."

"Yeah, but what about how Othello tries to kill him," Jordan added.

"But it says he stabs him," corrected Landen.

"So, if you're a devil, you can't die? Is that what they thought?"

"I don't know, but that's obviously not the case."

"Could you find out what the thinking might have been about the afterlife or good and evil?" I asked. Jordan looked at his book.

"This is not normal," he said.

I realized these two had not read the entire play, but they had read enough that they knew how Othello had been duped. They were confused at the end and wondered how this was a problem play. "Everyone's dead at the end," said Landen.

"No, they aren't," retorted Jordan. "What do you do about Iago? He's still out there. I know it says he will be tortured. But will it even hurt him if he can't be killed anyway? And why would the guy who's responsible be the one who lives while all those others who were his victims—even his own wife—be dead? It's just not fair."

"Agreed," I said. "Does that ever happen in real life?"

"Guess so," he said.

Mini-lessons on the structural components common to the problem plays were taught as part of the workshop model our English department adopted as part of a district initiative to teach reading and writing in ways that move students toward independence. We are a district that values choice. Classroom libraries, independent reading time, and collaborative practice with ongoing feedback is the hallmark of classrooms up through the twelfth grade.

Workshop Model

1. Ten-minute mini-lesson, including formative questions
2. Pull-out support during small-group collaborative work
3. Independent, ungraded formative practice
4. Summative assessment

Using student choice, mini-lessons, collaboration, and feedback as the foundational pillars of the Shakespeare Book Clubs project allowed students the time and practice needed to understand the common features of his problem plays. I began with a ten-minute Block to Love mini-lesson during which I used *The Taming of the Shrew* as a mentor text to explain how, in problem plays, a key character's desire for happiness was blocked by an authority figure or institution. I provided three pieces of evidence from the text that supported this block: in the first scene, when Baptista announces that Bianca must marry before Katherine (1.1.50–54); during Tranio's aside, when he realizes he must alert Lucentio to the situation at hand (183–87); and, finally, in act 2, when Baptista tells Petruchio that Katherine is "not for your turn, the more my grief" (2.1.66). My examples prompted a question to students about when blocks to love would mostly likely occur. Catelyn spoke up immediately: "Well, probably at the beginning."

"Why would that make sense to you?" I asked. She thought a minute first, but I saw sudden understanding when her eyes lit up.

"The block to love," she said, "is probably what starts the whole problem. Like in *Merchant of Venice,* Portia's dead father tries to block her right to choose her own husband by creating the casket riddle, but then she blocks Bassanio's love for Antonio at the end."

"How so?" I asked.

"Well, in the end, she makes him realize that he's got to be 'all in' in their marriage."

"And money is a block to love too," said Aidan. "Bassanio can't even try to marry her without some money, which is why he goes to Antonio in the first place." Other students were listening intently, and I could tell they were ready to talk about their own plays. In their book clubs, they discussed the types of blocks they saw and took notes in their journals. I walked around to listen to discussions and heard them talk about the characters who were blocked by an authority figure. Most talked about how the victims initially tried to push back but eventually were overcome by helplessness. I was amazed at how insightful they were about the plays after having read only a few acts. Many students realized how the block comes in the form of an authority figure, such as the father in *Merchant* and *Othello* or the King in *Winter's Tale* and *Measure for Measure.* The *Winter's Tale* group agreed that Leontes blocks his own love for his wife and blocks potential love for his children. Status or class becomes a block later in the play, so students realized that sometimes explicit and implicit blocks are at work. I heard Ailise talking to her group members about how Angelo in *Measure for Measure* actually sets up a self-block as he knowingly sets up an ultimatum and lewdly threatens Isabella. My excitement grew as I listened to these amazing young people share their thinking about Shakespeare's work. Their prereading and reading of the play had provided a new and interesting way of discussing the plays: through the lens of society's beliefs and mores. They considered how the key players were reacting to the restrictions placed on their personal lives, how the documents confirmed their obstinacies and desires, and how they were connecting with the play. Certainly, today's teenagers have felt their own love and friendships blocked. The pandemic, a force beyond their control, had done that.

Teaching structural components (Table 6.2) that tie the four book clubs together provides commonality among plays regardless of the differences in how the moral corruptors manipulate and vilipend or how the ambiguous endings confuse and discomfit. Using a mentor text as the instructional vehicle helps students follow an analysis model without leading students to answers. Discussions based on a common text are focused on one specific component, allowing students to delve into their own play and understand how the concepts work in other plays. The beauty of the workshop model lay in the adaptability of the how teaching and learning can occur. Some teachers may prefer to intersperse mini-lessons at various stopping points. Some may decide to wait until the reading is completed. Another idea is to insert the *block to love* and *moral corruptor* after the first two acts and use the final three after the completion of the plays. Teachers may also use student research to "tag" their discussions. If the moral corruptor is an authority figure, students may have found documents on the rights of kings to analyze how far he can go to control others. Students may also use various platforms for their discussions, such as Zoom, FaceTime, or Instagram after they watched recorded mini-lessons. Many of my students set up Google Docs to share their thinking. It was helpful for me to create a document (see Table 6.3) for students to guide their discussions, but it was also helpful to reflect on how the structural components lived in each play.[30]

TABLE 6.2. Problem plays' structural devices.

Block to love	A key character's desire for happiness is blocked by an authority figure or institution
Moral corruptor	A self-identified moral character who denigrates others identified and analyzed
Disguises and guile	Creative plans devised to overcome, hide, or trick an authority figure or system put into play
Framing devices and double plots	Nested stories and parallel plots explored and analyzed for their importance to overall meaning
Ambiguous resolution	Important speeches, discoveries, and untangling of complicated or misunderstood events lead to more questions and doubt

TABLE 6.3. Structural devices of two problem plays.

Title	*Taming of the Shrew* mentor text	Book club title: *Merchant of Venice* Book Club
Block to love	Baptista forbids Bianca from marrying until the elder daughter, Katherine, is married; he forbids Petruchio from marrying Katherine until she is in love with him.	Shylock is blocked from loving his life by the horrid abuse of Antonio and his daughter's decision to elope with a Christian. Portia is blocked from freedom and love by the dominance of her father's will and the shortsightedness of her suitors (sans Bassanio). Antonio is blocked from love and freedom due to the restrictions of the bond and loan between him and Shylock: if Antonio does not pay back three thousand ducats within three months, he will lose a pound of flesh nearest his heart.
Moral corruptor	Petruchio uses emotional and physical means to control "Kate." She must comply with his demands before he will allow her marry him and go to her sister's wedding.	Antonio continually verbally and physically abuses Shylock, even trying to guilt-trip him when Shylock is trying to propose fair terms to solidify their bond. Bassanio calls Shylock as having "a villain's mind," even after Antonio backhandedly compliments Shylock by saying "The Hebrew will turn Christian; he grows kind." Portia-as-Balthazar, in the court scene, refers to Shylock as an "alien" and heavily implies that he was never welcome in Venice. No matter what other qualities she may have, this statement clearly marks her as a moral corruptor.
Disguises and guile	Hortensio, Lucentio, and Tranio impersonate other men to gain admittance to Bianca and to set up the marriage; a lord disguises Sly, a drunken beggar, so he believes he is a lord.	Although it ends out well, Bassanio uses the lent money of Antonio to deliberately misrepresent his own wealth and stature in Venice in order to woo and marry Portia. Portia, on the other hand, does not have the freedom to use her cleverness in the beginning of her own story. She is bound by the terms and conditions of her father's will, but she branches and fleshes out her capacity for disguises and guile in act 4, scene 1, in order to successfully and legally weasel Antonio out of Shylock's hastily made and misworded bond.
Structural devices	*Nesting*: A play within a play (the "taming" story is told to Sly; parallel plot of Bianca's and Katherine's courting).	The closest *The Merchant of Venice* can get to either nesting or parallel plots is the tale of Antonio's ships. We first hear of them when Antonio offers to let Bassanio run him into debt so that Bassanio may woo and marry Portia. We next hear of Antonio's ships when we receive word that all of them have been lost at sea, thus making Antonio automatically default on his loan with Shylock. The last we hear of Antonio's ships is near the very end of *The Merchant of Venice*, when we are informed that some of Antonio's ships (presumed lost forever) have in fact made it back to the Venetian harbor safe and sound. (Antonio has also barely escaped his trial in one piece, so one could say that the return of his ships was a stroke of good fortune or too little, too late.)
Ambiguous ending	Kate's speech at the end about "obeying" her husband is questionable; it is unknown whether he has tamed her or if she has lost her spunk.	I don't actually think that *The Merchant of Venice* has a true ambiguous ending. Instead of having plot points unsatisfactorily wrapped up, it leaves the door open for *more* to happen within its world. What will happen with Shylock now that he has been forced to convert to Christianity? Now that Bassanio and Portia and Gratiano and Nerissa are happily married and good friends, what adventures will they have together? How will Jessica and Lorenzo fare now that they have eloped and have a swathe of Shylock's wealth in their possession? Many questions remain at the end of *The Merchant of Venice*, but not of the sort to make it an ambiguous ending.

Post-Reading

Throughout our two weeks of hybrid instruction, students learned as much as possible about the problem plays through documentaries, research, discussions, writing, and sketching. They read the plays, marked powerful moments, discussed structural components, and created common symbols for all the plays. My ultimate project goal was for students to create meaning and find relevance in the power of the problem plays. It was not often that I gave my students free rein to demonstrate their learning. The entire premise of the project was to give students time and space to decide if Shakespeare was still an important playwright today. Did he have something to offer twenty-first-century American teenagers? Does Shakespeare continue to speak to us today?

Does Shakespeare continue to speak to us today?

In a world where people around the globe feel isolated and alone, where our nation's youth feel dismissed and unimportant, where the innocent are often victimized and oppressed, how do four-hundred-year-old texts reach out to us and say, "#MeToo". . . "Black Lives Matter". . . "Justice! Justice! Justice!"? Would my students look to Shylock's resolve, "The villainy you teach me I will execute, and it will go hard but I will better the instruction" (*MV* 3.1.70–72), or would they forge other resolutions?

The Remix Project

For the final project, I chose the Multimedia Remix Project, because of the breadth and depth—and, let's face it, excitement!—it offers. Similar to how early modern playwrights and poets wrote within the context of an early modern European world, students also situated their own creativity and passion within today's popular culture. The only requirement was to "mix" meaningful connections between Shakespeare's world and ours. Book clubs were eager to search for twenty-first-century artifacts that hold sway against the forces of today's moral corruptors: song lyrics, movies, books, movements, art, slogans, quotes, memes, news reports, video clips, Instagram posts, tweets, and TikToks—evidence that early modern societal issues were similar to their own because human nature rarely changes. This was my students' sandbox. Their world. It was like unleashing an emotional whirlwind that pushed me back to give them space to think, talk, and create.

We did talk about how the rubric was *loose–tight*. I wanted them to fill empty spaces with how they felt about Shakespeare's work. The project description included the goal, to showcase how Shakespeare's problem plays are relevant and worthwhile literature for today's young adults, and the process, to illuminate the societal issues as the major connective tissue between our worlds. How students would present their ideas was dependent on their groups' skill sets. Some were adept at iMovie, some at TikTok, some at Screencast-O-Matic. The idea for a Multimedia Remix Project was the desire to give them freedom to experiment, time to think, and space to create. We reviewed the rubric and discussed how teams could divide the work:

Rubric

Remix projects of this caliber provide information about one of Shakespeare's problem plays through a variety of audio/visual media, such as text, film, podcasts, graphics, and music. All group members have worked collaboratively to select a platform that can serve as both a live presentation or a digital project sent electronically to a variety of real audiences. The *remix* of Shakespeare's work with contemporary artifacts reveals powerful connections and draws meaningful conclusions about why his work continues to be relevant today. Quotes from the play and other primary documents are well chosen and linked to a variety of appropriate contemporary references found in today's news, memes, posts, song lyrics, movies, art, ads, cartoons, laws, or social media. Projects that earn this score demonstrate excellence in time management, collaborative strategies, division of labor, and work ethic. Group members have completed all steps in the project and have reflected on the experience in a well-developed essay that outlines how their significant part has contributed to the quality of the whole project.

Students wondered about how many pieces of evidence were required, how long the videos had to be, if their voices needed to be included, and who were considered "real audiences." It was difficult yet refreshing to reassure them that my reasons for *not* specifying exact details was to provide the freedom they needed to work within the parameters of the rubric. They could present their idealized product representative of their learning. The most important question they had was one that many students have about group projects: "What happens if one of our group members does not contribute? Is that fair?" I was prepared for this question.

"Think of this as a collaborative project you are working on as part of your job. You have a team set in place by your employer who believes each member has a special skill set amenable to the task at hand. And you have a deadline. As John Donne said, 'No man is an island, and, in a perfect world, each team member should carry an equal share." I could see them nodding, so I was confident they had heard this speech before. "But I'd like you to approach this project with eyes and ears open to objection." Eyebrows went up.

"How can we do that?" asked Jordan. "It doesn't even make sense."

"Think about what you can gain from those who do not think, react, or plan like you. You will all stretch your personal boundaries by celebrating other viewpoints, especially those who are dragging their feet. Innovation is rarely found by following set patterns or concrete steps. Some of our best ideas come from stepping outside our circles of expectation."

"Well, that's easy to say, but what do we do if we make a plan, and *someone* doesn't do their part? It's frustrating!"

"No doubt. If we begin with the premise that we are all indispensable to each other, how can we build on those feelings during those first planning meetings?"

"Maybe we could make a list of things we are good at," offered Joe.

"What about making sure we have at least one idea from each person in the presentation?" added Anna.

"Those are great ways to begin," I said. "And, remember, much of what you are doing could be online without a teacher and ongoing feedback. It's easy to get frustrated and shut down [Graesser and D'Mello]."

"So is the idea to check in and give our own feedback?"

"That's a great idea, Joe, and could be one of the first things you talk about in your planning meetings. Along with *what* you want to include in your multimedia project, talk about *how* your process will play out the best. Who will take the lead on each section, who will check in with each member, who will remind members of the deadlines you set for each other?"

The knowledge I gained about project-based learning from Trevor Muir's *The Epic Classroom* was in full throttle. Cultures of collaboration are not instinctual and regardless of how much time is spent working on a project, working together toward a common goal is not without mishap. According to Muir, the best group outcomes will be based on individual accountability, including a "discussion about what they expect from each other throughout the process" (127).

Students had other struggles along the way but used their own strategies to solve them. Our hybrid schedule gifted them with two two-hour sessions to hammer out plans. Most groups perused the *sample schedule*[31] to use as a model and began dividing up the issues they wanted to explore and how they would store their information. One group discovered Clipchamp, the Chromebook version of iMovie, so one group member decided to concentrate on learning how to use it while the other two book club members researched quotes, song lyrics, and movie clips depicting sexual harassment. Students working on *Othello* were scouring the text for racial slurs and decided to include Iago's tainted words, "an old black ram / is tupping your white ewe" (1.1.97–98) and "your daughter and the Moor are (now) making the beast with two backs" (129–131), the first written in poetry and the second in prose. "Why have you chosen those two quotes?" I asked.

"Well," said Jenna, "It's so disgusting. I mean, it's so racist and is making them out to be animals when really they're married and in love."

"How are you connecting those comments to today?"

"I was thinking about Beyoncé's song 'Freedom.'"

"And I thought we could include some article quotes on racist police brutality," added Hannah.

"How would the quotes fit your ideas about *Othello*?" I asked.

Bryce spoke up immediately. "Well, I think Iago got away with this because he's white."

"Tell me more about that idea," I ventured.

"Well, we've been talking about it, and we've noticed all the lines that have to do with Othello's skin color. And how many times Iago has said, 'I hate the Moor.' It just makes sense that he hates him for that reason. Everyone else is white too, so how do we know they don't also feel that way?"

Bryce's words were impassioned and not without reason. Our own country's racial unrest had reached several crescendos within the several months since forty-six-year-old George Floyd was killed. Students wanted to talk about the hate crimes in our own country, so Iago's reasons—jealousy, greed, prejudice—were inconsequential. If and how he was punished for his actions were of utmost importance. "Iago got away with it," Bryce said. "Even if he got tortured at the end, he was still standing at the end."

"Yeah," said Hannah. It wasn't fair. Jenna looked down and shook her head.

Student Reflections

Student reflections were part of the final assessment. For each book club to earn a top score, members had to "complete all steps in the project and reflect on the experience in a well-developed essay that outlines how their significant part contributed to the quality of the whole project." As we reviewed the rubric together, I suggested accountability partners within the team to assure that students completed all parts and did not disappoint because they simply forgot. It happens. I was pleased—okay, ecstatic—that students internalized this piece of advice. All reflections were submitted. Every. Single. Student. I have never had that happen before. Their responses to the project were positive and reassuring. Most talked about what they thought of the book club approach, including their takeaways, and some commented on the differences between whole-class novels and book club approaches. They agreed that making their own meaning was the most important as well as how much support they received from each other.

> "We all took a risk in trying something that we had never done before."
>
> —James

> "Reading the plays the way we did made it easier to understand and make connections between themes in the book and what is going on in the world today."
>
> —Kara

> "I did do a little research on the other problem plays to see what themes were present. I also watched the different documentaries on the other plays to learn how these themes were presented."
>
> —DJ

> "Having discussions of the text helped to improve my comprehension of the early modern language and, most importantly, making connections to why the topics were relevant and important in my life."
>
> —Maddie

> "The research part allowed me to learn much more about Shakespeare than other approaches as it forced me to look deeper into the connections of his plays, his world at that time, and his person."
>
> —Aidan

Student writing and discussions gave me important information about their understanding of early modern society and Shakespeare's plays, but I had not expected feedback on my involvement in the project. Many students mentioned that, in past experiences, the teachers explained difficult sections, but Lindsey spoke about the freedom she felt to create her own meaning:

> I appreciate how you taught and guided us through this teaching of Shakespeare. In all other units of Shakespeare that I have encountered it almost felt like "church and the bible." It was all interpreted for me, laid out for me, I was just learning the components of what was already in front of me. This project however, you were "hands-off" in such a way that allowed us to truly interpret and come up

> with our own opinions/ ideas concerning the play I learned a lot more about how people in the early modern period thought and how that contrasts to familiar societal ideas currently. For example, I had no idea they were so superstitious and I learned a lot about how oppressive life was specifically for women during this time.

Lindsey's ideas shook me because I had not fully understood the powerlessness students felt trying to decipher Shakespeare's words. If each time we are confronted with new and difficult information, explanations leave us with few tools to become independent. What we need to approach difficult text is twofold. First, prereading is crucial because it provides background knowledge and language patterns that provide anticipation of what is to come. In other words, our predictions about a narrative structure become the anticipatory sets. We know when we have arrived, and we understand not only the meaning but also the significance. In short, comprehension builds when we reaffirm our preconceived beliefs about *what* we read *when* we read. In *The Winter's Tale*, for example, during prereading, students learn about Hermione's fall from grace when Leontes accuses her of infidelity. When they read the play in book clubs, students may add the details of the Oracle's decision relative to Hermione's guilt to their baseline of understanding. Adding cultural knowledge through artifacts, such as Anne Boleyn's trial record, adds texture and dimension to Hermione's reaction to Leontes's accusations. Second, collaborative practice builds confidence for independent, successful outcomes. How students feel about their ability to comprehend is more important than any unit of study. It is that feeling of "I know how to learn" rather than "I know what to do."

Even though we do not necessarily know Shakespeare's motives for writing or his process for setting quill to parchment, we do understand that he was writing within a society that experienced growing pains. He undoubtedly knew the consequences of staging political upheavals, religious strife, and tyrannical monarchs that were too close to home. But he also had a sixth sense about how to change the source plays he used to increase intensity, provide humor, and invoke tears. He was a businessman who understood how to fill the Globe and his pockets. Our students may not understand every word, catch each innuendo, or feel every *hamartia*, but they do take comfort and perhaps "take arms against a sea of troubles" in their own world. Reading becomes less about ways to pass the time and more about their appreciation for life beyond their own borders. Shakespeare offers us proof, not of a more evolved humanity or a growing mindset; instead, he offers us a challenge. We can find commonalities, develop empathy, and fight prejudice. Yes, Shakespeare's plays do entertain, inform, and sadden, but that is not enough to make a case for reading his poetry and plays in schools today. It must be more than required reading lists or Common Core Standards. Shakespeare lives within us long after the curtain closes or the final test is taken. We connect with his characters' fears of not being seen and cheer them on when they discover self-truths. We do indeed see ourselves in his imaginings of human frailty and solipsistic behavior. But we also have hope for a better tomorrow, one where tragedies and comedies are natural consequences of our actions. And we *are* in control of our own destinies.

Conclusion

There's Rosemary, that's for remembrance
Pray you, love, remember. And there is pansies,
That's for thoughts...
There's fennel for you, and columbines.
There's rue for you, and here's some for me
—OPHELIA (*Ham.* 4.5.199–205)

The document approach to teaching Shakespeare narrows the gap between early modern society and ours by helping students situate his plays and sonnets within a society fraught with tumultuous, searing political and religious upheaval—probably no different than our own world. Engaging in primary sources provides resources for discovery: Shakespeare and his contemporaries used art, pamphlets, speeches, scripts, sermons, and superstitious beliefs to speak their truths, the voices of that period. Their beautiful harmony is the backdrop of his stage.

Walking in Shakespeare's Shoes is a tool for today's teachers, a place to find solace if you sometimes struggle with how to teach difficult yet engaging poetry to today's teenagers. I'd like to think we are all on this road together and that this book can be used in conjunction with what you already do in the classroom. Early modern plant lore helped me understand Ophelia's plight in *Hamlet*. I've found that students are also intrigued with the green world and are much more able to empathize when they watch her give away plants and herbs to her brother and the King and Queen if they understand the symbolism and value of each. Polonius, her father, has been murdered, so Ophelia's dissembling seems justifiable. With some investigation, Gerard's *Herball* reveals that her choices are significant, and the audience standing in front of the Globe's stage would have readily understood the tragedy of her situation. Plant lore became Shakespeare's tool and an inroad into Ophelia's psyche, gifting his audiences the power of her behavior. They may have cried for this young woman who wove a crown out of the crow flowers and daisies that grew along the riverbank in spring but, when picked, wilted quickly and smelled putrid. The nettles she tied into the braided wreath made of supple willow branches were meant to sting her head, the antidote not far off but untouched. The long purples, too sexualized for a young woman of her age and standing, colored her death with longing and disappointment. When Gertrude reported Ophelia's death in act 4, scene 7, the audience would have been bereft.

This book evolved because I wanted to know what sixteenth-century men, women, and children might have felt as they stood in front of the stage for two hours or paid a penny to cushion their seats as they watched Shakespeare's stories unfold. I wondered if primary documents could tell today's students "the rest of the story" about the magnitude of regicide, the magic of the green world, or the mayhem in the city streets. Mostly, I wondered if my students would connect to Shakespeare's words in meaningful ways, if they would question his world the same way they question their own. Would they find the golden thread—the one that tautly spans our centuries—and wonder where it will take them next? The classroom stories in this book are real and punctuated with questions about early modern beliefs, showing how inquiry is part and parcel of the document approach.

Using primary and secondary sources to provide sundry voices has helped me situate Shakespeare's writing in much the same way that Lin-Manuel Miranda's *Hamilton* will be understood by future generations. Will they search for answers in today's artifacts to understand Miranda's writing? Will they watch our dissatisfaction with the world through memes, Twitter, and Instagram? Will they smile when they witness our spoken-word poetry, our medical procedures, our slang? Will they cry when they read about how we suffered during a deadly pandemic? Will our treatment of immigrants, the desire the rise to the top, and our "one shot" risky risk-taking be evident in the art, pamphlets, speeches, scripts, sermons, and the superstitious beliefs of our day? To understand Shakespeare's work, his tours de force, we must ingest not only his work but also his world.

Discovering the golden thread that connects the sixteenth and twenty-first centuries has shown me how we may become more comfortable in our discomfort as we catapult into the future. I hope we continue to teach our children and students to read widely and wisely. It is, after all, empathy we strive to gain. Understanding Shakespeare's world encompasses more than a single story. We need a variety of voices, from simple recipes to complex treatises, to help us understand the magnitude of his writing. His language has lasted over four hundred years, but his ability to permeate generations with his insight into the human soul has prompted us to catch the golden thread and hang on for as long as we can.

Pray you, love, remember.

Appendix A

Primary Documents

In addition to slides and lesson plans, all primary documents listed throughout this book can be accessed via the accompanying website *Teaching Shakespeare* (shakespearedocuments.info).

Romeo and Juliet

TABLE A.1. Act 1—Gender and clothing.

Proclamations	Queen Elizabeth I, *Proclamation Enforcing Statutes of Apparel*, 6 May 1562 (see Hughes and Larkin) Queen Elizabeth I, *Proclamation Prohibiting Unlawful Assembly under Martial Law*, 20 June 1594 (qtd. in Callaghan 232–33; see also Hughes and Larkin)
Poem	Samuel Rowlands, "The Humors that Haunt a Wife," *Humors Looking Glasse*, 1608
Essay	John Lyly, *Euphues: The Anatomy of Wit*, 1578, excerpt
Essays	Nicholas Breton, "A Virgin" (27) and "A Wanton Woman" (28) from *Descriptions of the Worthies, and Vnworthies of this Age*, 1616
Poems	Charles Pyrrye, "Here Beginneth the Disprayse of VVomen," *The Praise and Dispraise of Women*, 1569 Charles Pyrrye, "Here Beginneth the Prayse of VVomen," *The Praise and Dispraise of Women*, 1569
Essay	Jacques Ferrand, "Chapter 14: Signes Diagnosticke of Love- Melancholy," *Erotomania, or A Treatise Discoursing of the Essence, Causes, Symptomes, Prognosticks, and Cure of Love, or Erotique Melancholy*, 1640
Catalogue	John Gerard, "Feverfew" and "Black Hellebore," *The Herball, or Generall Historie of Plantes*, 1597
Excerpts	Katherine Usher Henderson and Barbara F. McManus, "The Pamphlet Wars in Renaissance England," *Half Humankind: Contexts And Texts of the Controversy about Women in England 1540–1640*, pp. 11, 51, 74
Pamphlets	Jane Anger, *Jane Anger Her Protection for Vvomen To defend Them Against the Scandalous Reportes of a Late Surfeiting Louer, and All Otherlike Venerians that Complaine so to Bee Ouercloyed with Womens Kindnesse*, 1589 Joseph Swetnam, *The Araignment of Leuud, Idle, Forward, and Vnconstant Women or the Vanitie of Them, Choose You Whether: With a Commendation of Wise, Vertuous and Honest Women: Pleasant for Married Men, Profitable for Young Men, and Hurtfull to None*, 1615

Frontispiece and sermon excerpt	William Whately, "Women's Roles," *A Bride-Bush, or A Vvedding Sermon Compendiously Describing the Duties of Married Persons*, 2nd ed., 1619
Poem	John Gough, "Encomiums on the Beauty of His Miftrefs," *The Academy of Complements. VVherin Ladyes Gentlewomen, Schollers, and Stranges May Accomodate Their Courtly Practice with Most Curious Ceremonies, Complementall, Amorous, High Expressions, and Formes of Speaking, or Writing. A Worke Perused and Most Exactly Perfected by the Author with Additions of Witty Amorous Poems*, 1640
Graphics	Harry Peacham, Four Humours, *Minerva Britanna: The Second Part, Or a Garden of Heroical Devises, Furnished, and Adorned with Emblemes and Impresa's of Sundry Natures*, 1612, pp. 126–29, woodcuts

TABLE A.2. Act 2—Marriage and sexuality.

Epic poem, excerpt	Edmund Spenser, *Faerie Queene*, 1590–96, lines 1.1.11–20
Sermons	William Whately, "Sermon on Marital Sex" and "On Rushing into Marriage," *A Bride-Bush, or A Vvedding Sermon Compendiously Describing the Duties of Married*, 2nd ed., 1619
Catalogue	John Gerard, "Of Sowbreade. Ch. 296," *The Herball or Generall Historie of Plantes*, 1597
Letter	William Miller, "A Letter of Advice Concerning Marriage by A. B.," 1676
Liturgy	"The Fourme of Solemnizacion of Matrimonye," *Book of Common Prayer*, edited by William Keatinge Clay, 1559 ed.
Treatise	Henry Swinburne, "Of Ripe or Lawful Age for Marriage" (sec. 9) and "Of Publick and Private Spousals" (sec. 14), *A Treatise of Spousals, or Matrimonial Contracts*, 1686
Chart	Copy from Peter Laslett, Table 1.2: Mean Age at First Marriage in England by Fifty-Year Periods, 1550–1849, *Family Life and Illicit Love in Earlier Generations: Essays in Historical Sociology*, 1981 (see also Young 470)
Letter	John Donne, "Letter to Sir George More," 1602
Scholarly article	Stephen Greenblatt, "Romeo and Juliet," *The Norton Shakespeare*, 1997. Includes visual *The Talk between Mafter Bradford, and Two Spanifh Friers* (woodcut held at the National Portrait Gallery, London)
Text comparisons	Arthur Brooke, "Tragicall Historye of Romeus and Juliet," 1562, and William Shakespeare, *Romeo and Juliet*, 1595

TABLE A.3. Act 3—Violence and death.

Frontispiece and explanation	Vincentio Saviolo, *His Practise*, 1595; and qtd. in Joan Ozark Holmer, 1994
Text comparisons	William Shakespeare, *Romeo and Juliet*, 1595, 2.4.6–35, 3.1.26–106; Vincentio Saviolo, *His Practise*, 1595 (with comments by Holmer, 1994)
Excerpt	Vincentio Saviolo, "When One Doth Call Another For an Offence Done vnto Him By a Third Person," *His Practise*, 1595, image 96
Woodcut	*O Wormes Meat: O Froath: O Vanitie: Why Art Thou So Insolent?* [copy from *The Mirror of Man's Lyfe* in Vincentio Saviolo, *His Practise*]
Handout	Matt McKay, "Parts of the Single Rapier, The Grippe, The Targets/Lines of Attack and Defense," 2005 (available from the *Teaching Shakespeare* website, shakespearedocuments.info)

TABLE A.4. Acts 4 and 5—Medicines and poison.

Article	Claudia Hammond, "Would Shakespeare's Poisons and Drugs Work in Reality?," 2014
Text comparisons of afterlife	*Book of Common Prayer*, 1549; *The Bible*; John Calvin's works in *Corpus Reformatorum* (see, e.g., Thompson; see also the act 5 documents on the *Teaching Shakespeare* website, shakespearedocuments.info); Edward Vaughan, *A Divine Discoverie of Death*, 1612 (qtd. in Targoff 20; see also Marshall 217); John Donne's letter of consolation to Lady Kingsmill, epitaphs, 1624; Ramie Targoff, "Mortal Love: Shakespeare's *Romeo and Juliet* and the Practice of Joint Burial," *Representations*, 2012
Catalogue	John Gerard, "Sleeping Nightshade," *The Herball, or Generall Historie of Plantes*, 1597
Catalogue	William Bullein, "Mandrakes" (41–42) and "Poppy" (25), *Bulleins Bulwarke of Defence*, 1579
Woodcuts (9)	Hans Holbein the Younger, *The Dance of Death* series, 1538 (see Pennant-Rea)
Article excerpt	Tanya Pollard, "'A Thing Like Death': Sleeping Potions and Poisons in 'Romeo and Juliet' and 'Antony and Cleopatra,'" *Renaissance Drama*, 2003
Article excerpt	Michael MacDonald and Terence R. Murphy, editors, "Suicides in the Early Modern Period," *Sleepless Souls: Suicide in the Early Modern Period*, 1996, including "Mortality Record: 'The Difeafes and Cafualities this Week,'" 1665
Catalogue	John Gerard, "Mandrake or Atropa Mandragora," "Garden Poppies," "Black Henbane," *The Herball, or Generall Historie of Plantes*, 1597

Hamlet

TABLE A.5. Act 1—Ghosts and afterlife.

Essay	Francis Bacon, "Of Revenge," *The Essays, or Councils, Civil and Moral, of Sir Francis Bacon, Lord Verulam, Viscount St. Alban*, 3rd ed., 1625
Pamphlet	Jane Owen, *Antidote against Purgatory*, 1634
Text comparisons on afterlife	St. Augustine, *De Civitate Dei Contra Paganos (Concerning the City of God Against the Pagans)*, circa 413–426 CE; Thomas Aquinas, *Summa Theologica*, 1265–1274; Ludwig Lavater, *Of Ghofts and Fpirits Walking by Nyght*, 1572; Thomas Nash, *The Terrors of the Night*, 1594; King James VI, *Daemonologie*, 1597; Reginald Scot, Appendix, *The Discoverie of Witchcraft*, 1584
Poem	Robert Southwell, "The Burning Babe," 1595
Drama	Thomas Kyd, *The Spanish Tragedy*, 1587, 1.5.98
Drama	William Shakespeare, *Hamlet*, 1.5.14–26, and Harold Jenkins, editor, "Notes," *Hamlet* (new Arden ed.), 1982
Treatises	Simon Fish, *A Supplicacyon for the Beggers*, 1529 Henry Brinkelow and Simon Fish, *A Supplicacyon of the Poore Commons Whereunto is Added the Supplication of Beggers* [a plea for Catholic reform], 1546
Scholarly article excerpt	Stephen Greenblatt, "The Death of Hamnet and the Making of Hamlet," *The New York Review*, 2004

TABLE A.6. Act 2—Madness and melancholy.

Catalogue	John Gerard, "Blacke Hellebore," *The Herball, or Generall Historie of Plantes*, 1597; including "Sweet Fruit" from Burton's *Anatomy*
Text	Robert Burton, *The Anatomy of Melancholy*, 1621
Visual	George Thomason, editor, *The Picture of an English Antick, with a Lift of his ridiculous Habits, and Apifh Geftures*, 1646
Text	Phillip Stubbes, "In Commendation of the Author, and His Booke," "The horrible Vice of pestiferous dauncing, vsed in Ailgna," "Beare baiting and other exercyses, vsed in vnlawfully in AILGNA," and "Of Musick in Ailgna, and how it allureth to vanitie," *The Anatomie of Abuses*, Part 1, 1583
Catalogue	Richard Amyas, "A Most Excellent Receipt against Melancholy," *An Antidote Against Melancholy*, 1659, p. 1
Lecture	John Taylor, "The Author's Advice on How to Tame a Shrew, or Vex Her," *A Juniper Lecture*, 1639
Sonnets	William Shakespeare, " Sonnet 45: The Other Two, Slight Air and Purging Fire," 1609 Ben Jonson, "On My First Sonne," 1616 (see Hunter 864)
Essay and poem	Amelia Lanyer, "To the Virtuous Reader" and "Eve's Apology in Defence of Women," *Salue Deus Rex Iudæorum*, 1611
Pamphlet frontispiece	*The Araignement and Burning of Margaret Ferne-Seede*, 1608
Scholarly article	Maria Isabel Barbudo "William Shakespeare and the Representation of Female Madness," 2015

TABLE A.7. Act 3—Theater and acting.

Scholarly text	James Shapiro, "The Globe Rises." *A Year in the Life of William Shakespeare: 1599*, 2005, pp. 107–09
Scholarly text	Andrew Gurr, "Bear-Baiting" [including a foreign visitor's 1584 witness], *The Shakespearean Stage 1574–1642*, 1992, p. 185
Pamphlet	Phillip Stubbes, "Of Stage-Playes and Enterluds, with Their Wickednes," *The Anatomie Of Abuses*, Part 1, 1583
Sonnet	William Shakespeare, "Sonnet 23" [and explanation], 1609 quarto ed.
Scholarly text	Andrew Gurr, "On Kemp and the Jig," *The Shakespearean Stage 1574–1642*, 1992, pp. 108, 214
Scholarly text	Andrew Gurr, "The Playhouses," *The Shakespearean Stage 1574–1642*, 1992, pp. 174–81
Essay	Sir Philip Sidney, "Poetry in England," *The Defence of Poesy* [originally titled *The Defence of Poesie* or *An Apologie for Poetrie*], 1595
Poem	Ben Jonson, "To the Memory of My Beloved the Author, Mr. William Shakespeare," 1623 (see Hunter 890)

TABLE A.8. Act 4—Gardens and lore.

Catalogue	John Gerard, "Of Crowfloures, or Wilde Williams," *The Herball, or Generall Historie of Plantes*, 1597
Scholarly text	Roy Strong, "Gardens for Queen Elizabeth I," *The Renaissance Garden in England*, 1998, pp. 50, 53 (including sketch of Kenilworth, 1656)
Visual	"Elizabeth I as *Rosa Electa*, flanked by the Tudor Rose and the Virgin Eglantine," 1590 (image from Henry Lyte's *The Light of Britayne; A Recorde of the Honorable Originall and Antiquitie of Britaine*, 1588; copy from Folger Shakespeare Library, image 3)
Pamphlet	*List of Fellows of the Royal College of Surgeons of Edinburgh from the Year 1581 to 31st December 1873*; with explanation from Trea Martyn's *Queen Elizabeth in the Garden*, 2008
Catalogues	John Gerard, *The Herball, or Generall Historie of Plantes*, 1597, and Thomas and Faircloth, 2016: "Rosemary," "Pansies," "Fennell," "Columbine," "Rue, or Herbe Grace," "Daisy," "Violets"
Sonnet	William Shakespeare, "Sonnet 15" [and explanation], 1609 quarto ed.
Manual	William Lawson, *The Country Housewifes Garden*, 1618
Poetry	Robert Herrick, "To Pansies," To Daisies Not to Shut so Soon," "To Violets," 1591–1674
Catalogue	Rembert Dodoens, "A Table Vvherein is Conteyened the Nature, Vertue, and Dangers, of Al the Herbes, Trees, and Plantes, of vvhich are spoken in the present Booke, or Herbal," *A Nievve Herball, or Historie Of Plantes Wherin is Contayned the Vvhole Discourse and Perfect Description of all Sortes of Herbes and Plantes*, translated by Henry Lyte, 1578

TABLE A.9. Act 5—Espionage and treason.

Narrative	Robert Wingfield, *From Narrative of the Execution of the Queen of Scots. In a letter to the Right Honorable Sir William Cecil*, 1587
Visual, letter, and essay	Nicholas Wolton, "Coded Letters," 1548, and Sir Francis Bacon, "Of Negotiating," 1597
Speech	Queen Elizabeth I, "Speech to the Troops at Tilbury," 1588
Scholarly article	Alexandra Briscoe, "Elizabeth's Spy Network," *BBC*, 2011
Essay	Qualities of an ambassador: Francis Thynne, 1578; Ortensio Landi, 1596; Alberico Gentili, 1585; Robert Hitchcock, 1590; including excerpt from Francis Thynne, "Trayterous Ambassadours," *The Perfect Ambassadour*, 1652, ch. 10
Scholarly article	Alexandra Briscoe, "Walsingham Traps Mary Queen of Scots," *BBC*, 2011
Letters	"Walsingham's Network," including letters from William Herle, 1587, and Nicholas Berden, 1586, to Walsingham
Painting of Elizabeth I	Formerly attributed to either Marcus Gheeraerts the Younger or Isaac Oliver, the *Rainbow Portrait*, circa 1600; including description by James Shapiro (*A Year in the Life* plate 3)

Macbeth

TABLE A.10. Act 1—Witchcraft and religion.

Indictment	*A Briefe Description of the Notorious Life of Iohn Lambe Otherwise Called Doctor Lambe. Together with His Ignominious Death*, 1628
Discourse	William Perkins, *A Discourse of the Damned Art of Witchcraft So Farre Forth As It Is Reuealed in the Scriptures, and Manifest by True Experience*, 1610
Dialogue	King James VI, *Daemonologie*, 1597
Catalogue	John Gerard, "Calves Snout, or SnapDragon," *The Herball, or Generall Historie of Plantes*, 1597
Visual	James Shapiro, "Demonic Possession," *The Year of Lear: Shakespeare in 1606*, 2015, p. 64
Proclamation	King James I, *An Act against Conjuration, Witchcraft, and Dealing with Evil and Wicked Spirits*, 1604
News report	James Carmichael, "The North Berwick Witch Trials," *Newes from Scotland*, 1592
Text comparisons on Lady Macbeth: Demonic or evil?	Dawn Saliba, *King James and the Theatre of Witches: Subversion upon the Jacobean Stage*, 2013; James Carmichael, *Newes from Scotland*, 1592; Daniel Swift, *Shakespeare's Common Prayers: The Book of Common Prayer and the Elizabethan Age*, 2013

TABLE A.11. Act 2—Government and freedom.

Dissertation excerpt	Paul Augustin Kottman, "Spectral Communities and Ghosts of Sovereignty: Interpreting Apparitions in *Hamlet* and *Macbeth*," 2000
Frontispiece	Article summary with quotes from *Machiavelli's Prince*, Rebecca Lemon, and Nicholas Machiavelli, *The Prince*, 1640
Speech and frontispiece	John Milton, *Areopagitica*, 1644
Woodcuts	Raphael Holinshed, *Macbeth and Banquo Meet the Witches*, "The Historie of Scotlande," *Chronicles of England, Scotlande and Irelande*, 1577, pp. 233–77 [copy in British Library, G.6006-7]
Treatise	King James VI, "The True Law of Free Monarchies," 1598
Treatise	John Milton, *The Tenure of Kings and Magistrates*, 1649
Confession and homily	*The Divine Right and the Irresistibility of Kings and Supreme Magistrates*, 1645, including "The Confession of Scotland"

TABLE A.12. Act 3—Manhood and customs.

Poem	Ben Jonson, "To Penshurst," 1616 (see Hunter 875–76)
Chapter excerpt	Charles Ross, "Macbeth's Future: 'A Thing of Custom,'" *The Custom of the Castle: From Malory to Macbeth*, 1997
Article	Judith Newmark, "Gender Lines Blur in this 'Macbeth.'" *McClatchy-Tribune Business News* (Washington), 19 July 2009
Essay	Count Baldassare Castiglione, *The Courtier*, 1561

Nonfiction excerpt	Roger Chartier, editor, *A History of Private Life: Volume 3, Passions of the Renaissance*, 2003, pp. 182–270
Diary	Simon Forman, *Book of Plays*, 1611
Manual	Desiderius Erasmus, "Of Manners at the Table," *De Civilitate Morum Puerilium* (*The Ciuilitie of Childehode with the Discipline and Institucion of Children*), translated by Robert Whittington, English ed., 1532
Poem and visual	Sir John Davis, "The Courtier," *Yet Other Twelve Wonders of the World*, 1602
Poems	Robert Herrick, "To the Virgins, to Make Much of Time," 1648, and Andrew Marvell, "To His Coy Mistress," 1650

TABLE A.13. Act 4—Equivocation and ambiguity.

Frontispiece	Francis Herring, *Mischeefes Mysterie*, 1617
Sonnet	William Shakespeare, "Sonnet 138," 1609
Scholarly text, including two prints	James Shapiro, "Remember, Remember," *The Year of Lear: Shakespeare in 1606*, 2015, pp. 119–33; *Execution of Guy Fawkes and Associates*, 1606; Crispijn de Passe The Elder, *The Gunpowder Plot Conspirators, 1605*, circa 1606 [reproduced in James Shapiro, *The Year of Lear: Shakespeare in 1606*, 2015, p. 118]
Treatises	Henry Garnet, "Treatise of Equivocation," 1598; Robert Parsons, "A Treatise Tending to Mitigation tovvardes Catholike-Subiectes in England," 1607
Treatise (chapter headings)	Robert Parsons, "A Treatise Tending to Mitigation tovvardes Catholike-Subiectes in England VVherin is Declared, That It Is Not Impossible for Subiects of Different Religion, (Especially Catholikes and Protestantes) to Liue Togeather in Dutifull Obedience and Subiection, vnder the Gouernment of his Maiesty of Great Britany," 1607
Pamphlet	*The Manner of Burning the Pope in Effigies in London, on the 5th of November, 1678*, 1678
Poem	Edward Hawes, "Trayterous Percyes and Catesbyes Prosopopoeia," 1606
Text comparisons	Andrew Sanders, editor, *The Short Oxford History of English Literature*, 3rd ed., 2004; Stephen Greenblatt, general editor, *The Norton Anthology of English Literature*, 8th ed., 2006

TABLE A.14. Act 5—Angst and insomnia.

Catalogue	John Gerard, *The Herball, or Generall Historie of Plantes*, 1597, and Rembert Dodoens, *A Nievve Herball*, 1578: "Rhubarb" and "The Vertues"
Play	William Shakespeare, *Henry IV, Part 2*, 3.1.4–31
Essay and frontispiece	John Sadler, *The Sicke VVomans Private Looking-Glasse*, 1636
Essay	Helkiah Crooke, *Mikrokosmographia: A Description of the Body of Man*, 1615
Treatise	*An Alarme to Awake Church-Sleepers*, 1644
Treatise	Thomas Hill, *The Moste Pleasuante Arte of the Interpretacion of Dreames*, 1576
Visuals	"A great perturbation in nature, to receive at once the benefit of sleep . . . in this slumb'ry agitation" (5.1.10–12): four different visual representations of the sleepwalking scene, all available from the *Teaching Shakespeare* website (shakespeare documents.info)
Scholarly article	Benjamin Parris, "'The Body is with the King, but the King is Not with the Body': Sovereign Sleep in Hamlet and Macbeth," *Shakespeare Studies*, 2012

A Midsummer Night's Dream

TABLE A.15. Act 1—Family and obligations.

Engraving	Levinus Hulsius, "Amazons Practicing Archery," 1598 [reproduced in Gail Kern Paster and Skiles Howard, editors, "Female Attachments and Family Ties," *A Midsummer Night's Dream: Texts and Contexts*, 1999, pp. 194–200]
Sermon	Thomas Adams, *A Divine Herball, Or the Prayse of Fertillitie*, 1616
Text comparisons	William Shakespeare, 1600; Thomas Adams, 1616; John Gerard, 1597; Robert Greene, 1592: Love-in-Idleness
Treatise	William Gouge, *Of Domesticall Duties*, 1622
Eulogy	Philip Stubbes, *A Crystal Glass for Christian Women*, 1592
Painting	Sandro Botticelli, *The Three Graces*, 1482
Poem	John Donne, "A Valediction Forbidding Mourning," 1633
Drama	William Shakespeare, *Romeo and Juliet*, 1595

TABLE A.16. Act 2—Conflict and resolution.

Painting	Hans Holbein, *The Ambassadors*, 1533
Poem	Ovid, "Pyramus and Thisbe," *Metamorphoses*, Book 4, 8 CE
Letter	Lady Jane Grey to her Father before her Execution, 1563
Poem	Sir Walter Raleigh, "The Lie," 1608
Poem	Edward Gosynhyll, *Here Begynneth a Lytle Boke named the Schole House of Women*, 1541
Frontispiece, title page, song	Gossips, 1619, 1654, 1690
Play	Desiderius Erasmus, *A Maid Hating Marriage*, 1523
Essay	"Nuns," Gail Kern Paster and Skiles Howard, editors, *A Midsummer Night's Dream: Texts and Contexts*, 1999, pp. 221–22

TABLE A.17. Act 3—Fairies and supernatural.

Text comparisons	Robert Burton, *The Anatomy of Melancholy*, 1621, and Reginald Scot, *The Discoverie of Witchcraft*, 1584
Pamphlet	*Robin Good-Fellow, His Mad Prankes, and Merry Iests*, 1639
Poem	Richard Corbett, "A Proper New Ballad Entitled The Fairies' Farewell: or God-A-Mercy Will," 1620
Lore	John Aubrey, "Fairies and Robin Goodfellow," *The Remains of Gentilism and Judaism*, 1688
Frontispiece	John Parkinson, *Paradisi in Sole*, 1629
Poem	Robert Herrick, "Oberon's Feast," 1648
Scholarly article	Marjorie Swann, "The Politics of Fairylore in Early Modern English Literature," *Renaissance Quarterly*, 2000
Paintings	Joseph Noel Paton, *The Quarrel of Oberon and Titania*, 1849; Amelia Jane Murray, *Fairies Floating Downstream In a Peapod* [reproduced in *Global Gallery*, www.globalgallery.com/search/subject/fairies, accessed 28 July 2016]; Edward Robert Hughes, *Midsummer Eve*, circa 1908

Scholarly chapter	Minor White Latham, "Shakespeare's Fairies," *The Elizabethan Fairies: The Fairies of Folklore and the Fairies of Shakespeare*, 1972 [originally published 1930], pp. 176–218

TABLE A.18. Act 4—Work and rank.

Director's notes	Ben Crystal, "The Mechanicals and Their Crafts," *Springboard Shakespeare: A Midsummer Night's Dream*, pp. 9–10
Blog post	S. A. Markham, "The Role of the Rude Mechanicals in *A Midsummer Night's Dream*, 2012
Statute	The House of Commons, "The Statute of Artificers 1562," 1563
Essay	William Harrison *The Description of England*, 1587
Treatise	Roger Ascham, *The Schoolmaster*, 1570
Title page	Attributed to George Turberville [probable author, Jacques du Fouilloux], *The Noble Art of Venery, or Hunting*, 1575
Portrait	Isaac Oliver, *Portrait of a Melancholy Young Man*, 1590–95
Epic poem	John Milton, Book 9, *Paradise Lost*, 1660
Drama	William Shakespeare, *Richard II*, 1597

TABLE A.19. Act 5—Celebrations and entertainment.

Scholarly article	Stephen Greenblatt, "Introduction: *A Midsummer Night's Dream*," *The Norton Shakespeare*, 1997, pp. 805–13
Poem	"A Midsummer Wish," 1670
Letter	Robert Laneham to Friend Humfrey Martin regarding the Queen at Kenilworth, 1575
Title page	George Gascoigne, *The VVhole Works of George Gascoigne Esquire*, 1587
Engraving	George Turberville, *Queen Elizabeth on a Hunt, The Booke of Falconrie*, 1611
Engraving	George Vertue, *Procession Portrait*, 1601
Excerpt	Trea Martyn, *Queen Elizabeth in the Garden*, 2008, p. 55
Masque	Ben Jonson, *The Irish Masque at Court*, 1616 [reproduced in Clark J. Holloway, *The Holloway Pages*, 2003, www.hollowaypages.com/jonson1692irish.htm]
Songs	"Young Man Put to His Dumps," 1686–1689; "May Day Country Mirth," 1684–1695

Appendix B

Shakespeare Teaching Strategies

3–2–1

This short but effective activity can be used anytime during the lesson to provide formative information about student needs. When teaching Shakespeare, it affords students opportunities to ask questions they may be reluctant to ask in front of their peers. One general version I use frequently is:

1. Name *three* things you understand about the play so far.
2. Name *two* things that do not make sense to you.
3. Ask *one* question that you still have.

I always take the time to read the questions—anonymously—to the class the next day. First, I want them to know the purpose for what I ask them to do. Second, I can clear up misconceptions about the play. And, third, my students understand that they are not alone in their confusions. We embrace them and move on.

Big Chunk, Little Chunk

This close reading activity allows for multiple readings of an excerpt. Students may read a scene, followed by one or two rereadings of a smaller chunk; first, with a partner, where one or both read aloud, and next independently. Students then follow up with summaries or analyses of specific word choices. Sharing with a partner or the entire class is the final step and one that should not be omitted.

Blocking Scenes

This activity is a shared reading experience where all partner or small groups receive the same scene to block, interpret, and act. First, students need a space large enough to imagine a stage, deciding where "players" stand, how they move, and when they speak. Plan for enough time to allow students to practice moves and speech sufficiently to be able to perform in class. The purpose of the activity is to break down language—especially in scenes where character placement is crucial, such as when Bernardo and Francisco are changing guard on the top of Elsinore Castle (1.1.1–12).

Cognitive Mind Maps

Mind mapping can take many forms, such as the character map shown in Figure B.1. But, often, maps that lay out themes in gradual complexity also work well, especially when working with intertextual thinking.

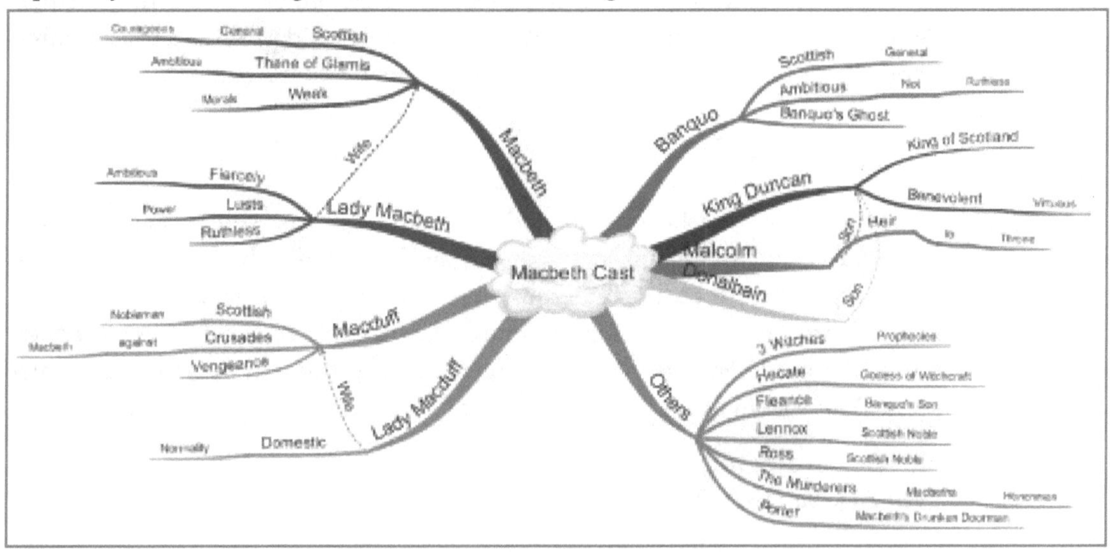

FIGURE B.1. Cognitive mind map.

Moving from a basic understanding of historical themes, such as describing primogeniture in *Hamlet*, followed by deeper understandings of how the theme compares to tanistry in *Macbeth* allows students to gradually synthesize ideas and draw conclusions about the tenuous relationships among characters and their deep-seated greed.

Generally, I model my own thinking before students begin work on their own examples in groups. This is one activity that moves students away from literal comprehension and toward deeper thinking about the plays.

Digital to Visual

Students take one scene, such as a soliloquy, and explicate its meaning through sketches only. This work can be expanded into symbols, which could be used for characters or big ideas.

Divide and Conquer

Divide up a scene into approximately fifty-line increments, assigning the number of students needed to act out the scene—which can go from one student, who may be speaking a soliloquy, to five students who are speaking to one another. Give students their section and time to practice. Having some props available makes this more fun. Groups perform their short scene clip sequentially in front of the class by reading their parts, blocking the movement, and acting the part. Before each group begins, a student in the group should provide a brief summary of what is happening. This is an interactive way to read, act, and view a scene.

Document Walk

After student groups have annotated a soliloquy or other short scene on poster-sized sticky note paper, place the papers on classroom or hallway walls spaced far enough apart that a group could stand in front to listen. It works best if students are working on different parts of the play that can be explained sequentially. Give students time to prepare a one-minute presentation of their annotated scene. Move from group to group as students unfold Shakespeare's work.

Explicate or Unfold

Students "close read" a passage and, using more modern language, unfold its meaning. Each line or section can be written as a contemporary poem—spoken word works well for this—and then do a Read-Around (a strategy described later in this Appendix), first reading the original and then the more modern version.

Family Tree

This activity provides a visual experience with figuring out "who's who" in a play. The idea works well when two families can be sorted out, such as the Capulets and Montagues in *Romeo and Juliet*. The same method also works with plays similar to *A Midsummer Night's Dream* to help students sort out which characters are in the three worlds: royal, rustic, and fairy. Simply type all the characters' names on a sheet of paper (16-point font size) and make a copy for each student. The easiest way is to have them cut the names into strips, so they can be moved around on a student's desktop. Try this method:

1. Before beginning the play, narrate the plot to the class while writing the names of the characters on the white-/blackboard. Students should each have an envelope with the names of the characters on strips and follow along with your placement of names on their desks.
2. After erasing the board, students put slips back in the envelopes and work with a partner. Collaboratively, they should make a tree of relationships from memory.
3. The next day, students work with a new partner to reassemble the names according to their relationships in the play.
4. The following day, each student should independently make a family/relationship tree.

Fishbowl Discussion

To demonstrate the dynamics of a conversation, try a *fishbowl* in a few different ways. Using one or two students and the teacher, read a short excerpt from a play, each taking a part. Depending on the age group, you may want to keep the reading to under two minutes. The most important part is the follow-up discussion of what you have just read. The teacher can guide the discussion by demonstrating how to return to the text as the source of discussion or questioning. The discussion should not exceed four minutes. After this activity, student groups should then read a different excerpt, to try the same technique. Another version of fishbowl is when student groups are given an extemporaneous question or excerpt to read. Four students sit in the middle and discuss the topic for up to two minutes. Each person in the class must take a turn. This second type of fishbowl works best when students are familiar with their small groups and have discussed with them several times before.

Foldables

This is an interactive note-taking system in which students can keep notes about a play. You will need three sheets of differently colored paper. Place them the "long way" vertically such that each color sheet is approximately one inch below the one under it.

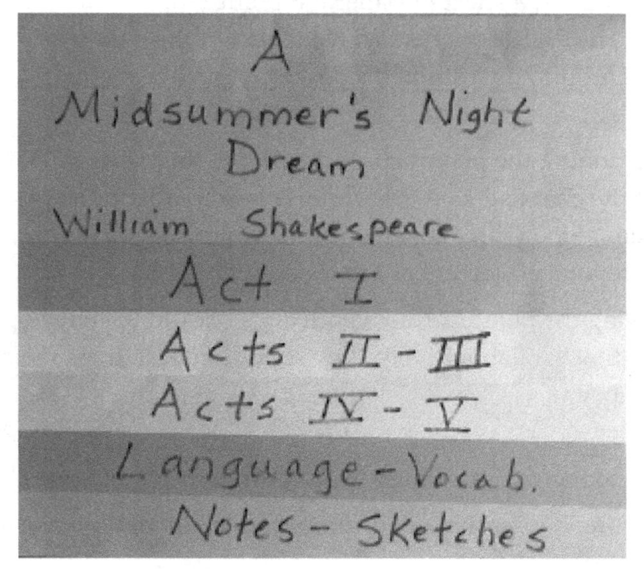

FIGURE B.2. *A Midsummer Night's Dream* foldable.

When you fold it, it will look like Figure B.2 with tabs that can be flipped open. Use one tab per act and one for language/vocabulary notes and sketches.

Students love making these and can decorate them accordingly. If your students have writer's notebooks, those pages can be limited to essays and quick-writes.

Inquiry Dive

Using a brief biographical video clip to highlight some general ideas about the early modern period, students create T-charts to compare popular culture from two time periods: sixteenth and twenty-first centuries. Students can then choose the specific areas they want to explore.

John Collins's "Five Types of Writing"

Experimenting with different types of writing helps students gain ideas and stamina for writing longer pieces. Brainstorming and writing thoughts within a specific amount of time helps students focus on topics in short spurts, providing impetus for later, longer pieces. The following are sample writing assignments corresponding to various Shakespeare plays.

Type 1

In three minutes, brainstorm fifteen historical or cultural ideas about Shakespeare you can share with your group.

Type 2

Describe briefly one incident when the ghost has appeared in *Hamlet* and the effects that it had through the viewpoint of one character.

Type 3

Write a two-page essay on why Macbeth decides to kill King Duncan. Be ready to read your draft aloud to your group. Make sure you attend to three focus correction areas: proper punctuation, detailed examples, and a conclusion.

Type 4

Write a first draft of an essay about the effect of the "play within a play" Shakespeare uses in *A Midsummer Night's Dream*. Your first draft will be critiqued by a peer before you write your second draft.

Type 5

Write a multi-draft persuasive essay on whether Shakespeare should be taught in American public high schools. After several opportunities for proofreading and revision, this essay should be in publishable form.

Jump-In Reading

Choose one section or soliloquy to review—one that you believe students would have fun reading aloud many times. First, ask a student to read through the selection entirely. Second, ask students to read it together *chorally*, to have the sense of many voices. Third, ask students to choose one or two lines they each like best and to practice reading only those lines with their partners. Finally, put it all together as follows:

1. The student who first read the entire selection in Step 1 reads the entire selection again.
2. The entire class reads the first line together.
3. Students "jump in" on their chosen two lines to read aloud.
4. The entire class reads the last line together.

This is both crazy and fun. You will notice that, sometimes, only the first student is reading, while, at other times, five or even twenty will join in on one or more lines. It's a great way to try some choral reading. Make a tape and play it back just for fun! (The Chicago Shakespeare Theater provides similar ideas during teacher trainings on activities to use when teaching Shakespeare.)

Page to Stage

This idea can be used as a follow-up to reading or as a replacement for reading independently. Divide up a scene or act into sections, assigning a number of students to each according to how many characters are in the selection. Student groups should leave the classroom and practice reading with as much expression as possible. When they return, student groups should perform sequentially. Make sure each group begins by summarizing what is happening in their section.

What is important about Page to Stage is that students learn a little about blocking and movement. Where should each character stand? How should they play the part? What is happening now? Appropriate props could make this come to life, so, if you have some in the classroom, make it work!

Another way to do this is to take the same scene and see how different groups would play it. Act 1, scene 1, in *Macbeth* works well because students can put their own spin on how to interpret the witches.

Play It Again, Sam!

Take only a few lines from the text to practice tone. In act 2, scene 3, of *Macbeth*, Macduff has just arrived at Macbeth's castle to ride with King Duncan to his next appointment. We know, however, that Macbeth has just slain the king. Ask two students to position themselves as it would happen on stage. Macduff will say, "Is the King stirring, worthy Thane?" six different times to Macbeth, but Macbeth will answer, "Not yet," using six different tones: calmly, annoyed, jittery, nervously, confidently, guiltily. Students can decide which tone conveys the message according to Macbeth's present state of mind. Students love this because it's fast, and the lines are easy to memorize.

Quick-Writes

In five-minute time allotments, students can reflect and express their thoughts for different purposes:

- at the beginning of class, to explain what was learned the day before
- during the middle of class, to assess learning formatively
- at the end of the class, to reflect on content
- to ask questions, to clarify, to predict

Read-Around

Students choose some section of their own writing that they believe to be good writing. It could be as brief as a vivid verb or as long as a sentence that contains a beautiful image. The activity is to prompt contribution from all students, especially those students who generally are too shy to say anything in class. Offering up one word usually sets the stage for a more confident voice later. Students can also do this with Shakespeare's language, where they choose specific lines to read aloud. See Jump-In (described earlier in this Appendix) for another version of this activity.

Reenactments

Using body motions only, students act out a scene segment while another student or the teacher reads the part aloud. This works particularly well if the language is confusing, such as in the stage directions "(*Tybalt under Romeo's arm stabs Mercutio*)" and when Mercutio claims, "Why the devil / came you between us? I was hurt under your arm" (3.1.101–02). The actions are most effective if they are done in slow motion.

Samoan Circle

Samoan Circles are different from Socratic Seminars (also described in this Appendix) in that the actual discussion involves a *temporary* small group that changes when an individual finishes having their "say." A circle of five in the middle of the room is where the discussion happens. A second circle of eight surrounds the inner circle, and a third circle of ten or more is the outer circle. The inner circle begins the discussion on a topic of interest. As individuals finish discussing, they move to the outer circle, and someone from the middle circle moves in. As the inner circle changes, so too do the discussion dynamics. New people bring new ideas, and often the focus changes direction. As students move from the middle circle to the inner circle, individuals must move from the outer circle to the middle. Teachers may need to keep track, encouraging those in the back to move forward. A few parameters to help discussions from becoming stagnant:

- Students in the inner circle may not stay long: add to the conversation, then move to the outer circle, allowing other voices to be heard.
- Students in the inner circle should leave individually—not more than one at a time—so the discussion does not change dramatically. The idea is that a new person adds to the conversation without changing course completely.
- Students may not "jump" from the outer circle to the inner circle without first "waiting" in the middle circle for a turn. Teachers may have to monitor this until students become familiar with the process.
- The process is not complete until each person has had an opportunity to speak.

Silent Annotations

Choose one section of a Shakespeare play or a sonnet. You may wish to enlarge the print to at least 18-point font size. Glue it to a large poster, chart paper, or giant sticky note. Provide various colors of markers, one per student in each group. Students must read and respond to the text with annotations, such as one-line summaries, definitions of words, meaningful sketches, questions, synonyms, or bubble comments. To hold students accountable for participation, ask them to print their names at the bottom in the same color they used for responses. Students can work on annotations in the classroom, out in the hall, at tables, or standing, as long as they know it is silent. They are, in essence, reading their group's annotations while they work, which is useful to initiate more comments. Timing this activity must take into account the time it will take for close reading. Sharing or reporting findings is as important as the activity itself. If the text is broken up in sequential part, such as excerpts from an act or longer scene, a Document Walk works well. Allow students five minutes to plan their "talk" and one minute to present before moving to the next group.

Socratic Seminar

Sometimes we forget the power of a circle. Most people think of Socratic Seminars as an opportunity to discuss a piece of writing, and this works extremely well. Students love sharing ideas and finding out what others think. Consider also how this might work as a "read through." Students may think of this as similar to what it must have been like to receive Shakespeare's script for the first time, and the players are reading the parts that Shakespeare has assigned. This works extremely well if you are doing an entire act with many different characters, thus involving as many students as possible.

Think-Aloud

Teachers can do Think-Alouds while they are reading a selection, stopping to comment on what comes to mind as they work through the text. The strategies we use when facing difficult language demonstrates to students how we build efficacy while reading. Another use for a Think-Aloud is to talk about your process as you write a piece in front of students. This is actually one you may wish to practice, simply because it is difficult to hold their attention if you pause for more than a few seconds. This process can be unnerving, but surprisingly advantageous. Students will generally pay attention, especially knowing that they will be writing immediately after you. Watching you struggle is a good reminder that all writing is ninety-nine percent perspiration! For another example of how this might work, see Chapter 4 on *Midsummer* for the description on writing about female power.

Three Ways to Have Fun with Shakespeare

The following post comes from the *Teaching Shakespeare!* blog provided by the Folger Shakespeare Library's education department:

> Listening to students speaking Shakespeare is certainly my favorite part of teaching Shakespeare, but I also love watching them play games. We've often ended a semester with Shakespeare-based games. (Perfect for this sunny time of year!) Student favorites have been "Who Am I?" and "Group Charades," though "Who Said That When?" can be good learning fun, too.
>
> A quick warm-up is "Who Am I?"—I type up a sheet or two of labels with the names of characters from the plays we have read during the last semester. So, after reading *Romeo and Juliet*, the labels might include characters like the Nurse, Capulet, Lady Capulet, Montague, Lady Montague, the Prince, Benvolio, Mercutio, Paris, and, of course, Romeo and Juliet.
>
> The students wear the labels on their backs and have to ask each other "yes" and "no" questions, trying to determine who they are. It's especially engaging when these questions involve direct quotations from the play (for deeper close reading, you can build this element into your instructions). I've had classes where the students would race to figure out their characters so that they could get another name.

Needless to say, "Who Am I?" can be engaging for students, but I think "Group Charades" is even more so. Plus, it's focused on the language itself. I generally give each group of four to six students a slip of paper with part of a scene from a play they've just read. Each group goes off to a different corner of the room to figure out how best to represent their assignment. (It might be the sword fighting scene from *Hamlet*, the balcony scene from *Romeo and Juliet*, or even the balcony scene from *Much Ado about Nothing*.)

My number one rule for the charades is that everyone in the group has to participate, even if it's just as a chair or a tree! Once the groups are ready, they take turns performing so that their classmates can guess what they are doing. If a scene is guessed too quickly, I do let the performing group finish their performance, as long as it doesn't take too long. (In a class full of especially imaginative, dramatic kids, performances take on a life of their own! During those situations, a time limit can help.)

Depending on the size of the class and what else we're doing that day, I generally have enough scenes selected for the groups to perform at least two or three times. But oftentimes, with a really enthusiastic group, they ask to make their own choices after they've done their first one. I love it when kids select, edit, and perform their own scenes!

The third bit of fun is great for review at the end of the play—or even as part of a final assessment itself. The challenge is called, "Who Said That and When?" Students can work solo or in groups to (a) deliver the lines and (b) guess the lines. I generally have a list already made up from the previous play(s). In this case, it's a list of lines or short scenes from the plays we've read—short excerpts that students have already read and studied closely. Points can be given for knowing who said the words, knowing who heard the words, summarizing or paraphrasing the words, explaining the dramatic context for the words, or doing something creative with the words, like imagining tone or props or even drawing an illustration. The points for one excerpt don't have to all be awarded to the same student or group—in fact, since the point of this is fun, not competition, it's best when everyone gets to win in some way. The whole point system might sound silly, but it's a great way to engage young people—ALL of the young people in your room—in speaking and listening to Shakespeare's words. (Jaime)

Turn and Talk

When students have an opportunity to talk about their learning, they are more likely to share their thinking with the entire class. This is a useful strategy when students are close reading or viewing a Shakespeare scene. *Partner-talk* throughout a lesson gives students time to voice their opinions as well as listen to others' ideas—it becomes the platform for later writing or discussion.

Verbal Fluency

This is a fun way to review the plot after the first three acts of a Shakespeare play. Students should number off by four in their groups, remembering their number. Ask, "Raise your hand if you are a '1'" and so on. Students will then go back to the beginning of the play to summarize what was happening. Each person has a certain number of seconds to summarize. Beginning with "1," give twenty seconds to summarize the beginning. When twenty seconds is over, the teacher yells "Stop," and then yells the next number—"2!" The next person summarizes the story from the point that their group's student "1" left off. Number 2 gets forty seconds. The teacher instructs "Stop" again and student number 3 takes over and summarizes the next section in sixty seconds. Finally, the last person must continue with a ninety-second summary. This is a fun way to review! The challenge is to see how much of the play can be summarized in this amount of time.

Whip-Around

Quickly moving from student to student, each reads or reports a few words in response to a writing prompt. Begin with students standing. As each responds, they sit.

Who Said What?

This is a great way to get students up and moving after the first act in any Shakespeare play. Choose three characters from the act and write their names on a large poster or piece of paper, placing them on three different walls of your classroom. Type up various lines from the act and hand one to each student. Make sure you have evenly divided how many are spoken by each character. Ask students to read their line aloud and go to that part of the room near the sign with their character's name. Once in the three groups, students can then confirm they are in the correct group by reading each line aloud in their groups. The discussion is the most important part of this activity.

The following *Teaching Channel* link shows how a drama teacher tried this activity with middle school students reading *Macbeth* (Broadbent): learn.teachingchannel.com/video/intro-to-teaching-macbeth.

Appendix C

Primary Document Teaching Strategies

Bubble Track

(See also Listen and Bubble in this Appendix.) While students listen to audios, discuss in groups, or annotate documents, roam the room with a clipboard, tracking responses in "character bubbles." Fill the page with bubbled student responses to share under a document camera, or, if you have a wireless keyboard or tablet, post the responses to the projected computer screen while you roam. Students will sometimes work hard to see their words in print!

Diminishing Maps/Notes

This strategy is extremely useful for struggling readers who need assistance in note-taking or comprehension. It provides a beginning template that students use as a model, which is filled out by the teacher, during the first half of the note-taking or comprehension activity. An audio version of a lecture or section of a play is an ideal activity because students are not reading and can thus participate while listening.

1. Create a map or outline based on a reading or audio lecture.
2. Fill in sections of the map/outline—more at the beginning and diminishing toward the end, leaving more and more geometric shapes empty.
3. Review the map/outline with students, carefully recounting *some* of the information.
4. Allow students to copy the filled-in portions before listening.
5. Play the audio, modeling when to fill in blank portions.
6. Stop filling in sections at the end—allow students to create their own meaning.

Document Walk

Using large sheets of rolled paper or poster-sized sticky notes, glue a primary document in the middle for students to annotate in small groups. Tape the documents to the wall or staple them to cork strips spaced far enough apart to allow larger groups of students to stand in front to listen. Students can then walk from document to document and listen to the creators explain and analyze content. Document Walks can also be interactive: place the documents on chart paper and allow students to annotate all of the documents as they wander from station to station. This activity can be loosely structured in this way or organized so students have specified time limits for each document.

Exit Slip

Exit slips are used during the final five minutes of class to check student understanding of the lesson you taught that period. Exit slips could be in the form of a slip of paper or a 3 × 5 card that you provide. One question usually is sufficient and can be used to drive your lesson the next day. Exit slips can also be in the form of a verbal answer, either from student desks, or, better yet, when they walk out the door. Stand by the door and ask each student a question that they must answer as they leave. You might be surprised at how much you learn from this quick activity!

Four Reads

This activity is one where students read the document four times. Each student has a copy of the document for an initial shared reading. To prepare, make sure you have read the document ahead of time, noting difficult vocabulary, structure, or content sections.

- first read: *origins and content*—significance of place and time
- second read: *meaning*—genre type and big issues presented
- third read: *argument*—how argument is structured
- fourth read: *historian*—treat like a mystery and dig deep (Faithfull)

Gradual Release of Responsibility

The components of the Gradual Release of Responsibility strategy encompass:

1. A short (ten-minute) mini-lesson where the teacher teaches a skill, modeling how to complete the task. During this time, the teacher can do a formative check by interspersing questions throughout.
2. Work through the task together as a large group. This may be an opportunity for the teacher to direct the activity with student help and feedback or with all students participating under direction of the teacher.
3. This step—collaboration—is when students work through the task together while the teacher works with small group on the side, providing direct instruction for students who seem to be struggling.
4. Finally, students try the task independently.

This process is extremely useful for working with documents. Students have told me that the collaboration step is most helpful, because students are sometimes more comfortable asking questions of peers. They can work out difficulty with language and purpose in smaller groups.

GRAPES

- G—genre
- R—rhetorical schemes
- A—audience
- P—purpose
- E—effect (on audience or tone)
- S—speaker, subject, situation (*kairos*)[32]

Jigsaw or Each Teach

It would be impossible for students to read as many primary documents as any teacher would like, so a Jigsaw activity works well because it provides an opportunity to hear about many documents. If you have eight documents, for example, students number off by eight and read the corresponding numbered document.

First, ask students to read and annotate independently, thus providing a baseline of understanding. Next, have students meet with other students—probably two to three—to reread the document together and to share annotations. This is where students will discuss the most important claims the author is making and how they relate to the historical/cultural theme. Each student should make bulleted points during this step, so they know exactly what they will share with their larger group. Third, students reconvene in their groups of eight. Students should share the major points while the others take notes on the documents. Make sure each student has a copy of all documents, especially if you believe they will use them later for writing.

What to Look For

Initially, students will share their documents, moving from one person to the next with little conversation. Eventually, students will move toward a more interactive discussion where questions will be raised and comparisons made about various documents. The goal is to see evidence of intertextual analysis. One way to demonstrate what this type of discussion looks like is to actually stage one in which the teacher is involved. It can be a Fishbowl experience (see Appendix B) where one group is in the middle of the room while others sit outside the circle taking notes. You may have to prep the Fishbowl participants ahead of time, but watching a discussion in peak form may help others understand the process.

Listen and Bubble

(See Bubble Track, described at the start of this Appendix.) While students are discussing the content of one or more documents, the teacher roams the room with a clipboard and writes down interesting comments they hear students say. After four or five comments, the teacher writes them on the board as dialogue bubbles, then continues roaming. Eventually, students notice what you are doing and will be more intentional in their comments. Fill the entire space with ideas. An alternative strategy is to create an entire page of bubble comments without stopping. Using the document camera, project this document after the discussion. A follow-up Quick-Write (see Appendix B) or Exit Slip activity might include choosing one bubble comment to reflect on in a well-developed paragraph.

Overview–Parts–Title–Interrelationships–Conclusion (OPTIC)

The following steps are used to help students approach visual texts:

- overview—write down a few notes on what the visual appears to be about
- parts—focus on parts of the visual, writing down any elements or details that seem important

- title—highlight the words of the title of the visual if one is available
- interrelationships—use the title as the theory and the parts of the visual as clues to detect and specify the interrelationships in the graphic
- conclusion—think about the visual as a whole, speculating the meaning and summarizing the visual in one or two sentences

PAPER

You can find numerous online ideas for reading primary documents, and, depending on your student group, these will be helpful. For example, one acronym for reading historical documents is *PAPER*:

- *p*urpose and motives of author
- *a*rgument and values in text and our own
- *p*resuppositions and values in text and our own
- *e*pistemology or evaluating truth
- *r*elate to other texts (Department of History, U of Iowa)

Students can also create acronyms of their own to share their strategies for reading documents. Try this one for *READ*: *r*ead, *e*valuate, *a*nnotate, *d*ecide.

Q&A Formative Checks for Understanding

The most effective Q&A experiences are when they are combined with a minilesson. During the first few experiences with documents, especially for those students who have never worked with them before, it is helpful for teachers to show students how they approach primary documents through a Think-Aloud (see Appendix B). Once this is underway, teachers can stop during their own self-questioning and ask students directly if any of them know where or how to find the answer. For example, in a document "An Indictment Preferred against Iohn Iambe," it is noted that he made a woman lift up her coat above her middle: "to the wonder of the company the woman began to take vp her cloathes, and by degrees lifted them vp aboue her middle" (10). After reading the document aloud and sharing my thinking, I asked why Lambe was stoned to death for witchcraft. Why was his behavior suspicious? As students interact while teachers model thinking, they become more than passive listeners and engage with their own shared copy of the document. The activity makes a great lead in to reading and annotating, followed by sharing with a small collaborative group.

Questioning

When students go through the first "run through" with a document, certain questions could guide their independent reading:

1. Look at the physical nature of your source. This is particularly important and powerful if you are dealing with an original source (i.e., an actual old letter, rather than a transcribed and published version of the same letter). What can you learn from the form of the source? (Was it written on fancy paper in elegant handwriting, or on scrap paper, scribbled in pencil?) What does this tell you?
2. Think about the purpose of the source. What was the author's message or argument? What were they trying to get across? Is the message explicit, or are there implicit messages as well?
3. How does the author try to get the message across? What methods do they use?
4. What do you know about the author? Race, sex, class, occupation, religion, age, region, political beliefs? Does any of this matter? How?
5. Who constituted the intended audience? Was this source meant for one person's eyes or for the public? How does that affect the source?
6. What can a careful reading of the text (even if it is an object) tell you? How does the language work? What are the important metaphors or symbols? What can the author's choice of words tell you? What about the silences—what does the author choose *not* to talk about? (Ladd-Taylor et al.)

Say Something

Students form trios and alternately read a difficult portion from text. After each reading, the listeners synthesize and summarize what they heard in the reading. The second person may not repeat what has already been stated.

Shared Reading

Students have a copy of primary document, and the document is enlarged and on the screen in front of the classroom. The teacher is able to annotate and walk students through portions of the reading in a Think-Aloud. Students interact with text and with teacher, allowing the experience to be a formative assessment of student comprehension. This is one of the first steps of the Gradual Release model (also described in this Appendix) during the mini-lesson.

Shift and Share

Begin with approximately five to six readings students can read independently to share with others. Form three large groups, each group containing ten students with two lines of five desks facing each other. Partners sit across from each other. First, each partner group reads one article/poem/story/essay, annotating the key points, followed by an opportunity to share the details and conclusions of their reading. The next section of this activity is to "shift" to the right—students may need to physically get up and move to a different seat. (Options may include "rolling," if desks have casters, or sitting on the floor and scooting to the right.) New partner groups take approximately four minutes to each share their article and take notes.

Student Writing

After students have written about documents, put them under the document camera or scan several to put up from the computer. Students love to see their work highlighted as good models. Explain why the writing is particularly good by pointing out strong verbs, insightful thinking, and clear writing. The secondary effects of this strategy are that students will often write more and better if they believe their work will be projected.

Subject–Occasion–Audience–Purpose–Speaker–Tone (SOAPSTone)[33]

SOAPSTone is a text analysis strategy for initially teaching students how to analyze nonfiction, as follows:

- *s*ubject—the general topic or main idea
- *o*ccasion—the event or catalyst causing the writing
- *a*udience—the group of readers to whom the piece is directed
- *p*urpose—the reason behind the text
- *s*peaker—the individual or collective voice
- *tone*—the attitude of the author

T-Square Notes

Comparing primary documents using the template depicted in Figure C.1 helps students scaffold thinking about multiple, competing voices on the same issue.

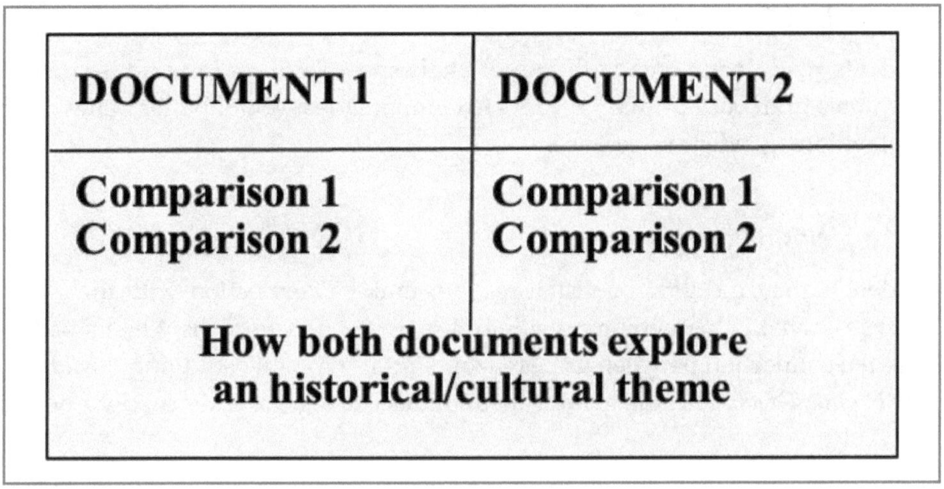

DOCUMENT 1	DOCUMENT 2
Comparison 1 Comparison 2	Comparison 1 Comparison 2
How both documents explore an historical/cultural theme	

FIGURE C.1. T-square notes template for primary documents.

Students could compare an article from the *Newes from Scotland* (Carmichael) and *Daemonologie*, a play written by James VI, to compare ideas about early modern fears about witchcraft. Working in pairs or small groups helps students work through documents first before sharing thoughts about multiple ideas. The analysis of how both documents explore an issue is how you would like students to approach documents, but this may take considerable practice before seeing ease and confidence. Students do best when they make their own T-square notes in their writer's notebooks. Passing out a template for students to fill in is actually restrictive, in that students are not making meaning in the way that makes sense to them.

Text Comparison

On one page, place two document excerpts side by side. When students read, they should look for what the author is saying about the subject, as well as how the writing is structured. After some practice with this skill, ask them to analyze *how* the author is conveying the information. Is it in narrative form? Does visual text, such as graphs, charts, or diagrams, illuminate the main points? Students should be given time to work through this on their own before discussing in small groups. This is best done using the Gradual Release model, comprising the mini-lesson (teacher to student), formative (checking for understanding), collaborative (students together), and independent (students alone) stages.

Text-to-Text Connections

Students read documents with one of Shakespeare's plays in mind, searching for quotes from both primary sources to compare ideas about larger issues, such as plant lore, gender, or violence.

Text-to-World Connections

Students analyze digital or visual texts to make a connection with the world at large—what is happening outside of the text. An example is when students note the connection between the Amazon engraving while studying *A Midsummer Night's Dream* and the gender inequalities during the early modern period (*MND* 10).

Visual Text Analysis

Students analyze visuals, such as charts, graphs, illustrations, paintings, and sketches, according to the following systematic approach.

Step One: Introducing Visual Text Analysis

1. If using a projector, dim the lights. It is easier not only to see the visual, but also to quiet the group.
2. Give students one to two minutes to simply look at the visual in silence. This may seem like a long time, but it is the most important step. Students may first look but, given more time, will begin to focus on the details.
3. Ask students, "What do you notice?" Students may begin slowly but will build more confidence when they realize no "correct" answer is necessary. Voicing diverse ideas will spur more of the same. This is the step where many students will participate, more than in other class discussions.
4. Provide writing time for students to reflect on the visual and what they learned from others' viewpoints that they had not noticed during the first two minutes of quiet observation.

Step Two: Releasing Responsibility through Partnership

1. Project a second visual. If you are working with primary documents, the visuals may all fall under the same category, such as family relationships or normative gender roles.

2. Observe the visual in silence for one to two minutes.
3. Each student talks with an "elbow partner" about what they noticed in relation to theme. This step is important in that it builds confidence and content. Students find that some observations coincide with those of others, but they also learn about diverse lenses. Their partners can provide insights that become springboards for new ideas.
4. The teacher asks each partner group to report. Each person in the group must say something they noticed or learned.
5. Writing time—students need at least five minutes to reflect on their learning.

Step Three: Moving toward Independence

1. Project a third visual.
2. Students observe it for one to two minutes, then move immediately into partner groups for discussion.
3. Partner groups combine into groups of four to six, where they share ideas about what they observed. This can be divided into two sections in which students have approximately ten minutes to share and then ten minutes to direct their conversations toward a specific open-ended question, such as *How does this document provide context for the Macbeth's relationship?* or *How does this document provide evidence for the religious significance of ghosts?* Students should jot down their findings in their critical-reading journals. During this step, the teacher visits each group to listen and to write down a few comments in a bubble sheet (see also Listen and Bubble, discussed earlier in this Appendix). Using one sheet of printer paper, draw at least ten circles. Fill in at least two bubbles for each group with a student comment.
4. Using the projector, teacher shares ideas that bubbled up from observing groups. This can be the ice breaker, when some of the more unique ideas are shared.
5. Large group reports—each group should select a spokesperson to share one conclusion that bubbled up from the discussions in both partner and small groups.
6. Writing time—each student needs to reflect on how their confidence with visual texts is increasing. What are they noticing about their own efficacy?

Step Four: Independent Work

1. Project visual text.
2. Quiet observation for one to two minutes.
3. Partner share for one to two minutes.
4. Writing time for fifteen minutes.

Step Five: Transferring Knowledge (Optional)

1. Students research visual texts on a specific topic. This step can be more successfully done with partners or in small groups to encourage immediate feedback on research results. It should be a noisy activity with vocal engagement.
2. Students take notes on observations, specifically focused on connections among visuals.
3. Students create contextual questions for each visual.
4. Students share their findings.

Write–Think–Pair–Share

Asking students to write about how primary documents speak to specific cultural ideas helps them formulate their own thinking. Once they get ideas down on paper, they are then able to share their writing with a partner. Teachers can begin by asking partner groups to share how their combined writing describes Shakespeare's cultural beliefs on a topic. Students can pair up with students who are reading other documents to compare authors' slants, tone, and wording.

Appendix D

Researching Primary and Secondary Documents

The best part about teaching Shakespeare using primary documents is finding the documents! The adventure lies within the search, and there is no better feeling when you find something unexpected. Two sources I have found to be extremely useful and open to students are, first, the Folger Shakespeare Library, and, second, the Chicago Shakespeare Theater.

Folger Shakespeare Library

The Folger Library may be the most underused goldmine by secondary teachers, primarily because teachers do not know about the wealth it houses. Moreover, most do not know that the Folger Education team's primary goal is to help teachers teach Shakespeare's plays and sonnets (see, e.g., the *Folger Teaching* home page: teaching.folger.edu). If you are working with documents, you will want to take advantage of the databases for scholarship and documents, but a plethora of other sources, such as weekly blog posts and podcasts, are a rich source of daily classroom ideas too.

You may wish to include research in your Shakespeare unit, so students have the opportunity to find their own early modern documents based on specific historical/cultural issues. You can access the "Research and Scholars" site using the following URL: www.folger.edu/research-scholars. Then, use either *Hamnet*, for secondary documents, or *LUNA*, for primary. Take time to peruse the site to see all the treasures. It's best to find a few nuggets yourself, so you will be able to best advise your students.

The Collation: Research and Exploration at the Folger

The Collation is the new Folger "go to" for scholarship and learning and is considered a "gathering of useful information and observations from staff and researchers" (https://collation.folger.edu). Set up in blog form, writers share modern glimpses into the Folger's early modern treasure troves. My own maiden voyage uncovered a recent post about *Macbeth* and slavery in the United States that collates ideas about witches, the Civil War, and slavery. Once you begin, you will be exquisitely lost in Shakespeare's world through varying lenses.

This site is open for students and teachers.

LUNA

LUNA is a platform for primary visual and digital documents like no other: luna.folger.edu/luna/servlet. Tens of thousands of digitized original documents will be of vital importance to teachers and students who have specific interests. The Folger Education team will help any teacher who is planning research projects.

Folgerpedia

Folgerpedia is the Folger Shakespeare Library's encyclopedia of anything Folger: folgerpedia.folger.edu. It describes not only the library offerings but also the theatrical performances and teacher trainings.

You may find it difficult to leave this site because of the many opportunities for anything Shakespeare or early modern. At the time of writing this book, for example, the newest exhibits and information are all about Elizabeth I and her court.

What I have found works best is to decide on a few themes or ideas from the play you are teaching. If you have a projector, you can demonstrate your detective skills as you think through an idea.

Romeo and Juliet

Let's say a student in your ninth-grade English class is interested in apothecaries. She wants to know something about their role in early modern society. You decide to log on to the *LUNA* site at the Folger Library to see if you can find any pictures or descriptions of their work. You type in *apothecary* in the search bar at the top. The first thing you see are two rows of drawings from scenes during the eighteenth and nineteenth centuries. As you place your curser over each picture, the citation pops up, providing the image number and description. Other pictures show handwritten documents, and you find a 1619 letter written by Sir George More requesting payment for medicine. Another visual is an apothecary's bill from 1591. The writing is difficult to read, so you click on the picture to enlarge it and click on the bar in the lower-right corner to slide the picture up and down. Now you can see the writing, but this isn't quite what you wanted. You go back to the search bar and type in *medicine*. Bingo! Look at all the pictures of skeletons and plants that look like people and books about medicine. One of these books from the 1600s is about "the new, safe, and powerful way of physick . . . to cure themselves." This could be fun!

A Midsummer Night's Dream

You teach general eighth-grade English and have students who want to know more about the play when it first came out in 1600, especially how the characters were portrayed. You go to Folger's *Shakespeare Documented* website (shakespearedocumented.folger.edu) and type in the title of the play in the search bar. You find a handwritten copy of when it was approved by the stationer (plays had to be approved before they could be staged). It was entered as "A Mydsommer Nightes Dreame." From there, you decide to look at some pictures of Bottom: What did he look like? What costume did he wear? You return to *LUNA* and find numerous sketches of Bottom from a variety of productions. One catches your eye. It's a pen-and-ink drawing of Bottom and Titania, drawn by George Cruikshank from the early nineteenth century. What's interesting here is that Bottom is *huge*—while Titania is a tiny little fairy, similar to Tinkerbell. Your students decide to make their own sketches of how they envision the sizes of the fairies compared to Bottom.

The first thing you will notice about early modern documents is the writing. It can sometimes be difficult to read. Sometimes, the writing is transcribed for you, or you can search for more information at the top of the page. The most important thing to remember is to give yourself and your students time to explore. And have fun!

Teaching Modules

You can also find primary documents on the *Teaching Modules* site: folger.edu/teaching-modules. Under each play's title, you will find resources, such as "PRIMARY SOURCE SPOTLIGHT," featuring specific documents that go with each play. Holinshed's *Chronicles*, for example, are listed in sections under *Macbeth*, making it easy for teachers to align the original source with different parts of the play. The Folger staff team provides resources in conjunction with lesson plans, which is extremely helpful.

Chicago Shakespeare Theater

Short Shakespeare!

The Chicago Shakespeare Theater on Navy Pier in Chicago offers much more than plays on their thrust stage (see, e.g., the *Education* site: www.chicagoshakes.com/education). Teachers who organize student field trips can purchase more economical tickets for "Short Shakespeare!," ninety-minute productions followed by "talk-backs" during which students can ask questions about the performance. (Combining a Short Shakespeare! production with a shopping trip on the Miracle Mile is a good way to spend your day!) Teachers are also invited to an all-day workshop where they can learn how to teach the play, a "hands-on" experience that focuses on how to get students out of their seats and have fun with the language. In addition, you will be treated to a rehearsal of the actual play your students will see, which I find to be one of the most valuable experiences of the day. They will generally choose one scene to rehearse where the director works with them on specific movements, expressions, and language. Blocking the scene is helpful, but observing how the scene can be performed several different ways, depending on the director's choice, lends credence to multiple practice runs.

Education

You will find extremely useful *Teacher Handbooks* (www.chicagoshakes.com/education/teaching_resources/teacher_handbooks) for each play containing student activities, critical commentaries, performance descriptions, and plot summaries.

Essays on Elizabethan England and early modern theater experiences are also available for background information as you begin your work with primary documents.

Researching Secondary Documents

Sometimes, teachers would like to share ideas for researching information about early modern culture using more contemporary sources. From past experiences with students on the internet, I often have had to search myriad sites, wishing I had everything in one place. The following are user-friendly links you might want to explore.

First, "96 Incredibly Useful Links for Teaching and Studying Shakespeare" (www.onlinecollege.org/2009/12/16/100-incredibly-useful-links-for-teaching-and-studying-shakespeare). If you want everything all in one spot, this is it. It categorizes links by topics: articles, quizzes, teacher's guides, and audio/video resources. Students may wish to use this site for more modern references to Shakespeare's plays. Some links do take you to early modern sources, though.

Next, some historical and cultural websites:

- "Teaching Shakespeare with the *New York Times*," learning.blogs.nytimes.com/2010/08/02/teaching-shakespeare-with-the-new-york-times/?mcubz=1—"top-shelf" resource and at the top of my list
- "Clothing in Elizabethan England," www.bl.uk/shakespeare/articles/clothing-in-elizabethan-england
- "Daily Life in the Elizabethan Era," www.encyclopedia.com/humanities/news-wires-white-papers-and-books/daily-life-elizabethan-era
- *Elizabethan Era*, www.elizabethan-era.org.uk
- "Elizabethan Era Daily Life: Food, Education, Marriage, Family, Fashion," schoolworkhelper.net/elizabethan-era-daily-life-food-education-marriage-family-fashion
- *History of the Present* journal, historyofthepresent.org/1.1/introduction.html
- "Life in 16th Century England," www.localhistories.org/tudor.html
- "Life in Shakespeare's London," www.shakespeare-online.com/biography/londonlife.html
- *The Norton Anthology of English Literature: Core Selections Ebook*, 10th ed., digital.wwnorton.com/englishlit10core
- *Renaissance Sites and Elizabethan Resources*, www.elizabethan.org/sites.html
- *Shakespeare and the Elizabethan Age in England*, lfanet.libguides.com/content.php?pid=638991&sid=5286776
- *Shakespeare Resource Center*, www.bardweb.net/england.html
- *Shakespeare's World*, www.folger.edu/shakespeares-world
- *The Social Structure in Elizabethan England*, www.bl.uk/shakespeare/articles/the-social-structure-in-elizabethan-england

Appendix E

Sonnet Project Presentation Ideas

Blogs

Blogging can be a way for students to have ongoing discussions throughout their project, especially if students enjoy reading and writing while they are exploring Shakespeare's work. Blogging is good for students who enjoy writing in sentence format rather than concentrating on graphics. Students can post questions to create interactive blogs. One blogger who likes to dabble in fiction and fact is Grace Tiffany, a Shakespeare scholar from Western Michigan University. She has written numerous young adult fiction books about real early modern issues, such as *Gunpowder Percy*, a novel about the Gunpowder Plot. According to her blog, she "uses fiction as additional medium for exploring the early modern world" (Tiffany "About"). A *Behind the Story* interview with Tiffany originally broadcast on the NPR radio station KWBU is available online here: kwbu.org/post/behind-story-interview-grace-tiffany.

Class Book

Create a virtual or digital class book of sonnets and responses. Responses could include music, contemporary poetry, visuals, sketches, or research. Divide the class into pairs, trios, or larger groups of four to six. As they self-select their favorite sonnets, ask them to add pages to the book. A Google Doc works well for this because of its "share" feature, whereby many students can work at one time.

Facebook Page

Create a Facebook page for Shakespeare where you can ask him questions about his sonnets. Create a profile and add pictures of his family. Get creative: he can post where he's been and what he's doing while he goes on vacation. Include work on his sonnets, such as where he got his ideas and what they are about. See the BBC Shakespeare Facebook page for an example (www.facebook.com/BBCShakespeare).

Group Websites

Create a sonnet website where Shakespeare's sonnets are shared and discussed. Specific sonnets can be posted and discussed with scholarly articles, lectures, primary documents, and graphics. Websites do not have to be serious. You could do a Valentine's Day website that showcases his love sonnets, for example

Interviews

Students can set up an interview with Shakespeare and/or different sonneteers. This can be done live or recorded. Students make a list of questions regarding Shakespeare and his sonnets. The best part of this is when students decide to dress the part of Shakespeare and his contemporaries (Figure E.2).

FIGURE E.2. Interviews.

Name That Sonnet

Creating titles for poetry is difficult because students need to know the poems well enough to create a title that is both unique and telling. A challenge to this activity is to take the titles of fourteen sonnets to create another sonnet, using Shakespeare's structure and rhyme scheme. The beauty of this project is that you can divide the class in a variety of ways to work and present.

Panel Discussions

A panel discussion can be a different experience if the panel incorporates a Fishbowl discussion format (see Appendix B) for at least a portion of the discussion. We often expect panels to be similar to a speech, except that more than one person speaks at a time. Consider a panel where the members have a natural discussion in front of the class, rather than in a group where, Fishbowl-like, members are surrounded by the audience to listen and learn.

Poster Walk

This presentation will get all of your students up and walking. Presenters can use either tables to set up a project or large poster-sized sticky notes to put on the wall as their station. Divide the class into as many groups as you have presenters. Groups walk through the hall or classroom, stopping for at least five minutes at each station to hear the presenter speak about their findings.

RealtimeBoard

RealtimeBoard (now rebranded as Miro) is a whiteboard that can be remotely and collaboratively shared by a team working on a project. Think of it as a whiteboard you would use either at school or in an office but one that is online and can be revised and enhanced by a group of learners. Begin with a few ideas and let the fun begin. You can choose a template or create your own (check out Matt Mulholland's quick tutorial on YouTube). Ideas can be developed by everyone in the group anytime and anyplace. Add clips, pictures, audios, sticky notes—research you have gathered to develop this idea. For example, if you are working on a hunch about the identity of the "dark lady" of Shakespeare's sonnets, add a few possibilities, and then send it out to your team. Each person can research a possible name and add to the board. The presentation is where you project your board to share your findings.

Roaming Team Leaders

This presentation works well for group projects. Instead of students standing up in front of the class, students present to small groups. An example might include a group of four students who decide to divide up the poems into types, such as those written to another man, those written to a mistress, those written to a rival poet, and those written about self-recrimination. After students have researched and discussed their roles and findings, they divide the class into four groups. Each member of the group, or team leader, rotates through each small group, presenting for approximately ten minutes each. Vertical whiteboards can be used as separators between groups or students can convene around large round tables.

If classes are smaller, a laptop can be used to show a clip or PowerPoint presentation to a group of six to eight.

Shakespeare Kahoot!

Creating a Kahoot! game is intuitive, and students love playing. It works well for learning just about anything and takes on a multiple-choice format (see kahoot .com). Students first set up an account and then make a list of what should be learned. They must make up the questions, foils, and correct answers. What students love are the music, sound effects, and stopwatch elements. Students access the site on their phones by signing in, and respond to each question within a set number of seconds.

FIGURE E.1. The VoiceThread cloud application enables video, voice, and text commenting.

Points are earned for each correct answer, with a winner declared at the end. Very competitive and great fun!

Triad Presentations

A three-person group is perfect. It's not too small, yet it's not too big where members can get lost in the shuffle. Moreover, it works especially well for students who are less likely to feel comfortable sharing in front of a large group. You can try a few different types of triads to see which you like the best.

In this project, each group has the same three different topics. For example, you could ask students in each group to research the background of the sonnet, Shakespeare's sonnet structure, and contemporary sonnets. Once each triad has decided who will take which part, groups can then break apart, such that those students who are working on the same projects can work together to research their part. In addition to collaborating on ideas, they should also decide how to create a fifteen-minute presentation on their topic. This may take four days. On the fifth day, students reconvene in their original triads to present. End with a reflection on what they learned. The results are generally amazing!

Another approach to the triad presentation is to have each group of three research collaboratively one self-selected idea. They will work together to create something that can be shared with other groups in a fifteen-minute presentation. To present, split up the triad to work with three other triads, so that each member of the triad is teaching their product to two other students from other groups. A final reflection could include a panel discussion where each triad shares their process with the rest of the class.

VoiceThread

This is an amazing way to add voice to your PowerPoint slide, visual, or any other document that needs explaining. VoiceThreads can be added to your work by phone, webcam, microphone, text, or file upload (see voicethread.com) (Figure E.1). Students who do not like to speak in front of class and are comfortable hearing themselves on a recorder will love this project type.

Appendix F

Contemporary Fiction Based on Shakespeare Plays

Hamlet

- *The Black Prince*, Iris Murdoch, 1973—a depiction of obsessive love
- *The Dead Fathers Club*, Matt Haig, 2006—Matt joins a club where members' dead fathers are ghosts
- *Falling for Hamlet*, Michelle Ray, 2012—Ophelia, high school senior, is ruled by Hamlet's fame and father's death
- *Gertrude and Claudius*, John Updike, 2000—imaginative prequel to the play
- *A Girl, a Ghost, and the Hollywood Hills*, Lizabeth Zindel, 2010—Holly's mom dies, and her ghost provides the truth
- *Hamlet, A Novel*, John Marsden, 2008—an Australian author reimagines *Hamlet*
- *Hamnet*, Maggie O'Farrell, 2020—the story of Shakespeare's son and twin, Judith
- *The Lunatic, the Lover, and the Poet*, Merlyn A. Hermes, 2010—the story of Horatio who believes in philosophy until he meets the Prince of Denmark
- *Nutshell*, Ian McEwan, 2016—Hamlet, an unborn child, tells his sordid story from Trudy's womb
- *Ophelia*, Lisa M. Klein, 2007—*Hamlet* told through Ophelia's point of view
- *Ophelia: Queen of Denmark*, Jackie French, 2015—a novel about a strong, determined Ophelia
- *Rosencrantz and Guildenstern Are Dead*, Tom Stoppard, 1966—a quirky, comedic play about R and G

- *Saving Hamlet*, Molly Booth, 2016—a stage trapdoor is the entry to time travel
- *Simon*, Michael Mullin, 2015—nineteen-year-old film student avenges father's ghost
- *Something Rotten*, Alan Gratz, 2007—detective fiction set in Tennessee
- *The Steep and Thorny Way*, Cat Winters, 2016—supernatural retelling set in 1920s' Oregon
- *The Story of Edgar Sawtelle*, David Wroblewski, 2009—a mute boy finds out how his uncle killed his father
- *The Total Tragedy of a Girl Named Hamlet*, Erin Dionne, 2010—Hamlet Kennedy lives an unordinary life with Shakespeare scholar parents
- *To Be or Not To Be: A Chooseable-Path Adventure*, Ryan North, 2016—take control of the *Hamlet* ending by choosing how you want events to unfold
- *A Wounded Name*, Dot Hutchinson, 2013—story of Hamlet through Ophelia's eyes

Julius Caesar

- *The Dogs of War*, Frederick Forsyth, 1974—ruthless men operate by their own code

King Lear

- *Fool*, Christopher Moore, 2009—Lear's story told through the jester's eyes
- *Moby-Dick*, Herman Melville, 1851—Ahab takes on nature to kill his prey; greed and foolishness quash his success
- *A Thousand Acres*, Jane Smiley, 1991—three daughters stand to gain when their father gives up the farm

Macbeth

- *As I Descended*, Robin Talley, 2016—Lily and Maria are willing to do anything to make their dream come true
- *Enter Three Witches*, Caroline B. Cooney, 2008—told from the perspective of the daughter of Lady Macbeth's Lady in Waiting

- *Lady Macbeth*, Susan Fraser King, 2009—vivid portrait of a woman maligned by history
- *Lady Macbeth's Daughter*, Lisa M. Klein, 2010—Albia is raised by three strange sisters
- *Mac / Beth: The Price of Fame Shouldn't Be Murder*, Michelle Ray, 2015—a contemporary Hollywood accidental murder
- *Something Wicked*, Alan Gratz, 2008—police arrest Malcolm for a murder
- *The Talented Mr. Ripley*, Patricia Highsmith, 1955—Mr. Ripley wants what someone else has
- *Third Witch*, Jackie French, 2017—a retelling with balance of good and evil
- *The Third Witch*, Rebecca Reisert, 2002—fast-paced tale of revenge told by the third witch
- *Weird Sisters*, Eleanor Brown, 2012—three sisters return to their home to find their mother sick and their father speaking in verse
- *The Wyrd Sisters*, Terry Pratchett, 1988—story of Granny Weatherwax, the unleader of a group of social witches

The Merchant of Venice

- *The Serpent of Venice*, Christopher Moore, 2014—a satiric Venetian gothic mystery

A Midsummer Night's Dream

- *Dreamers Often Lie*, Jacqueline West, 2016—a girl who dreams about Shakespeare characters
- *Eyes Like Stars*, Lisa Mantchev, 2010—characters from many plays are trapped in an unusual theater
- *The Great Night*, Chris Adrian, 2011—fairy tale of love, magic, and human yearning
- *Ill Met By Moonlight*, Sarah A. Hoyt, 2002—a transparent castle in another world
- *King of Shadows*, Susan Cooper, 2005—Nat joins an American troop to perform *Midsummer* in London

- *Love in Idleness*, Amanda Craig, 2004—set in contemporary Tuscany and exposes the frailties of love and marriage
- *A Midsummer Tights Dream*, Louise Rennison, 2012—Tallulah is admitted to a performing arts school and tries to keep it open
- *Station 11*, Emily St. John Mandel, 2014—pandemic causes the world to appreciate Shakespeare
- *This Must Be Love*, Tui T. Sutherland, 2005—Hermia and Helena search for their soulmates
- *The Treachery of Beautiful Things*, Ruth Frances Long, 2012—Jenny struggles to navigate a fairy world
- *Wings: A Fairy Tale*, E. D. Baker, 2008—Tamisin learns she was adopted from Fairyland when wings sprout from her back

Much Ado about Nothing

- *Confessions of a Triple Shot Betty*, Jody Gehrman, 2008—story of mistaken identities and just enough romance
- *Manga Shakespeare: Much Ado about Nothing*, Richard Appignanesi and Emma Vieceli, 2009—a graphic novel
- *Much Ado about Murder: A Shakespeare in the Catskills Mystery*, Simon Hawke, 2017—complications arise when a British actress arrives to play the role of Beatrice

Othello

- *Exposure*, Mal Peet, 2010—soccer player falls for white pop star
- *I, Iago*, Nicole Galland, 2012—Iago takes center stage and reveals his motivation for ruining Othello
- *Iago: A Novel*, David Snodin, 2012—an adventure story where *Othello* leaves off

Richard III

- *The Daughter of Time*, Richard Tey, 1995—detective Alan Grant takes an interest in a much-maligned king
- *Requiem of Rose King*, Aya Kanno, 2017—graphic novel

- *Richard Revisited*, Els Launspach, 2014—novel based on the recent finding of Richard's skeleton

Romeo and Juliet

- *Anyone but You*, Kim Askew, 2014—the Montes are still fighting the Caps
- *Arcadia Awakens*, Kai Meyer, 2012—New Yorker Rosa falls in love with Mafia son in Sicily
- *I Am Juliet*, Jackie French, 2014—Juliet as helpless victim
- *The Juliet Club*, Suzanne Harper, 2010—Kate travels to Verona after she is burned by love
- *Juliet Immortal*, Stacey Jay, 2012—Juliet doesn't kill herself; she is murdered by Romeo
- *Juliet's Nurse*, Lois Leveen, 2015—tragicomedy about Juliet's nurse who still mourns her own daughter
- *Letters to Juliet*, Lise Friedman, 2010—letters come to Verona from romantics seeking advice
- *Prince of Cats*, Ron Wimberly, 2016—hip-hop retelling
- *Romeo x Juliet Omnibus*, illustrated by COM, 2010—Juliet survives a massacre and turns on the Montagues
- *Ronit and Jamil*, Pamela L. Laskin, 2017—contemporary retelling in verse
- *Saving Juliet*, Suzanne Selfors, 2009—time travel transports Mimi to early modern period
- *Still Star-Crossed*, Melinda Taub, 2013—the story of Rosaline and Benvolio after R and J
- *Sung in Shadow*, Tanith Lee, 1983—parallel-world retelling
- *Warm Bodies*, Isaac Marion, 2012—zombie apocalypse version
- *When You Were Mine*, Rebecca Serle, 2013—modern recounting through Rosaline's eyes

Shakespeare (General)

- *All Night Awake*, Sarah A. Hoyt, 2003—Fairy Lady Silver tracks a supernatural beast
- *Any Man So Daring*, Sarah A. Hoyt, 2004—Hamnet disappears in the realm of an Elvin King

- *Interred with Their Bones*, Jennifer Lee Carrell, 2008—a killer reenacts the most bloody Shakespeare murders
- *Kill Shakespeare, Vol. 1: A Sea of Troubles*, Conor McCreery et al., 2010—the Bard's heroes are pitted against his villains
- *The Late Mr. Shakespeare*, Robert Nye, 2000—Pickleherring, an old friend, writes Shakespeare's story
- *Loving Will Shakespeare*, Carolyn Meyer, 2008—the story of Anne Hathaway and her love for Shakespeare
- *The Man Who Built the Castle*, M. Wellman, 2016—two people meet and connect by their love of art
- *My Father Had a Daughter*, Grace Tiffany, 2004—Judith Shakespeare runs away to London to find her father
- *My Name Is Will*, Jess Winfield, 2008—grad student Willie Shakespeare meets playwright William
- *Perchance to Dream: Classic Tales from the Bard's World in New Skins*, edited by Lyssa Chiavari, 2015

New Takes on Several Plays

- *Playing with My Heart*, Valerie Wilding, 2014—romance at the Globe
- *Serenissima: A Novel of Venice*, Erica Jong, 1997—Venice Film Festival just senses something mysterious
- *Shakespeare's Daughter*, Peter W. Hassinger, 2004—Suzanna yearns to travel
- *Soliloquies: The Lady Doth Indeed Protest*, Chris Wind, 2011—a collection of female characters' soliloquies
- *Shakespeare Makes the Playoffs*, Ron Koertge, 2010—Kevin meets a girl who shares his love of verse at Mic Night
- *Shakespeare Undead*, Lori Handeland, 2010—questions Shakespeare's authorship
- *Swan Town: The Secret Journal of Susanna Shakespeare*, Michael J. Ortiz, 2006—Susanna longs for excitement
- *The Tragedy of Arthur*, Arthur Phillips, 2012—family drama about a long-lost Shakespeare play
- *William Shakespeare's* Star Wars, Ian Doescher, 2013—*Star Wars* told in iambic pentameter

Sonnets

- *Fortune and Men's Eyes Two Plays*, John Herbert, 1967, 1971—an off-Broadway play based on sonnet 29
- *Paint*, Grace Tiffany, 2016—Emilia Bassano strategizes how to preserve her own solitude

The Taming of the Shrew

- *The Taming of the Drew*, Stephanie Kate Strohm, 2016—Cass lands the role she is meant to play
- *Vinegar Girl*, Anne Tyler, 2017—doctor schemes to have his daughter marry his lab assistant
- *Wise Children*, Angela Carter, 2007—twins, doubles, and paradoxes

The Tempest

- *Ariel*, Grace Tiffany, 2005—Ariel entices Prospero with her visions
- *Blast of Tempest*, Kyo Shirodaira et al., 2010—a sorceress promises to help find a family's killer
- *The Chosen Prince*, Diane Stanley, 2015—two princes and a mysterious girl on a magical island
- *Dream of Perpetual Motion*, Dexter Palmer, 2011—steampunk retelling
- *Hagseed*, Margaret Atwood, 2017—an ousted stage director brings *The Tempest* to life in a revenge plot
- *The Gentleman Poet*, Kathryn Johnson, 2010—astonishing events that may have led Shakespeare to write *The Tempest*
- *Brave New World*, Aldous Huxley, 1932—an outcast is despised for his appearance
- *Mama Day*, Gloria Naylor, 1989—emancipated woman tested by Island's dark forces
- *Prospero Lost*, L. Jagi Lamplighter, 2009—contemporary Miranda discovers her father missing
- *Prospero's Daughter*, Elisabeth Nunez, 2006—set on Caribbean island during height of tensions between natives and British colonists
- *Rough Magic*, Caryl Cude Mullin, 2009—both prequel and sequel to *Tempest*

Twelfth Night

- *Cakes and Ale*, W. Somerset Maugham, 1930—a novel about literary snobbery
- *The Fool's Girl*, Celia Rees, 2010—an adventure tale with Shakespeare, Violetta, pirates, social issues, and love
- *The Madness of Love*, Katharine Davies, 2005—an interwoven love story

Two Gentlemen of Verona

- *Two Gentlemen of Lebowski*, Adam Bertocci, 2010—tale of ridiculousness, bowling, and mistaken identity

The Winter's Tale

- *Exit, Pursued by a Bear*, E. K. Johnston, 2016—cheerleading captain faces obstacles when someone slips something into her drink
- *The Gap of Time*, Jeanette Winterson, 2016—takes place in London after a storm-ravaged the American South
- *The Winter's Song*, Jeana Watters, 2017—mismatched couple find letters addressed to a dead baby

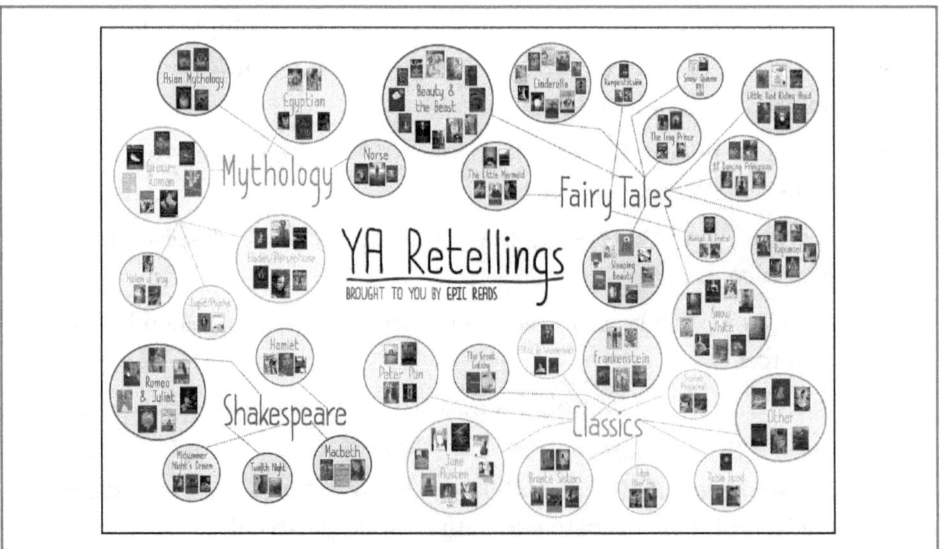

FIGURE F.1. "YA Retellings": 162 young adult books that are retellings or reimaginings of myths, fairy tales, Shakespeare plays, and popular classic literature ("An Epic Chart").

Appendix G

Teacher Online Resources

All the resources listed below and elsewhere in this book can be accessed directly through the accompanying website *Teaching Shakespeare* (shakespearedocuments .info).

Hamlet

"5 Hamlet To Be Or Not To Be Soliloquies." *YouTube*, uploaded by moenieful, 19 June 2016, www.dailymotion.com/video/x2xb0hd

Five different performances of Hamlet's famous soliloquy in one place.

Bhaneja, Raoul. *Hamlet (Solo). Hope and Hell Theatre Company*, 2006, www.raoulbhaneja .com/hamletsolo/index.php#trailer

Performance of *Hamlet* where Bhaneja performs all parts.

Blake, William. "Portraits Inspired by Shakespeare." *Shakespeare Magazine*, 2014, www.shakespearemagazine.com/2014/12/gaze-in-wonder-at-visionary-poet-and-artist-william-blakes-spellbinding-paintings-inspired-by-the-works-of-william-shakespeare

Blake, William. Hamlet and His Father's Ghost. britishmuseum.org/collection/object/P_1954-1113-1-27

Illustration in pen and gray ink of Hamlet and his father's ghost.

"Character List." *Folger Shakespeare Library*, www.folger.edu/sites/default/files/TM4%20-%20Enter%20Players%20handout.pdf

Two handouts: character list from folio (Folger Shakespeare Library ed.) and character map.

Boyle, Francis. ". . . Or Not To Be" *Shakespeare Magazine*, 8 Mar. 2015, pp. 38–43, issuu.com/shakespearemagazine/docs/shakespeare_magazine_06

Collins, John. "Five Types of Writing." *Collins Writing Program*, Collins Educational Associates, 5 Sept. 2017, collinsed.com/approach/five-types-of-writing

Steps for developing skill in process writing.

Crystal, Ben. "Original Pronunciation: *Hamlet* 'To Be or Not To Be.'" *YouTube*, uploaded by Shakespeare on Toast, 25 Nov. 2014, www.youtube.com/watch?v=qYiYd9RcK5M

Famous soliloquy in original pronunciation.

"Decoding Films." *Royal Shakespeare Company*, nextshoot.com/video/royal-shakespeare-company-video-production

Strategies from RSC actors on how to deliver monologues, duologues, soliloquys

Dylan, Bob. "Where Am I Going to Get a Human Skull?" Nobel Banquet speech, 10 Dec. 2016, *Nobel Prize Outreach*, www.nobelprize.org/prizes/literature/2016/dylan/speech

Bob Dylan discusses the goals of an artist, referencing Shakespeare.

"Elizabethan Theater: Shakespeare and the Globe." *YouTube*, uploaded by mistersato 411, 28 Dec. 2017, www.youtube.com/watch?v=U1p8iS7_kZc

Slide presentation on the Globe and early modern culture.

Experiencing Shakespeare. PBS in partnership with Folger Library. *PBS LearingMedia*, www.pbslearningmedia.org/resource/775df496-31b0-45e1-9270-b44f069857b/experiencing-shakespeare/#.WV-q_dPyv-Y

Explores the Folger Library's deep vaults.

"Famous Last Words from Shakespeare." *Folger Shakespeare Library*, www.folger.edu/sites/default/files/TM20%20-%20Famous%20Death%20Lines.pdf

Quotes from death scenes from a variety of plays.

French, Esther. "Shakespeare and Early Modern Girlhood." *Shakespeare and Beyond*, 8 Nov. 2016, shakespeareandbeyond.folger.edu/2016/11/08/shakespeare-early-modern-girl

Garber, Megan. "How Kanye's Vocabulary Stacks Up to Shakespeare's." *The Atlantic*, 24 May 2014, www.theatlantic.com/technology/archive/2014/05/kanyes-vocabulary-compared-to-shakespeares/361697

How hip-hop artists often out-rhyme Shakespeare.

Gaze, Christopher. "Shakespeare is Everywhere." *YouTube*, uploaded by TEDx Talks, 21 Mar. 2012, www.youtube.com/watch?v=LsESSyMnwmU

Discusses sonnet eulogy to Hamnet "Shall I Compare Thee to a Summer's Day?"

Gheeraerts, Marcus [attributed to]. *Rainbow Portrait*. Circa 1600, Hatfield House. *Wikipedia*, en.wikipedia.org/wiki/File:Elizabeth_I_Rainbow_Portrait.jpg

Portrait of Queen Elizabeth I in gown covered with eyes and ears.

Green, John. "Ghosts, Murder, and More Murder – *Hamlet* Part 1: Crash Course Literature 203." *YouTube*, uploaded by CrashCourse, 14 Mar. 2014, www.youtube.com/watch?v=My14mZa-eq8

A fast-paced John Green "rant" about *Hamlet*.

Greenblatt, Stephen. "Episode 100: Stephen Greenblatt on Shakespeare's Tyrants." Interview conducted by Barbara Bogaev. *Folger Shakespeare Library: Shakespeare Unlimited*, 12 Jun. 2018, podcasts.apple.com/us/podcast/stephen-greenblatt-on-shakespeares-tyrants/id1082457631?i=1000414676378&mt=2. *iTunes* app.

Hamlet. Directed by Franco Zeffirelli, performances by Mel Gibson and Glenn Close. Warner Bros., 1990, *Decider*, decider.com/movie/hamlet-1990

Mel Gibson as Hamlet.

Kastan, David Scott. "Episode 49: Shakespeare and Religion." Interview conducted by Neva Grant. *Folger Shakespeare Library: Shakespeare Unlimited*, 31 May 2016, podcasts.apple.com/us/podcast/shakespeare-and-religion/id1082457631?i=1000369769843&mt=2. *iTunes* app.

"Kenneth Branagh ~ Hamlet ~ Gravediggers Scene ~ Part 2 ~ Imperious Caesar, Dead and Turned to Clay." Performance by Kenneth Branagh. *YouTube*, uploaded by Jay Rickards, 20 June 2011, www.youtube.com/watch?v=dBpGgB1NTYg

Film performance of gravedigger scene in Act 5.

"Hamlet – To Be Or Not To Be – Mel Gibson." *YouTube*, uploaded by Jay Rickards, 20 June 2011, www.youtube.com/watch?v=jdp6dpiK8Ko

Film performance of Hamlet's famous soliloquy.

"Hamlet": To Be or Not To Be. Performance by Adrian Lester. *The Guardian*, 1 Feb. 2016, www.theguardian.com/stage/video/2016/feb/01/adrian-lester-hamlet-to-be-or-not-to-be-shakespeare-solos-video

Film monologue performance of Hamlet's famous soliloquy.

The Hamlets. *This American Life*, 9 Aug. 2002, www.thisamericanlife.org/radio-archives/episode/218/act-v?act=1

Prisoners perform Hamlet.

Hovde, Sarah. "Hamlet on the (Very) Small Stage." *Shakespeare and Beyond*, 16 Dec. 2016. shakespeareandbeyond.folger.edu/2016/12/16/hamlet-laurence-olivier-toy-theater-more-4466

"Hamlet – The Life of Ophelia in 4 Different Film Versions." *YouTube*, uploaded by Max Partain, 18 Dec. 2013, www.youtube.com/watch?v=GC5lmDDs4ZQ

Four different directors' versions of Ophelia in a thirteen-minute clip.

"If Shakespearean Insults Were Used Today – Anglophenia, Ep. 13." Performance by Siobhan Thompson. *YouTube*, uploaded by Anglophenia, 24 Sept. 2014. www.youtube.com/watch?v=P_Uej8LJ48Q

Spoof on Shakespearean insults.

"Insults by Shakespeare." Lesson by April Gudenrath, narration by Juliet Blake. *YouTube*, uploaded by TED-Ed, 4 May 2012, www.youtube.com/watch?v=vdCjKH5IKJ8

Animated video on language with background on "fishmonger."

"London Tour: The Globe Theater." *YouTube*, uploaded by DaltonHistory, 29 Apr. 2010. www.youtube.com/watch?v=ZarqSs1odXE

Informational video on history of the Globe.

Menzer, Paul. "Episode 57: Anecdotal Shakespeare" (begin at 14:55 for narratives about the skull from act V and David Tennant). Interview conducted by Neva Grant. *Folger Shakespeare Library: Shakespeare Unlimited*, 20 Sept. 2016, podcasts.apple.com/us/podcast/anecdotal-shakespeare/id1082457631?i=1000375553962&mt=2. *iTunes* app.

"Monty Python's Flying Circus S04E04 Hamlet." *Dailymotion*, uploaded by mitsuglerfoss18yah51, 2018, www.dailymotion.com/video/x6gf7r2

Spoof on Oedipal Hamlet.

"Ophelia and Madness." *YouTube*, uploaded by FolgerLibrary, 26 May 2010, www.youtube.com/watch?v=MhJWwoWCD4w

Educational four-minute video exploring Ophelia's madness.

Paster, Gail Kern, and Barbara Traister. "Episode 55: Elizabethan Medicine." Interview conducted by Neva Grant. *Folger Shakespeare Library: Shakespeare Unlimited*, 23 Aug. 2016, podcasts.apple.com/us/podcast/elizabethan-medicine/id1082457631?i=1000374466965&mt=2. *iTunes* app.

Poltrack, Emma. "A World of Poison: The Overbury Scandal." *Shakespeare and Beyond*, 16 Oct. 2018, shakespeareandbeyond.folger.edu/2018/10/16/a-world-of-poison-the-overbury-scandal/#more-8233

Overbury is mysteriously killed in the Tower of London when he becomes too involved in Robert Carr's involvement with Frances Howard, a married woman.

Pat Reid, editor. *Shakespeare Magazine*, www.shakespearemagazine.com

Reiss, Benjamin. "Episode 9: Shakespeare and Insane Asylums." Interview conducted by Rebecca Sheir. *Folger Shakespeare Library: Shakespeare Unlimited*, 27 Aug. 2014, podcasts.apple.com/us/podcast/shakespeare-insane-asylums/id1082457631?i=1000362436156. *iTunes* app.

Representation and Abstraction: Milais' Ophelia and Newman's Vir Heroicus Sublimis. Conversation with Sal Khan, Beth Harris, and Stephen Zucker. *Khan Academy*, www.khanacademy.org/humanities/art-1010/beginners-guide-20-21/v/representation-abstraction-looking-at-millais-and-newman

Art history lesson.

"Robin Williams' Hilarious Shakespeare Improvisation, Johnny Carson's *Tonight Show*." *YouTube*, uploaded by Johnny Carson, 7 Jan. 2014, www.youtube.com/watch?v=oU73kj5Sw9M

Johnny Carson's interview with Robin Williams about Mel Gibson's Hamlet.

"The Rose Theater Virtual Environment." *YouTube*, uploaded by Ortelia Interactive Spaces, 9 May 2012, www.youtube.com/watch?v=EApTZ1QuoHs

Computer-animated virtual tour of the Rose Theater during early 1600s.

Schoch, Richard. "Portraits in Hamlet: 'Look Here upon This Picture, and on This. . ." *Shakespeare and Beyond*, 8 Apr. 2016, shakespeareandbeyond.folger.edu/2016/04/08/portraits-in-hamlet-shakespeare

Blog posts on historical/cultural significance of *Hamlet*.

"Shakespeare: The Globe Theater London Tour." *YouTube*, uploaded by i2iTravel, 9 Dec. 2013, www.youtube.com/watch?v=m3VGa6Fp3zI

Live tour of the Globe.

Shakespeare Unlimited. Produced by Richard Paul, edited by Gail Kern Paster, *Folger Shakespeare Library*, 1996–, www.folger.edu/shakespeare-unlimited. Podcast.

Shapiro, James. "The Question of Hamlet." *The New York Review*, 19 Apr. 2018, www.nybooks.com/articles/2018/04/19/the-question-of-hamlet

Book review of *Hamlet and the Vision of Darkness* by Rhodri Lewis.

Shea, Christopher D. "Shakespeare's Globe is Winding Up a 'Hamlet' World Tour." *New York Times*, 22 Mar. 2016, www.nytimes.com/2016/03/23/arts/international/londons-globe-theater-is-winding-up-hamlet-world-tour.html?_r=1

Article on 400th anniversary world tour of *Hamlet*.

"Sir John Everett Millais, Ophelia." Created by Beth Harris and Steven Zucker. *YouTube*, uploaded by Smarthistory, 2 Apr. 2012, www.youtube.com/watch?v=I2M7U8eCeHA

Lecture on famous Millais painting.

Slings and Arrows. Performance by Paul Gross, season 1, Acorn Media, 2006. *Amazon Prime*, www.amazon.com/Slings-Arrows-Season-1/dp/B003NDPPY2

Modern interpretation of *Hamlet*.

Smith, Emma. "Podcast 10: 'Hamlet?'" *Approaching Shakespeare*, 23 Oct. 2012, podcasts.apple.com/us/podcast/hamlet/id399194760?i=1000410372226. *iTunes* app.

Podcast lectures on all Shakespeare plays; this one asks the question "Why is Hamlet called 'Hamlet'?"

"Tom Hiddleston is Hamlet." Images courtesy of Marvel Studios and the BBC. *Shakespeare Magazine*, 25 Oct. 2016, pp. 32–35, issuu.com/shakespearemagazine/docs/shakespeare_magazine_11/48

Free online magazine dedicated to exploring and celebrating Shakespeare.

Teaching Shakespeare: A Folger Education Blog, teachingshakespeareblog.folger.edu. Burdick-Zupancic, Jill. "Hamlet's Ophelia: How Imagery Supports Characterization." *Teaching Shakespeare*, 6 May 2014, teachingshakespeareblog.folger.edu/2014/05/06/hamlets-ophelia-how-imagery-supports-characterization

Historical and cultural ideas for and by teachers.

"Toby Stephens Talks about Hamlet." *YouTube*, uploaded by Lissaveta, 9 June 2008, www.youtube.com/watch?v=WydsuDrbCE0

Toby Stephens on playing the title role in Michael Boyd's 2004 Royal Shakespeare Company production.

Tomlinson, Jane. "The Shakespeare Triptych: Three Paintings to Celebrate the Bard's Genius." *Jane Tomlinson*, 10 Feb. 2019, janetomlinson.com/shakespeare-plays-map

Artistic renditions of maps indicating the settings of Shakespeare's plays.

"Who the Hell is Shakespeare?" *Shakespeare Magazine*, issue 14, 26 Jul. 2018, issuu.com/shakespearemagazine/docs/shakespeare_magazine_14/5

Issue focused on Hamlet, including articles, productions, and Ophelia movie.

"Why and How We Read Literature: A Cognitive Journey." *Annenberg Learner*, www.learner.org/workshops/conversations/conversation/rethinking

Various perspectives on reading *Hamlet* from a cognitive standpoint.

"William Shakespeare – Playwright." *YouTube*, uploaded by Biography, 12 Dec. 2012, www.youtube.com/watch?v=geev441vbMI

Short biography on Shakespeare.

Williams, Deanne. "Episode 60: Shakespeare and Girlhood." Interview conducted by Neva Grant. *Folger Shakespeare Library: Shakespeare Unlimited*, 1 Nov. 2016, podcasts.apple.com/us/podcast/shakespeare-and-girlhood/id1082457631?i=1000377389646. *iTunes* app.

Folger Shakespeare Library podcasts covering an array of historical/cultural topics.

"Working in the Theatre: The Globe." Narrated by Dr. Farrah Karim-Cooper. *YouTube*, uploaded by American Theatre Wing, 8 Apr. 2015, www.youtube.com/watch?v=DzCs1nGprXA

Karim-Cooper, Head of Higher Education and Research at the Globe, provides historical background.

Macbeth

Anecdotal Shakespeare. SoundCloud, 20 Sept. 2016, soundcloud.com/folgershakespeare library/anecdotal-shakespeare?in=folgershakespearelibrary/sets/shakespeare-unlimited [section on Macbeth begins at 11:00].

Anecdote about the curse of *Macbeth*.

Broadbent, Sabrina. "Analyzing *Macbeth*." *Teaching Channel*, 9 Mar. 2021, learn.teaching channel.com/video/intro-to-teaching-macbeth

Two lessons on teaching *Macbeth* with drama teacher.

Blake, William. *Pity*. Painting, 1795. *Shakespeare Magazine*. @ShakespeareUK. "From the archives: Gaze in wonder at visionary poet & artist William Blake's magical Shakespeare-inspired paintings." Twitter, 18 June 2017, https://twitter.com/ukshakespeare/status/876578566640676864?lang=en

Inspired from lines, "And pity, like a new-born babe, Striding the blast."

Bruff, Andrew. "William Shakespeare's 'Macbeth' Act 1 Scene 1 Analysis." *YouTube*, uploaded by Mr Bruff, 25 Jul. 2014, www.youtube.com/watch?v=EPhB8AzAnlk

Analysis of the first scene with the witches.

"Cast Talks Davenant's MACBETH." *YouTube*, uploaded by FolgerLibrary, 29 Aug. 2018, www.youtube.com/watch?v=CA7Q3PE-fWw

Restoration period *Macbeth* with added scenes and set to music.

Dench, Judy. "On Playing Lady Macbeth." *BBC*, 24 Mar. 2016, www.bbc.co.uk/programmes/p03nxwmw

Dench podcast and her analysis of Lady M.

"Inside the Collection: 'Macbeth and the Vision of the Armed Head.'" Narrated by curator Erin Blake. *YouTube*, uploaded by FolgerLibrary, 17 July 2017, www.you tube.com/watch?v=9PVScj9DJKM

Description of the eighteenth-century painting.

Garber, Megan. "How Kanye's Vocabulary Stacks Up to Shakespeare's." *The Atlantic*, 24 May 2014, www.theatlantic.com/technology/archive/2014/05/kanyes-vocabulary-compared-to-shakespeares/361697

How hip-hop artists often out-rhyme Shakespeare.

Gibson, Susan. "Primary Source Spotlight: Holinshed's *Chronicles*." *Teaching Modules*, 20 Apr. 2020, www.folger.edu/primary-source-spotlight-holinsheds-chronicles

Shakespeare's source play in sections.

Ginther, Ronald. *The Emmaus Walker Presents: "Witchcraft in America—How Bad Is It?"* Part II, The Poverty/Witchcraft Connection in American Society. *Butterfly Productions*, 2006, theemmauswalk.tripod.com/witchcraftinamericaparttwo.html

A Bible-based article on witchcraft as responsible for poverty.

Goldstein, David B. "Toil and Trouble: Recipes and Witches in *Macbeth*." *Shakespeare and Beyond*, 18 Sept. 2018, shakespeareandbeyond.folger.edu/2018/09/18/recipe-witches-macbeth-witchcraft

Hovde, Sarah. "A Manual for Witch-Hunters." *Shakespeare and Beyond*, 25 Oct. 2016, shakespeareandbeyond.folger.edu/2016/10/25/manual-hunting-witches/#more-4319

Copy of *Malleus Maleficarium*, or *Hammer of Witches*, written by Catholic witch hunters in fifteenth century.

Luong, Thai. "Climate Change: The Zombie Apocalypse?" 17 Aug. 2016. *SciTechConnect*, scitechconnect.elsevier.com/climate-change-zombie-apocalypse

Effects of climate change.

"*Macbeth* – The Three Witches Exclusive Clip – Digital Theatre." *YouTube*, uploaded by Digital Theatre, 7 Nov. 2013, www.youtube.com/watch?v=hnc0pOjr1qY

Macbeth at the Globe—meeting the witches.

"*Macbeth*." *Folger Shakespeare Library*, 10 Aug. 2020, folgerpedia.folger.edu/Macbeth

Web page listing a variety of primary and secondary teaching and scholarly resources.

"*Macbeth*: An Insider's Guide." *Archive-It Wayback Machine/Folgerpedia, Folger Shakespeare Library*, wayback.archive-it.org/2873/20141219015339/http:/www.folger.edu/documents/macbeth_An_Insiders_Guide.mp3

Podcast with sound effects of play with famous directors and actors.

"Mapping the Study of Macbeth." From the files of Mary Magnusson, shared at Narrative Writing Workshop, UNH, Jul. 2018, docs.google.com/document/d/1seSDhvHRIkQrk5AM33HxRRt2R8EXqQdGe3YtLpnA-A4/edit

Unit of study with mini-lessons and quick-writes.

"*Macbeth* and the Restoration." *YouTube*, uploaded by FolgerLibrary, 12 Jul. 2018, www.youtube.com/watch?v=P04KU3WPkDg

Project to present a Restoration version of Shakespeare set to music.

Moore, Stewart Kenneth. "Heart of Darkness." Interview conducted by Pat Reid. *Shakespeare Magazine*, 25 Oct. 2016, pp. 13–19, issuu.com/shakespearemagazine/docs/shakespeare_magazine_11

Graphic novel brings *Macbeth* to life.

Rawls, Kristin. "What Does Our Obsession with Zombie Stories Tell Us about Our Politics?" *AlterNet*, 6 June 2016, www.alternet.org/story/155783/what_does_our_obsession_with_zombie_stories_tell_us_about_our_politics

Apocalyptic/supernatural images in popular culture.

Supernatural and Shakespeare. PBS LearningMedia, www.pbslearningmedia.org/asset/shak13_vid_witchmac

The supernatural and Shakespeare's world.

Broadbent, Sabrina. "Analyzing *Macbeth*." *Teaching Channel*, 9 Mar. 2021, learn.teachingchannel.com/video/intro-to-teaching-macbeth

British drama teacher demonstrates strategies for middle school students.

Teaching Shakespeare, teachingshakespeareblog.folger.edu.

Jochman, Stephanie. "An Alternative to the Traditional Literary Essay." *Teaching Shakespeare*, 29 Mar. 2016. teachingshakespeareblog.folger.edu/2016/03/29/an-alternative-to-the-traditional-literary-essay

Ideas for teachers by teachers.

Thomas, Catherine E. "(Un)Sexing Lady Macbeth: Gender Power, and Visual." *The Upstart Crow*, vol. 31, 2012, pp. 81–102. *The Free Library*, 2012, www.thefreelibrary.com/(Un)sexing+Lady+Macbeth%3a+gender%2c+power%2c+and+visual+rhetoric+in+her...-a0323037688

Representations of Lady Macbeth.

Toyra, Kayleight. "My Nation Underground." Illustrations by Graham Burke and Jon Craig. *Shakespeare Magazine*, 25 Oct. 2016, pp. 58–62, issuu.com/shakespearemagazine/docs/shakespeare_magazine_11

Performing Macbeth in a cave.

Tomlinson, Jane. "The Shakespeare Triptych: Three Paintings to Celebrate the Bard's Genius." *Jane Tomlinson*, 10 Feb. 2019, janetomlinson.com/shakespeare-plays-map

Artistic renditions of maps indicating the settings of Shakespeare's plays

V for Vendetta. Directed by James McTeigue, performances by Hugo Weaving and Natalie Portman, Warner Bros. Entertainment, 2006. *YouTube*, uploaded by YouTube Movies & Shows, 6 Apr. 2011, www.youtube.com/watch?v=Et6M2r3yTAw

Pop culture movie on vigilante groups (anon) using Guy Fawkes masks as symbol of retribution.

Webber, Michael E. "World War G: Zombies, Energy, and the Geosciences." *Earth*, 22 Nov. 2013, www.earthmagazine.org/article/world-war-g-zombies-energy-and-geosciences

Book review.

Witchcraft in Shakespeare's World. PBS LearningMedia, www.pbslearningmedia.org/asset/witchcraft-mezz.mp4

Shakespeare's audiences and witches.

A Midsummer Night's Dream

The Ambassadors. Discussion with Beth Harris and Steven Zucker. *Khan Academy*, www.khanacademy.org/humanities/renaissance-reformation/northern/holbein/v/hans-holbein-the-younger-the-ambassadors-1533

Art criticism of Holbein painting.

Blake, William. "Portraits Inspired by Shakespeare." *Shakespeare Magazine*, 2014, www.shakespearemagazine.com/2014/12/gaze-in-wonder-at-visionary-poet-and-artist-william-blakes-spellbinding-paintings-inspired-by-the-works-of-william-shakespeare

Beautiful paintings by Blake.

British Council. "William Shakespeare." *LearnEnglish Kids*, learnenglishkids.britishcouncil.org/en/short-stories/william-shakespeare

Brief biography of William Shakespeare.

Folger Theater's *A Midsummer Night's Dream*, www.folger.edu/events/midsummer-nights-dream

Actors/actresses talk about their roles in the Folger production.

"Shakespeare: *A Midsummer Night's Dream* (Shakespeare's Globe)." *YouTube*, uploaded by Opus Arte, 7 Aug. 2014, www.youtube.com/watch?v=oqmoIyIPEcc

Fight scene with Helena and Hermia.

A Midsommer Nights Dreame, first folio copy, 1600. *Folger Shakespeare Library*, www.shakespearedocumented.org/exhibition/document/midsummer-nights-dream-first-edition

Original 1600 copy of *A Midsummer Night's Dream*.

A Midsummer Night's Dream: The Love Potion. Shakespeare Uncovered, PBS LearningMedia, www.pbslearningmedia.org/resource/shak15.ela.lit.lovepo/a-midsummer-nights-dream-the-love-potion-shakespeare-uncovered

Love potion origins.

A Midsummer Night's Dream. Online script. docs.google.com/a/nvps.net/document/d/1TBkCzoVNKV-CS60DV6QdDBCbBoRJwpiX6Xxmt1Jts0/edit?usp=sharing

Student copy of play.

Murray, Al. "Show Us Your Bottom." Interview with Pat Reid. 25 Oct. 2016, *Shakespeare Magazine*, pp. 28–34, issuu.com/shakespearemagazine/docs/shakespeare_magazine_11

Magazine articles for "all the Will in the world."

"*A Midsummer Night's Dream* (Shakespeare) – Thug Notes Summary & Analysis." *YouTube*, uploaded by Wisecrack, 23 June 2015, www.youtube.com/watch?v=CpLqTC2-HuA

Thug Notes plot summary (some swearing).

Murray, Al. "Show Us Your Bottom." Interview with Pat Reid. 25 Oct. 2016, *Shakespeare Magazine*, pp. 28–34, issuu.com/shakespearemagazine/docs/shakespeare_magazine_11

Magazine articles for "all the Will in the world."

"Puck/Oberon." *YouTube*, uploaded by gentlemenoftheshade, 24 Oct. 2014, www.youtube.com/watch?v=GC9jq4ZHw4Q

Oberon tells Puck to put juice in Athenian's eye.

"Video SparkNotes: Shakespeare's *A Midsummer Night's Dream* summary." *YouTube*, uploaded by VideoSparkNotes, 29 Oct. 2010, www.youtube.com/watch?v=M1wMfOwlAZ8

SparkNotes plot summary.

Rude Mechanicals in Shakespeare's *A Midsummer Night's Dream. Study*, study.com/academy/lesson/rude-mechanicals-in-shakespeares-a-midsummer-night-dream.html

Explains the job of each rustic.

Shakespeare Magazine. Shakespearemagazine.com

"Shakespeare Steps Out." *YouTube*, uploaded by FolgerLibrary, 15 July 2011, www.youtube.com/watch?v=rIrxvB9Rigs

Teaching Shakespeare in middle school.

Tomlinson, Jane. "The Shakespeare Triptych: Three Paintings to Celebrate the Bard's Genius." *Jane Tomlinson*, 10 Feb. 2019, janetomlinson.com/shakespeare-plays-map

Artistic renditions of maps indicating the settings of Shakespeare's plays.

Romeo and Juliet

Adichie, Chimamanda Ngozi. "The Danger of a Single Story." *TED*, July 2009, www.ted.com/talks/chimamanda_ngozi_adichie_the_danger_of_a_single_story

Barton, Michaella. *Much Ado About Nothing*. Monologue. 13 Dec. 2016. drive.google.com/file/d/0BzRxAi1ZXZv1U19rZzcwWlZiVHM/view

High school senior delivers monologue from Act 4, scene 1, lines 292–316.

"Blunt & Corden in Pop-Music Version of *Romeo & Juliet*." Performances by Emily Blunt and James Corden. *YouTube*, uploaded by CBS New York, 9 June 2017, www.youtube.com/watch?v=1Zgykm9mCbs

Soundtrack to *Romeo and Juliet* with Emily Blunt.

Claybourne, Anna, and Rebecca Treays. *The Usborne World of Shakespeare. Usborne*, 1996. www.usborne.com/quicklinks/eng

Resource book on Elizabethan England with accompanying website.

"Damian Lewis Interview – *Romeo and Juliet* (2013)." *YouTube*, uploaded by Movie Interview, 25 Sept. 2013, www.youtube.com/watch?v=9oNxOYc3j4Y

Interview with Damian Lewis about playing Capulet in 2013 film adaptation.

"Five Modern Day Shakespeares Whose Legacies Will Live On." Illustrations by Leigh Cox. *Vulture*, 2017, www.vulture.com/2017/06/five-modern-shakespeares.html

Illustrations and short biographies of current popular culture artists.

Garber, Megan. "How Kanye's Vocabulary Stacks Up to Shakespeare's." *The Atlantic*, 24 May 2014, www.theatlantic.com/technology/archive/2014/05/kanyes-vocabulary-compared-to-shakespeares/361697

How hip-hop artists often out-rhyme Shakespeare.

Grundhauser, Eric. "When High Class Ladies Wore Masks That Made It Impossible to Speak." 27 Feb. 2017, *Atlas Obscura*, www.atlasobscura.com/articles/visard-mask-elizabethan-visor-blank-16th-century

Article on sixteenth-century women wearing visards to avoid sun.

Hammond, Claudia. "Would Shakespeare's Poisons and Drugs Work in Reality?" *BBC Future*, 16 Apr. 2014, www.bbc.com/future/article/20140416-do-shakespeares-poisons-work

Accessible article on poisons used in Shakespeare's plays.

Huff, Dana. "Shakespeare: To Teach or Not to Teach?" *HuffEnglish*, 15 June 2015, www.huffenglish.com/shakespeare-to-teach-or-not-to-teach

Article reflecting on pros and cons for teaching Shakespeare in high school English.

Koyczan, Shane L. "TED Talk – Shane Koyczan – Bullying." *YouTube*, uploaded by Mary Anne Moran, 23 Sept. 2014, www.youtube.com/watch?v=AOtsNMCRYG0

Spoken word poet on bullying.

Lyon, Karen. "The Well Dressed Elizabethan: Renaissance Fashions as Social Markers." *Shakespeare and Beyond*, 5 Sept. 2017, shakespeareandbeyond.folger.edu/2017/09/05/renaissance-fashion-elizabethan-clothing

Clothing and its effect on social standing for the upper class.

McMahon, Vanessa. "Episode 24: Elizabethan Street Fighting." Interview conducted by Rebecca Sheir. *Folger Shakespeare Library: Shakespeare Unlimited*, 6 May 2015, www.folger.edu/shakespeare-unlimited/elizabethan-street-fighting

Merrill, Lisa. "Episode 13: When Romeo Was a Woman." Interview conducted by Rebecca Sheir. *Folger Shakespeare Library: Shakespeare Unlimited*, 24 Oct. 2014, www.folger.edu/shakespeare-unlimited/romeo-charlotte-cushman

"*Romeo and Juliet* Trailer 2013 Movie – Official [HD]." Directed by Carlos Carlei, performances by Hailee Steinfeld and Douglas Booth. *YouTube*, uploaded by Stream Movie Trailers, 28 July 2013, www.youtube.com/watch?v=mu-lMzHSNNk

Trailer for 2013 version of *Romeo and Juliet* adapted by Julian Fellowes.

"Romeo and Juliet: Who's to Blame?" DBQ Project, teacher version, 2013, drive.google.com/file/d/0B0PfVHmkcjUAaWNvT1lZRHEyb2c/view?usp=sharing

Complete lesson plan for Mini-Qs in Literature and all resources.

"Romeo and Juliet: Who's to Blame?" DBQ Project, enhanced student version, 2013, drive.google.com/file/d/0B0PfVHmkcjUANE5fZ1NJTmxMcTQ/view?usp=sharing

Student copy for Mini-Qs in Literature.

Shakespeare Unlimited. *Folger Shakespeare Library*, www.folger.edu/shakespeare-unlimited

Sheir, Rebecca, host. "Episode 12: Romeo and Juliet through the Ages." *Folger Shakespeare Library: Shakespeare Unlimited*, 8 Oct. 2014, www.folger.edu/shakespeare-unlimited/romeo-juliet

Strauss, Valerie. "Student: Why Teachers Should Not Assign Shakespeare's *Romeo and Juliet*." *The Huffington Post*, 22 June 2015, www.washingtonpost.com/news/

answer-sheet/wp/2015/06/22/student-why-teachers-should-not-assign-shakespeares-romeo-and-juliet/?utm_term=.9bbc6c5d509c

College student's reflection on high school experiences with Shakespeare.

"Thirteen Reasons Why Not: Shakespeare, Netflix, and a Teachable Moment." *Teaching Shakespeare*, 17 May 2017, teachingshakespeareblog.folger.edu/2017/05/17/thirteen-reasons-not-shakespeare-netflix-teachable-moment

Blog post on runaway brides or marriage where the female uses marriage as rebellion, including *Othello*, *Merchant of Venice*, and *Romeo and Juliet*.

Williams, Deanne. "Episode 60: Shakespeare and Girlhood." Interview conducted by Neva Grant, based on *Shakespeare and the Performance of Girlhood*, 2014. *Folger Shakespeare Library: Shakespeare Unlimited*, 1 Nov. 2016, www.folger.edu/shakespeare-unlimited/girlhood

Williams, Deanna, and Graham Holderness. "Episode 25: Shakespeare's France and Italy." Interview conducted by Rebecca Sheir. *Folger Shakespeare Library: Shakespeare Unlimited*, 20 May 2015, www.folger.edu/shakespeare-unlimited/france-italy

Forty-five-minute podcasts on timely topics.

Tomlinson, Jane. "The Shakespeare Triptych: Three Paintings to Celebrate the Bard's Genius." *Jane Tomlinson*, 10 Feb. 2019, janetomlinson.com/shakespeare-plays-map

Artistic renditions of maps indicating the settings of Shakespeare's plays.

Trendacosta, Katharine. "An Infographic That Keeps Track of all of Shakespeare's Deaths for You." *io9*, 2 Mar. 2014, io9.gizmodo.com/an-infographic-that-keeps-track-of-all-of-shakespeares-1534516437

Infographic displaying deaths in Shakespeare's tragedies.

Sonnets

Biondo-Hench, Susan. "'But then Begins a Journey in My Head': Stepping into Sonnets." *Teaching Shakespeare*, 24 May 2017, teachingshakespeareblog.folger.edu/2017/05/24/begins-journey-head-stepping-sonnets

Ideas for teaching sonnets.

"Building Websites." *GoDaddy*, www.godaddy.com

Purchasing new domain names (ideas for projects).

Didriksen, Erik. "Episode 41: Pop Sonnets." *Folger Shakespeare Library: Shakespeare Unlimited*, 10 Feb. 2016, www.folger.edu/shakespeare-unlimited/pop-sonnets.

Podcast on Didriksen's transformation of popular music into sonnet form.

Guerrero, Laurie Ann. "What I Learned From My City." *YouTube*, uploaded by TEDx Talks, 13 Nov. 2014, www.youtube.com/watch?v=5EYGtTnPJ4c

TED Talk on how communities shape poetry.

Hill, Fran. "Final Word: O How My Bard Was Botched." *The Times Educational Supplement*, no. 4852, 14 Aug. 2009, p. 44, *Tes*, www.tes.com/magazine/archive/final-word-fran-hill

Article on teaching Shakespeare.

Neal10. "iRubric: Song Lyric/Sonnet Project Rubric." *Rcampus*, 2022, www.rcampus.com/rubricshowc.cfm?code=D3W436&sp=true

Kingslee James Dalee (Akala). "Episode 78: Akala and Hip-Hop Shakespeare." Interview conducted by Barbara Bogaev. *Folger Shakespeare Library: Shakespeare Unlimited*, 25 July 2017, www.folger.edu/shakespeare-unlimited/akala-hip-hop-shakespeare

Shakespeare as popular culture hip-hop artist.

"Shakespeare's Sonnets: Crash Course Literature 304." Presented by John Green. *YouTube*, uploaded by CrashCourse, 28 July 2016, www.youtube.com/watch?v=bDpW1sHrBaU

Background on the sonnets, including sonnets 18, 116, and 130.

"Shakespeare: The Sonnets." *Pinterest*, www.pinterest.com/pin/110267890854775162

Sonnets set to contemporary music.

Smith, Bruce. "How Should One Read a Sonnet?" *Early Modern Literary Studies*, Special Issue, vol. 19, no. 2, pp. 1–39, purl.oclc.org/emls/si-19/smitsonn.htm

Reading the sonnets in American Sign Language.

The Harriet W. Sheridan Center for Teaching and Learning. "Designing Grading Rubrics." *Brown U*, 2022, www.brown.edu/sheridan/teaching-learning-resources/teaching-resources/course-design/classroom-assessment/grading-criteria/designing-rubrics

Wolf, Kenneth, et al. "Rubrics! A Digital Resource." *The Regents of the U of Colorado*, www.ucdenver.edu/offices/assessmentoffice/rubrics!-a-digital-resource

Sonnet Project rubric templates (see Chapter 5 and Appendix E).

Starbuck, George. "The Essential Shakespeare, Vol. 12: Space Saver Sonnets." *Poetry Foundation*, www.poetryfoundation.org/poems/47051/the-essential-shakespeare-volume-xii-space-saver-sonnets

Starbuck's attempt to rewrite sonnets in brief form.

"VoiceThread Workshops." Basics 2 and 3. *Ed.VoiceThread*, 2021, voicethread.com/workshop-categories/basics

Creating VoiceThread projects.

Whittemore, Hank. *The Monument*, new.shakespearesmonument.com. Accessed 12 July 2022.

Website devoted to the sonnets, with a focus on the dark lady and the fair youth.

Notes

1. The *Rainbow Portrait*. Circa 1600. Formerly attributed to either Marcus Gheeraerts the Younger or Isaac Oliver. Elizabeth's garment is covered with eyes and ears, suggesting she sees and hears all. She holds a rainbow in her right hand bearing the words *Non sine sole iris* or "There is no rainbow without the sun" (description of painting from Shapiro, *A Year in the Life* plate 3).

2. Until 2020, the Chicago Shakespeare Theater's education department offered 90-minute "Short Shakes" performances to students each year. The abridged program is now called "Short Shakespeare!"

3. Text printed in the margin next to the woodcut in Holinshed's source story refers to the women as otherworldly by using the descriptions "weird sisters" and "feiries" (Kersey).

4. See Question 1, Section II, of the AP English Language and Composition: Free-Response Questions (College Board).

5. See College Board sample questions, such as the SAT Practice Essay #1: satsuite.collegeboard.org/media/pdf/sat-practice-test-1-essay.pdf.

6. See the *Teaching Shakespeare* website (shakespearedocuments.info) for visuals, video clips, and handouts about stage combat.

7. Bullein, Barrough, and du Laurens all speak to the effects of sleeping nightshade in an excerpted document filed on the *Teaching Shakespeare* website (shakespearedocuments.info), under "*Romeo and Juliet* Documents, act 4."

8. In full, *The Book of Common Prayer and Administration of the Sacraments, and Other Rites and Ceremonies of the Church*. The 1549 *Book of Common Prayer* is also referred to as the "First Book of Edward VI," while the 1559 edition (itself a modification of the 1552 "Second Book of Edward VI") is called the "First Book of Queen Elizabeth."

9. See competing ideas about the afterlife catalogued on the *Teaching Shakespeare* website (shakespearedocuments.info), within the *Romeo and Juliet* act 5 documents (Steelman).

10. See *Teaching Shakespeare* (shakespearedocuments.info) for Silent Annotations handouts.

11. See Appendix C, "Bubble Track."

12. See Appendix B, "Blocking Scenes."

13. See Appendix D for steps to research early modern documents.

14. See Appendix B, "Digital to Visual."

15. See Appendix C, "Text to Text."

16. See *Teaching Shakespeare* (shakespearedocuments.info) for formative and summative assessments and a rubric.

17. If you haven't introduced sketch-noting to your students, use Doug Neill's *YouTube* tutorial to get started: www.youtube.com/watch?v=y_fn2fpO5cU.

18. Observed by modern pagans as a seasonal festival as well as a gathering of witches.

19. James reigned as James VI, King of Scotland, from 1567, and as James I, King of England and Ireland, from 1603.

20. See Appendix C, "Shift and Share."

21. Teachers can access all recorded mini-lessons on the *Teaching Shakespeare* website (shakespearedocuments.info) or via my *AP Literature* website: steelmancafe.weebly.com.

22. The British Council offers short animated clips for younger students, including one on *Midsummer.* See Online Resources (Appendix G) for a full list of teaching ideas to use while teaching this play.

23. When students write short, numerous pieces in their writer's notebooks or foldables, they can build stamina for writing longer pieces in one sitting. Quick-writes also serve as prediscussion strategies to use before sharing with an elbow partner, small groups, or the entire class.

24. Appendixes B and C provide classroom strategies for teaching Shakespeare and for incorporated documents.

25. A 3–2–1 activity can be used as an entrance or exit slip, as well as a way to check learning after a mini-lesson. Students reflect on *three* things they know, *two* things they are unsure about, and *one* question they still have (see also Appendix B). Teachers can use the question section to review the next day. Misconceptions can be cleared up without students knowing who asked which questions.

26. In Elizabethan England, beggars and unemployed people were whipped for begging; a second offence meant hanging. In the sketch—a copy of which can be accessed on the *Teaching Shakespeare* website (shakespearedocuments.info)—the beggar is on his way to the gallows.

27. See *Teaching Shakespeare* (shakespearedocuments.info) for assessments and rubrics.

28. See *Teaching Shakespeare* (shakespearedocuments.info) for all sonnet teaching materials.

29. See Appendix G for classroom strategies and activities to strengthen research skills.

30. See *Teaching Shakespeare* (shakespearedocuments.info) for all documents, video tutorials, lesson plans, slides, and project samples.

31. The sample schedule provides an organizational tool for completing the project in one week. See *Teaching Shakespeare* (shakespearedocuments.info).

32. Thank you to Audra Whetstone, AP Language and Composition instructor at Northview High School in Grand Rapids, Michigan, who devised this method for reading nonfiction pieces.

33. The SOAPSTone strategy, developed by Tommy Boley, is included in the College Board workshop Pre-AP: Interdisciplinary Strategies for English and Social Studies, for use in analyzing prose and visual texts.

Works Cited

1h) Act I, Scene V - Hamlet with his father's ghost (Branagh). *Vimeo*, uploaded by Peabody Humanities, 2013, vimeo.com/52799318.

"96 Incredibly Useful Links for Teaching and Studying Shakespeare." *OnlineCollege.org*, 16 Dec. 2009, www.onlinecollege.org/2009/12/16/100-incredibly-useful-links-for-teaching-and-studying-shakespeare.

Adichie, Chimamanda Ngozi. "The Danger of a Single Story." *TED*, July 2009, www.ted.com/talks/chimamanda_ngozi_adichie_the_danger_of_a_single_story.

Amyas, Richard. *An Antidote against Melancholy. Or, A Treasury of 53 Rare Secrets and Arts Discovered, By an Expert Artist, Richard Amyas*. 1659. *Early English Books Online*, Wing (2nd ed. 1994), A3032A, name.umdl.umich.edu/A25314.0001.001.

Anger, Jane. *Jane Anger Her Protection for Vvomen to Defend Them against the Scandalous Reportes of a Late Surfeiting Louer, and All Otherlike Venerians that Complaine so to Bee Ouercloyed with Womens Kindnesse*. Printed by Richard Jones and Thomas Orwin, 1589. *Early English Books Online*, STC (2nd ed.), 644, name.umdl.umich.edu/B11194.0001.001.

Appleman, Deborah. *Critical Encounters in High School English: Teaching Literary Theory to Adolescents*. 2nd ed., Teachers College Press, 2009.

The Araignement and Burning of Margaret Ferne-Seede, for the Murther of Her Late Husband Anthony Ferne-Seede, Found Deade in Peckham Field Neere Lambeth, Hauing Once Before Attempted to Poyson Him with Broth, Being Executed in S. Georges-Field the Last of Februarie, 1608. Henry Gosson, 1608. *Early English Books Online*, STC, 10826, name.umdl.umich.edu/A00692.0001.001.

Atwell, Nancie. *In the Middle: A Lifetime of Learning about Writing, Reading and Adolescents*. 3rd ed., Heinemann, 2014.

Bacon, Francis. *The Essays of Francis Bacon*. Edited with introduction and notes by Mary A. Scott, Scribner, 1908.

———. "Of Marriage and Single Life." 1553. *The Norton Anthology of English Literature*, edited by Stephen Greenblatt, 8th ed., vol. B, W. W. Norton, 2006, pp. 1553–54.

Barbudo, Maria Isabel. "William Shakespeare and the Representation of Female Madness." *Creative Dialogues, Narrative and Medicine*, edited by Isabel Fernandes et al., Cambridge Scholars, 2015, pp. 150–55.

Barrough, Philip. *The Methode of Phisicke Conteyning the Causes, Signes, and Cures of Invvard Diseases in Mans Body from the Head to the Foote. VVhereunto is Added, the Forme and Rule of Making Remedies and Medicines, Which Our Phisitians Commonly Vse at this Day, with the Proportion, Quantitie, & Names of Ech [sic] Medicine.* Imprinted by Thomas Vautroullier, 1583. *Early English Books Online*, STC, 1508, name.umdl.umich.edu/A04936.0001.001.

Bell, Marvin. "To Dorothy." *Nightworks: Poems 1962–2000*, Copper Canyon Press, 2000, p. 105.

Blau, Sheridan. *The Literature Workshop: Teaching Texts and Their Readers*. Heinemann, 2003.

Boaistuau, Pierre, et al. "Demonic Possession." 1598. *Histoires Prodigieuses*. *The Year of Lear: Shakespeare in 1606*, by James Shapiro, Simon and Schuster, 2015, p. 65.

Breton, Nicholas. *The Good and the Badde, or Descriptions of the Vvorthies, and Vnworthies of this Age Where the Best May See Their Graces, and the Worst Discerne Their Basenesse*. Iohn Budge, 1616. *Early English Books Online*, STC, 3656, name.umdl.umich.edu/A16748.0001.001.

A Briefe Description of the Notorious Life of Iohn Lambe Otherwise Called Doctor Lambe. Together with his Ignominious Death. G. Miller, 1628. *Early English Books Online*, STC (2nd ed.), 15177, name.umdl.umich.edu/A05033.0001.001.

Brinkelow, Henry, and Simon Fish. *A Supplicacyon of the Poore Commons Whereunto is Added the Supplication of Beggers*. Printed by John Day, 1546. *Early English Books Online*, STC (2nd ed.), 10884, name.umdl.umich.edu/A00758.0001.001.

British Library. "Venetian Gold Ducat." 1523–1538. *British Museum*, www.britishmuseum.org/collection/object/C_1849-1121-567.

Britton, James. *Language and Learning*. U of Miami P, 1970.

Broadbent, Sabrina. "Analyzing *Macbeth*." *Teaching Channel*, 9 Mar. 2021, learn.teachingchannel.com/video/intro-to-teaching-macbeth.

Buccola, Regina. *Fairies, Fractious Women, and the Old Faith: Fairy Lore in Early Modern British Drama and Culture*. Susquehanna UP, 2006.

Bullein, William. *Bulleins Bulwarke of Defence against all Sicknesse, Soarenesse, and Vvoundes that Doe Dayly Assaulte Mankinde: Which Bulwarke is Kept with Hilarius the Gardener, [and] Health the Phisicion, with the Chirurgian to Helpe the Wounded Souldiours. Gathered and Practised from the Most Worthy Learned, Both Olde and New: To the Great Comfort of Mankinde*. Thomas Marshe, 1579. *Early English Books Online*, STC, 4034, name.umdl.umich.edu/A17156.0001.001.

Burton, Robert. *The Anatomy of Melancholy: Vvhat It Is. VVith All the Kindes, Causes, Symptomes, Prognostickes, and Seuerall Cures of It. In Three Maine Partitions with Their Seuerall Sections, Members, and Subsections. Philosophically, Medicinally, Historically, Opened and Cut Vp. By Democritus Iunior.* Henry Cripps, 1621. [Copy from British Library.] *Early English Books Online*, STC (2nd ed.), 4159, name.umdl.umich.edu/A17310.0001.001.

Callaghan, Dympna, editor. *Romeo and Juliet: Texts and Contexts*. Bedford/St. Martin's, 2003.

Carey-Webb, Allen (also Webb, Allen). Interview. Conducted by Sheridan Steelman, 10 Sept. 2017.

———. "National and Colonial Education in Shakespeare's *The Tempest*." *Early Modern Literary Studies*, vol. 5, no. 1, May 1999, paras. 1–39.

Carlei, Carlo, director. *Romeo and Juliet*. Performances by Douglas Booth and Hailee Steinfeld, Echo Lake Entertainment, 2013.

Carlsen, G. Robert, et al., editors. *Insights: Themes in Literature*. Webster Division, McGraw Hill, 1985.

Carmichael, James. *Newes from Scotland, Declaring the Damnable Life and Death of Doctor Fian a Notable Sorcerer, who was Burned at Edenbrough in Ianuary last. 1591. Which doctor was Regester to the Diuell that Sundry Times Preached at North Barrick Kirke, to a Number of Notorious Witches. With the True Examination of the Saide Doctor and Witches, as They Vttered Them in the Presence of the Scottish king. Discouering how they Pretended to Bewitch and Drowne his Maiestie in the Sea Comming from Denmarke, with Such Other Wonderfull Matters as the Like Hath Not been Heard of At Any Time*. 1592. [Copy from Bodleian Library.] *Early English Books Online*, STC (2nd ed.), 10841a, name.umdl.umich.edu/A00710.0001.001.

Castiglione, Count Baldassare. "Book 4," *The Courtier*. 1561. *The Norton Anthology of English Literature*, edited by Stephen Greenblatt, 8th ed., vol. B, W. W. Norton, 2006, pp. 650–57.

Claybourne, Anna, and Rebecca Treays. *The World of Shakespeare*. Usborne, 1996.

Cohen, Paula Marantz. *Of Human Kindness: What Shakespeare Teaches Us about Empathy*. Yale UP, 2021.

———. "What Shakespeare Can Teach Us About Empathy." *Wall Street Journal*, 13 Feb. 2021. C4, pp. 13–14.

College Board. "AP English Language and Composition Free-Response Questions." *AP Central*, 2021, apcentral.collegeboard.org/pdf/ap21-frq-english-language.pdf.

———. "The SAT Practice Essay #1" (5LS05E). *SAT Suite of Assessments*, 18 Oct. 2018, satsuite.collegeboard.org/media/pdf/sat-practice-test-1-essay.pdf.

Collins, John. "Five Types of Writing." *Collins Writing Program*, Collins Educational Associates, 5 Sept. 2017, collinsed.com/approach/five-types-of-writing.

Cramner, Thomas, editor. *An Homilie against Disobedience and Wilfull Rebellion*. By John Jewel, John Bill, 1571. *Anglican Library*, Book 2, XXI, www.anglicanlibrary.org/homilies/bk2hom21.htm.

Crystal, Ben. "Original Pronunciation: *Hamlet* 'To Be or Not To Be.'" *YouTube*, uploaded by Shakespeare on Toast, 25 Nov. 2014, www.youtube.com/watch?v=qYiYd9RcK5M.

———. *Shakespeare on Toast: Getting a Taste for the Bard*. Icon, 2008.

———. *Springboard Shakespeare: A Midsummer Night's Dream*. Bloomsbury, 2013.

Dakin, Mary Ellen. *Reading Shakespeare: Film First*. National Council of Teachers of English, 2012.

———. *Reading Shakespeare with Young Adults*. National Council of Teachers of English, 2009.

David Harewood on the Racial Prejudice in Othello. Shakespeare Uncovered, 6 Feb. 2015, www.pbs.org/video/shakespeare-uncovered-david-harewood-racial-prejudice-othello.

Day, Richard. *A Booke of Christian Prayers, Collected Out of the Auncie[n]t Writers, and Best Learned in Our Tyme, Worthy To Be Read with an Earnest Mynde of all Christians, in These Daungerous and Troublesome Dayes, that God for Christes Sake will Yet still be Mercyfull Vnto Vs*. John Day, 1578. Early English Books Online, STC, 6429, name.umdl.umich.edu/A19989.0001.001.

Delahoyde, Michael. "Shake-speare's Sonnets." *Shakespeare*. Washington State U, 12 Dec. 2017, public.wsu.edu/~delahoyd/shakespeare/sonnets.html.

Department of History, U of Iowa. "How to Read a Primary Source." *Teaching and Writing Center*, 2004, clas.uiowa.edu/history/teaching-and-writing-center/guides/source-identification/primary-source.

de Passe (the Elder), Crispijn. *The Gunpowder Plot Conspirators, 1605*. Circa 1605. [See also Passe, *Eygentliche Abbildung*.] *National Portrait Gallery*, www.npg.org.uk/collections/search/portrait/mw00381/The-Gunpowder-Plot-Conspirators-1605.

di Grassi, Giacomo. *Di Grassi, His True Arte of Defence*. Translated by Thomas Churchyard, Iohn Iaggard, 1594. *Early English Books Online*, STC (2nd ed.), 12190, reel 344:06, name.umdl.umich.edu/A02044.0001.001.

The Divine Right and Irresistibility of Kings and Supreme Magistrates Clearly Evidenced, Not from Any Private Authority, But from the Publique Confessions of the Reformed Churches, and the Homilies of the Church of England. Leonard Lichfield, 1645. [Copy from Bodleian Library.] *Early English Books Online*, Wing, D1732, name.umdl.umich.edu/A36175.0001.001.

"Elizabeth: March 1973, 16–31." *Calendar of State Papers Foreign: Elizabeth, Volume 10, 1572–1574*. Edited by Allan James Crosby, Her Majesty's Stationery Office, 1876.

"An Epic Chart of 162 Young Adult Retellings." *Epic Reads*, 26 Feb. 2014, www.epicreads.com/blog/an-epic-chart-of-162-young-adult-retellings.

Erasmus, Desidarius. "A Maid Hating Marriage." 1523. *A Midsummer Night's Dream: Texts and Contexts*, edited by Gail Kern Paster and Skiles Howard, Bedford/St. Martin's, 1999, pp. 227–31. Originally published in *The Colloquies, or Familiar Discourses of Desidarius Erasmus of Rotterdam, Rendered into English*, translated by H. M. Gent, H. Brome, B. Tooke, and T. Sawbridge, 1671, pp. 140–48. *Early English Books Online*, STC, 12316.

"Execution of Guy Fawkes and Associates" [from *Verratheren in England*]. 1606. Lambeth Palace Library, *Bridgeman Images*, www.bridgemanimages.com/en/german-school/execution-of-guy-fawkes-and-associates-from-verratheren-in-england-1606-engraving/engraving/asset/234056.

Faithfull, Bayard. "Four Reads: Learning to Read Primary Documents." Roy Rosenzweig Center for History and New Media at George Mason U, 2018. *Teaching History*, teachinghistory.org/teaching-materials/teaching-guides/25690.

Fish, Simon. *A Supplicacyon for the Beggers*. Johannes Grapheus, 1529. *Early English Books Online*, STC, 10883, name.umdl.umich.edu/A00757.0001.001.

Garnet, Henry. "A Treatise of Equivocation." 1598. *Macbeth: Texts and Contexts*, edited by William C. Carroll, Bedford/St. Martin's, 1999, pp. 266–68.

Gerard, John. *The Herball, or Generall Historie of Plantes. Gathered by Iohn Gerarde of London Master in Chirurgerie*. Imprinted by John Norton, 1597. [Copy from Henry E. Huntington and Art Gallery and Bodleian Library.] *Early English Books Online*, 1633 ed., enlarged and extended by Thomas Johnson, STC (2nd ed.), 11750, name.umdl.umich.edu/A01622.0001.001.

Gibson, Mel, performer. *Hamlet*. Directed by Franco Zeffirelli, Warner Bros., 1990.

Gibson, Rex. *Teaching Shakespeare*. Cambridge UP, 1998.

Goodman, Nicholas. *Hollands Leaguer: Or, an Historical Discourse of the Life and Actions of Dona Britanica Hollandia the Arch-Mistris of the Wicked Women of Utopia. Wherein is Detected the Notorious Sinne of Panderisme, and the Execrable Life of the Luxurious Impudent*. 1632. *British Library*, www.bl.uk/collection-items/17th-century-brothel-in-nicholas-goodmans-hollands-leaguer.

Gouge, William. "The Third Treatise: Of Wiues Particular Duties." *Of Domesticall Duties: Eight Treatises*, William Bladen, 1622, sec. 43 (Of a Wives Active Obedience), p. 315. [Copy from Folger Shakespeare Library.] *Early English Books Online*, STC (2nd ed.), 12119, reel 801:07, name.umdl.umich.edu/A68107.0001.001.

Graesser, Arthur C., and Sidney K. D'Mello. "Emotions during the Learning of Difficult Material." *Psychology of Learning and Motivation: Advances in Research and Theory*, vol. 57, 2012, pp. 183–225.

Greenblatt, Stephen. "Culture." *The Greenblatt Reader*. 1995. Edited by Michael Payne, Blackwell, 2005, p. 13.

———. "The Death of Hamnet and the Making of Hamlet." *The New York Review*, Oct. 21 2004, www.nybooks.com/articles/2004/10/21/the-death-of-hamnet-and-the-making-of-hamlet.

———, editor. *The Norton Anthology of English Literature*. 8th ed., vol. B, W. W. Norton, 2006.

———, editor. *The Norton Anthology of English Literature: Core Selections Ebook*. 10th ed., W. W. Norton, 2021, digital.wwnorton.com/englishlit10core.

———. *Tyrant: Shakespeare on Politics*. W.W. Norton and Company, 2018.

Gurr, Andrew. *The Shakespearean Stage: 1574–1642*. Cambridge UP, 1992.

Hammond, Claudia. "Would Shakespeare's Poisons and Drugs Work in Reality?" *BBC Future*, 16 Apr. 2014, www.bbc.com/future/article/20140416-do-shakespeares-poisons-work.

Harner, James. *World Shakespeare Bibliography Online*. Edited by Heidi Craig, Texas A&M U/Folger Shakespeare Library/Oxford UP, 2022, www.worldshakesbib.org.

Hedeen, Timothy. "The Reverse Jigsaw: A Process of Cooperative Learning and Discussion." *Teaching Sociology*, vol. 31, no. 3, 2003, pp. 325–32.

Henderson, Katherine U., and Barbara F. McManus. *Half Humankind: Contexts and Texts of the Controversy about Women in England, 1540–1640*. U of Illinois P, 1985.

Henning, Megan. Interview. Conducted by Sheridan Steelman, 20 Sept. 2017.

Herring, Francis. *Mischeefes Mysterie: or, Treasons Master-Peece, the Powder-Plot Inuented by Hellish Malice, Preuented by Heauenly Mercy: Truely Related. And from the Latine of the Learned and Reuerend Doctour Herring Translated, and Very Much Dilated. By Iohn Vicars*. Printed by E. Griffin, 1617. [Copy in Henry E. Huntington Library and Art Gallery.] *Early English Books Online*, STC (2nd ed.), 13247, reel 962:01, name.umdl.umich.edu/A03116.0001.001.

Hoffman, Michael, director. *A Midsummer Night's Dream*. Performances by Kevin Kline and Michelle Pfeiffer, Twentieth Century Fox, 1999.

Holbein (the Younger), Hans. *The Ambassadors*. 1533. *National Gallery*, www.nationalgallery.org.uk/paintings/hans-holbein-the-younger-the-ambassadors.

Holinshed, Raphael. *The Firste [Laste] Volume of the Chronicles of England, Scotlande, and Irelande Conteyning the Description and Chronicles of England, from the First Inhabiting vnto the Conquest: the Description and Chronicles of Scotland, from the First Original of the Scottes Nation Till the Yeare of our Lorde 1571: the Description and Chronicles of Yrelande, Likewise from the First Originall of That Nation Untill the Yeare 1571 / Faithfully Gathered and Set Forth by Raphaell Holinshed*. Vol. 1, imprinted for John Hunne, 1577. *Early English Books Online*, STC (2nd ed.), 13568b, name.umdl.umich.edu/A03448.0001.001.

Holmer, Joan Ozark. "'Draw, If You Be Men': Saviolo's Significance for *Romeo and Juliet*." *Shakespeare Quarterly*, vol. 45, no. 2, summer 1994, pp. 163–68.

House of Commons. "The Statute of Artificers 1562." 1563. *A Midsummer Night's Dream: Texts and Contexts*, edited by Gail Kern Paster and Skiles Howard, Bedford/St. Martin's, 1999, pp. 182–85.

Hughes, Paul L., and James F. Larkin, editors. "Proclamation 735: Prohibiting Unlawful Assembly under Martial Law (June 20, 1591)." *Tudor Royal Proclamations: Vol. 3*. Yale UP, 1969, pp. 82–83.

Hulsius, Levinus. "Amazons Practicing Archery on Their Prisoners and Preparing to Roast Their Victims, 1497." *The Discovery of Guiana*, German ed., by Sir Walter Raleigh, Robert Robinson, 1598. Reprod. in "Female Attachments and Family Ties," *A Midsummer Night's Dream: Texts and Contexts*. Eds. Gail Kern Paster and Skiles Howard, Bedford/St. Martin's, 1999, pp. 194–200.

Hunter, John C., editor. *Renaissance Literature: An Anthology of Poetry and Prose*. Wiley-Blackwell, 2010.

Innocent III, Pope. *The Mirror of Man's Lyfe Plainely Describing, What Weake Moulde We Are Made of: What Miseries We Are Subiect vnto: Howe Vncertaine This Life Is: and What Shal Be Our Ende*. Translated by H. Kirton, Henry Bynneman, 1576. *Early English Books Online*, STC (2nd ed.), 14094.5, name.umdl.umich.edu/A04036.0001.001.

Jaime, Catherine. "Three Ways to Have Fun with Shakespeare." *Teaching Shakespeare!*, 7 June 2017, teachingshakespeareblog.folger.edu/2017/06/07/three-ways-fun-shakespeare.

James I, King of England. *An Act against Conjuration, Witchcraft and Dealing with Evil and Wicked Spirits* [1 James 1 c.12]. 1604. *The Statutes Project*, 11 June 2018, statutes.org.uk/site/the-statutes/seventeenth-century/1604-1-james-1-c-12-an-act-against-witchcraft.

James VI, King of Scotland. *Daemonologie, in Forme of a Dialogue, Diuided into Three Bookes*. Printed by Robert Walde Graue, printer to the Kings Majestie, 1597. [Copy from Henry E. Huntington Library and Art Gallery.] *Early English Books Online*, STC (2nd ed.), 14364, name.umdl.umich.edu/A04243.0001.001.

———. *The Trve Lawe of Free Monarchies: Or, the Reciprock and Mvtvall Dvtie betwixt a Free King, and his Naturall Subiectes*. 1598. "*The True Law of Free Monarchies* by King James VI and I," *British Library*, 2022, www.bl.uk/collection-items/the-true-law-of-free-monarchies-by-king-james-vi-and-i.

Kay, Dave. "The Four Temperaments." *Guardian Defence*, 28 Jan. 2020, krav-maga-self-defence.com/the-four-temperaments.

Kersey, Harriet. "Holinshed's Chronicles: Macbeth, Banquo and Three Weird Sisters (CCL, W/G-5-15)." *Canterbury Cathedral*, 1 Oct. 2018, www.canterbury-cathedral.org/heritage/archives/picture-this/holinsheds-chronicles-macbeth-banquo-and-three-weird-sisters-ccl-w-g-5-15.

The Kingdomes Monster Vncloaked From Heaven the Popish Conspirators, Malignant Plotters, and Cruell Irish, in One Body to Destroy Kingdome, Religion and Lawes: But under Colour to Defend Them, Especially the Irish, Who Having Destroyed the Protestants There, Flye Hither to Defend the Protestant Religion Here. 1643. *Early English Books Online*, Wing, K587, name.umdl.umich.edu/A87775.0001.001.

Kinney, Arthur F. *Lies Like Truth: Shakespeare, Macbeth, and the Cultural Moment*. Wayne State UP, 2001.

Kinney, Clare R. "Lecture 5: Hamlet III—Difficult Women." *Shakespeare's Tragedies*, Part 1. Teaching Company, 2007.

Kottman, Paul A. *Spectral Communities and Ghosts of Sovereignty: Interpreting Apparitions in Hamlet and Macbeth*. 2000. U of California, Berkeley, PhD dissertation.

Kyd, Thomas. *The Spanish Tragedie, or Hieronimo is Mad Againe*. 1587. *Four Revenge Tragedies*. Edited and introduced by Katharine Eisaman Maus, Oxford UP, 1995, pp. 1–91.

Ladd-Taylor, Molly, et al. "How to Analyze a Primary Source." *Carleton College Department of History*, 25 Mar. 2021, www.carleton.edu/history/resources/history-study-guides/primary.

Lamb, Mary Ellen. "Book Review: Anthony Fletcher. *Gender, Sex, and Subordination in England: 1500–1800*." *Renaissance Quarterly*, vol. 51, no. 1, spring 1998, pp. 278–81.

Lambert, Tim. "Tudor Society." *Local Histories*, 14 Mar. 2021, localhistories.org/life-in-the-16th-century.

Lanyer, Amelia. "Eve's Apology in Defense of Women." 1611. *The Norton Anthology of English Literature*, edited by Stephen Greenblatt, 8th ed., vol. B, W. W. Norton, 2006, pp. 1317–19.

———. *Salue Deus Rex Iudæorum Containing, 1. The Passion of Christ, 2. Eues Apologie in Defence of Women, 3. The Teares of the Daughters of Ierusalem, 4. The Salutation and Sorrow of the Virgine Marie: with Diuers Other Things Not Vnfit to Be Read*. Richard Bonian, 1611. *Early English Books Online*, STC (2nd ed.), 15227.5, name.umdl.umich.edu/A05085.0001.001.

Laslett, Peter. *Family Life and Illicit Love in Earlier Generations: Essays in Historical Sociology*. Cambridge UP, 1981.

Lavater, Ludwig. *Of Ghostes and Spirites Walking by Nyght, and of Strange Noyses, Crackes, and Sundry Forewarnynges, which Commonly Happen Before the Death of Menne, Great Slaughters & Alterations of Kyngdomes*. Translated by Robert Harrison, R. Watkins, 1572. *Early English Books Online*, STC (2nd ed.), 15320, name.umdl.umich.edu/A05186.0001.001.

Lemon, Rebecca. "Sovereignty and Treason in Macbeth." *New Critical Essays*, edited by Nick Moschovakis, 2008, pp. 73–87.

Long, Kevin, and Mary T. Christel. *Bring on the Bard: Active Approaches for Shakespeare's Diverse Student Readers*. National Council of Teachers of English, 2019.

MAISA Disciplinary Literacy Task Force. "Essential Practices for Disciplinary Literacy Instruction in the Secondary Classroom: Grades 6 to 12." *MAISA*, 6 Nov. 2019, www.gomaisa.org/downloads/le_files/dle_6-12_110619_electronic.pdf.

Marshall, Peter. *Beliefs and the Dead in Reformation England*. Oxford UP, 2002.

Michigan Department of Education. *Standards for the Preparation of Teachers of English Language Arts: Middle Grades (5–9) and High School (7–12)*. 11 Aug. 2020, www.michigan.gov/mde//mde/-/media/Project/Websites/mde/educator_services/prep/standards/ela_standards_59_712.pdf.

"*A Midsummer Night's Dream*: Act 2, Scene 1." Performances by Blake Harrison, Trajik, and Miss Netty. *Flocabulary*, www.flocabulary.com/unit/a-midsummer-nights-dream-the-merry-wanderer.

Millais, John Everett. *Ophelia*. 1851–52. *Tate Britain*, www.tate.org.uk/art/artworks/millais-ophelia-n01506.

Miller, William. "A Letter of Advice Concerning Marriage by A. B." Printed for William Miller, 1676. *Early English Books Online*, Wing, B15, name.umdl.umich.edu/A27103.0001.001.

Milton, John. *Areopagitica; A Speech of Mr. John Milton for the Liberty of Vnlicenc'd Printing, to the Parlament of England*. 1644. *Early English Books Online*, Wing (2nd ed.), M2092, name.umdl.umich.edu/A50883.0001.001.

Muir, Trevor. *The Epic Classroom: How to Boost Engagement, Make Learning Memorable, and Transform Lives*. Blend Education, 2017.

Mulholland, Matt. "Getting Started with Miro." *YouTube*, uploaded by Miro, 23 Mar. 2020, www.youtube.com/watch?v=pULLAEmhSho.

Nafisi, Azar. *Reading Lolita in Tehran*. Random House, 2003.

Nash, Thomas. *Terrors of the Night Or, A Discourse of Apparitions*. William Iones, 1594. *Early English Books Online*, STC (2nd ed.), 18379, name.umdl.umich.edu/A08014.0001.001.

National Endowment for the Arts. "Shakespeare in Our Time." *YouTube*, uploaded by Michele Leuthold, 7 Apr. 2014, www.youtube.com/watch?v=cZYtIYoKOc0.

Neill, Doug. "Getting Started with Sketchnoting." *YouTube*, uploaded by Verbal to Visual, 7 Nov. 2017, www.youtube.com/watch?v=y_fn2fpO5cU.

Ovid. "Book 4." *The Metamorphoses*. 8 CE. Translated by A. S. Kline, *Poetry in Translation*, 2000, www.poetryintranslation.com/PITBR/Latin/Metamorph8.php.

Owen, Jane. *Antidote against Purgatory. Or Discourse, Wherein is Shewed that Good-Workes, and Almes-Deeds, Performed in the Name of Christ, Are a Chiefe Meanes for the Preuenting, or Migatating the Torments of Purgatory. Written by that Vertuous, and Rightworthy Gentle-Woman (the Honour of Her Sexe for Learning in England) Ms. Iane Owen, late of God-stow, in Oxfordshire, Deceased, and Now Published after Her Death.* English College Press, 1634. [Dedicatory 4, copy in Bodleian Library.] *Early English Books Online*, STC, 18984, name.umdl.umich.edu/A08680.0001.001.

Parsons, Robert. *A Treatise Tending to Mitigation towards Catholic Subjects in England*. 1607. *Macbeth: Texts and Contexts*, edited by William C. Carroll, Bedford/St. Martin's, 1999, pp. 269–70.

———. *A Treatise Tending to Mitigation tovvardes Catholike-Subiectes in England VVherin is Declared, that it is Not Impossible for Subiects of Different Religion, (Especially Catholikes and Protestantes) to Liue Togeather in Dutifull Obedience and Subiection, vnder the Gouernment of his Maiesty of Great Britany. Against the Seditions Wrytings of Thomas Morton Minister, & Some Others to the Contrary. Whose Two False and Slaunderous Groundes, Pretended to be Dravvne from Catholike Doctrine & Practice, Concerning Rebellion and Equiuocation, are Ouerthrowne, and Cast vpon Himselfe.* Printed by F. Bellet, 1607. *Early English Books Online* (Phase 1), STC, 19417, name.umdl.umich.edu/A09111.0001.001.

Passe, Crispijn van de. *Eygentliche Abbildung wie Ettlich Englische Edelleut einen Raht Schliessen den König sampt dem Gantzen Parlament mit Pulfer Zuvertilgen*. Circa 1606. *Folger Shakespeare Library*, luna.folger.edu/luna/servlet/detail/FOLGERCM1~6~6~113534~107492:Eygentliche-Abbildung-wie-ettlich.

Paster, Gail Kern, and Skiles Howard, editors. *A Midsummer Night's Dream: Texts and Contexts*. Bedford/St. Martin's, 1999.

Pennant-Rea, Ned. "Hans Holbein's *Dance of Death* (1523–25)." *Public Domain Review*, 17 Apr. 2018, publicdomainreview.org/collection/hans-holbeins-dance-of-death-1523-5. 41 woodcuts. Originally published in French as *Les Simulachres & Historiees Faces de la Mort* (Holbein, 1538).

Pollard, Tanya. *Drugs and Theater in Early Modern England*. Oxford UP, 2005.

———. "'A Thing Like Death': Sleeping Potions and Poisons in 'Romeo and Juliet' and 'Antony and Cleopatra.'" *Renaissance Drama*, vol. 32, 2003, pp. 95–121.

Pyrrye, Charles. *The Praise and Dispraise of Women Very Fruitfull to the Well Disposed Minde, and Delectable to the Readers Therof. And a Fruitfull Shorte Dialogue vppon the Sentence, Know before Thou Knitte*. Imprinted by William How, 1569, copy at Henry E. Huntington Library and Art Gallery. *Early English Books Online*, STC (2nd ed.), 20523, name.umdl.umich.edu/A10244.0001.001.

Rainbow Portrait [formerly attributed to Marcus Gheeraerts the Younger or Isaac Oliver]. Circa 1600, Hatfield House. *Wikipedia*, en.wikipedia.org/wiki/File:Elizabeth_I_Rainbow_Portrait.jpg.

Raleigh, Walter. *The Discouerie of the Large, Rich, and Bevvtiful Empyre of Guiana: With a Relation of the Great and Golden Citie of Manoa (which the Spanyards Call El Dorado) and the Prouinces of Emeria, Arromaia, Amapaia, and Other Countries, with Their Riuers, Adioyning: Performed in the Yeare 1595 by Sir W. Ralegh Knight, Captaine of Her Maiesties Guard, Lo. Warden of the Stanneries, and Her Highnesse Lieutenant Generall of the Countie of Cornewall*. Imprinted by Robert Robinson, 1596. *Early English Books Online*, STC (2nd ed.), 20635, name.umdl.umich.edu/ARZ7311.0001.001.

Raleigh, Walter, et al. *The Poems of Sir Walter Raleigh: Collected and Authenticated, with Those of Sir Henry Wotton and Other Courtly Poets from 1540 to 1650*. Edited by George Bell and Sons, 1892. *Forgotten Books*, 2016, www.forgottenbooks.com/en/download/ThePoemsofSirWalterRaleigh_10154352.pdf.

"Research and Scholars." *Folger Shakespeare Library*, 18 Nov. 2014, www.folger.edu/research-scholars.

Robin Good-Fellow, His Mad Prankes and Merry Iests. Full of Honest Mirth, and Is a Fit Medicine for Melancholy. 2nd ed., printed by Thomas Cotes, 1639. [Copy at Folger Shakespeare Library.] *Early English Books Online*, STC (2nd ed.), 12017.

Rocklin, Edward. *Performance Approaches to Teaching Shakespeare*. National Council of Teachers of English, 2005.

Rosenblatt, Louise. *Literature as Exploration*. Modern Language Association, 1938.

Rowlands, Samuel. *Humors Looking Glasse*. William Ferebrand, 1608. *Early English Books Online*, STC (2nd ed.), 21386, name.umdl.umich.edu/A11119.0001.001.

———. *Well Met Gofsip: Or, Tis Merrie When Gofsips Meete*. John Deane, 1609. *Online Books*, edited by John Mark Ockerbloom, onlinebooks.library.upenn.edu/webbin/book/lookupid?key=ha009246960.

Saviolo, Vincentio. *Vincentio Saviolo, His Practise. In Two Bookes. The First Intreating of the Vse of the Rapier and Dagger. The Second, of Honor and Honorable Quarrels*. Iohn Wolff, 1595. *The Raymond J. Lord Collection of Historical Combat Treatises and Fencing Manuals* (in conjunction with the Massachusetts Center for Renaissance Studies), 15 Dec. 2009, www.umass.edu/renaissance/sites/default/files/assets/renaissance/lord/Saviolo_1595.pdf.

Scot, Reginald. *The Discoverie of Witchcraft, Wherein the Lewde Dealing of Witches and Witchmongers is Notablie Detected, in Sixteen Books . . . Whereunto Is Added a Treatise upon the Nature and Substance of Spirits and Devils*. William Brome, 1584. [Quarto, copy in British Library, G.19129.]

Shakespeare Uncovered. Seasons 1–3. Produced by Blakeway Productions, 116 Films, and Thirteen Productions, 2012–2018. *PBS*, www.pbs.org/wnet/shakespeare-uncovered.

Shakespeare, William. *Measure for Measure*. Edited by Barbara A. Mowat and Paul Werstine, Simon and Schuster, 2009. Folger Shakespeare Library. Formerly published in *Mr. William Shakespeare's Comedies, Histories, & Tragedies*, edited by John Heminges and Henry Condell, Edward Blount and Isaac Jaggard, 1623.

———. *Merchant of Venice*. Edited by Barbara A. Mowat and Paul Werstine, Simon and Schuster, 1992. New Folger Library Shakespeare. Formerly published in *Mr. William Shakespeare's Comedies, Histories, & Tragedies*, edited by John Heminges and Henry Condell, Edward Blount and Isaac Jaggard, 1623.

———. *Much Ado about Nothing*. Circa 1598/1599. Edited by Barbara A. Mowat and Paul Werstine. *Folger Shakespeare Library*, 25 June 2020, shakespeare.folger.edu/shakespeares-works/much-ado-about-nothing.

———. *Othello*. Edited by Barbara A. Mowat and Paul Werstine, Simon and Schuster, 1993. New Folger Library Shakespeare. Formerly published in *Mr. William Shakespeare's Comedies, Histories, & Tragedies*, edited by John Heminges and Henry Condell, Edward Blount and Isaac Jaggard, 1623.

Shakespeare, William. *Romeo and Juliet*. Circa 1591–1595. Edited by David Bevington and David Scot Kastan, Pearson Education, 2004. Formerly published in *Mr. William Shakespeare's Comedies, Histories, & Tragedies*, edited by John Heminges and Henry Condell, Edward Blount and Isaac Jaggard, 1623.

Shakespeare, William. "*Romeo and Juliet*." *Insights: Themes in Literature*, edited by G. Robert Carlsen et al., Webster Division, McGraw Hill, 1985.

Shakespeare, William. "*Romeo and Juliet*." *The Norton Shakespeare: Tragedies*, edited by Stephen Greenblatt, W.W. Norton, 1997, pp. 872–939.

Shakespeare, William. "Sonnet 23: As an Unperfect Actor on the Stage." 1609, Thomas Thorpe. *Shakespeare's Sonnets*, edited by Barbara A. Mowat and Paul Werstine. *Folger Shakespeare Library*, 25 June 2020, shakespeare.folger.edu/shakespeares-works/shakespeares-sonnets/sonnet-23.

———. "Sonnet 45: The Other Two, Slight Air and Purging Fire." 1609, Thomas Thorpe. *Shakespeare's Sonnets*, edited by Barbara A. Mowat and Paul Werstine. *Folger Shakespeare Library*, 25 June 2020, shakespeare.folger.edu/shakespeares-works/shakespeares-sonnets/sonnet-45.

Shakespeare, William. "Sonnet 55: Not Marble Nor the Gilded Monuments." 1609, Thomas Thorpe. *The Norton Anthology of English Literature*, edited by Stephen Greenblatt, 8th ed., vol. B, W. W. Norton, 2006, p. 1066. *Poetry Foundation*, www.poetryfoundation.org/poems/46455/sonnet-55-not-marble-nor-the-gilded-monuments.

Shakespeare, William. *The Taming of the Shrew*. Edited by Barbara A. Mowat and Paul Werstine, Simon and Schuster, 1992. New Folger Library Shakespeare. Formerly published in *Mr. William Shakespeare's Comedies, Histories, & Tragedies*, edited by John Heminges and Henry Condell, Edward Blount and Isaac Jaggard, 1623.

———. *The Tragedy of Hamlet: Prince of Denmark*. Edited by Barbara A. Mowat and Paul Werstine, Washington Sq. P, 1992. Folger Shakespeare Library. Formerly published in *Mr. William Shakespeare's Comedies, Histories, & Tragedies*, edited by John Heminges and Henry Condell, Edward Blount and Isaac Jaggard, 1623.

———. *The Tragedy of Macbeth*. Edited by Barbara A. Mowat and Paul Werstine, Simon and Schuster, 1992. New Folger Library Shakespeare. Formerly published in *Mr. William Shakespeare's Comedies, Histories, & Tragedies*, edited by John Heminges and Henry Condell, Edward Blount and Isaac Jaggard, 1623.

———. *The Winter's Tale*. Edited by Barbara A. Mowat and Paul Werstine, Washington Sq. P., 1998. New Folger Library Shakespeare. Formerly published in *Mr. William Shakespeare's Comedies, Histories, & Tragedies*, edited by John Heminges and Henry Condell, Edward Blount and Isaac Jaggard, 1623.

Shapiro, James. *A Year in the Life of William Shakespeare: 1599*. HarperCollins, 2005.

———. *The Year of Lear: Shakespeare in 1606*. Simon and Schuster, 2015.

———. "The Question of Hamlet." *The New York Review*, 19 Apr. 2018, www.nybooks.com/articles/2018/04/19/the-question-of-hamlet.

———. *Shakespeare in a Divided America*. Faber and Faber, 2020.

Sharpe, James. "In Search of the English Sabbat: Popular Conceptions of Witches' Meetings in Early Modern England." *Journal of Early Modern Studies*, vol. 2, 2013, p. 164.

Sidney, Philip. *An Apologie for Poetrie. VVritten by the Right Noble, Vertuous, and Learned, Sir Phillip Sidney, Knight*. Henry Olney, 1595. *Early English Books Online*, STC (2nd ed.), 22534, name.umdl.umich.edu/A12224.0001.001.

———. *The Defense of Poesy*. 1595. *The Norton Anthology of English Literature*, edited by Stephen Greenblatt, 8th ed., vol. B, W. W. Norton, 2006, pp. 970–71.

Slater, Dashka. *The 57 Bus*. Farrar, Straus and Giroux Books for Younger Readers, 2017.

Smith, Emma. "Podcast 10: 'Hamlet?'" *Approaching Shakespeare*, 23 Oct. 2012, podcasts.apple.com/us/podcast/hamlet/id399194760?i=1000410372226. *iTunes* app.

———. *This Is Shakespeare*. US ed., Pantheon Books, 2020.

Steelman, Sheridan. *Teaching Shakespeare*, 2017, shakespearedocuments.info.

Strong, Roy. *The Renaissance Garden in England*. Thames and Hudson, 1998.

Stubbes, Phillip. *The Anatomie of Abuses Contayning A Discouerie, or Briefe Summarie of Such Notable Vices and Imperfections, As Now Raigne in Many Christian Countreyes of the Worlde: But (Especiallie) in a Verie Famous Ilande called Ailgna: Together, with Most Fearefull Examples of Gods Iudgementes, Executed vpon the Wicked for the Same, Aswell in Ailgna of Late, as in Other Places, Elsewhere. Verie Godly, to be Read of all True Christians, Euerie Where: But Most Needefull, to Be Regarded in Englande*, Part 1. Richard Jones, 1583. *Early English Books Online*, STC, 23377, name.umdl.umich.edu/A13086.0001.001.

———. *A Christal Glasse for Christian Vvomen Containing, a Most Excellent Discourse, of the Godly Life and Christian Death of Mistresse Katherine Stubs, Who Departed This Life in Burton Vpon Trent, in Staffordshire the 14. Day of December. 1590. With a Most Heauenly Confession of the Christian Faith, Which Shee Made a little Before Her Departure: As Also a Wonderfull Combate Betwixt Sathan and Her Soule: Worthie to be Imprinted in Letters of Golde, and Are to Be Engrauen in the Tables of Euery Christian Heart. Set Downe Word For Word, as She Spake It, as Neere as Could Be Gathered: by Phillip Stubbes*. Richard Jones, 1592. *Early English Books Online*, STC, 23382, name.umdl.umich.edu/A13094.0001.001.

Swinburne, Henry. "Section 9: Of Ripe or Lawful Age for Marriage." *A Treatise of Spousals, or Matrimonial Contracts Wherein All the Questions Relating to That Subject Are*

Ingeniously Debated and Resolved, Robert Clavell, 1686, pp. 45–54. *Early English Books Online*, STC, S6260, name.umdl.umich.edu/A62036.0001.001.

The Talk between Mafter Bradford and Two Spanifh Friers. 1601. *National Portrait Gallery*, www.npg.org.uk/collections/search/portrait/mw19955/The-talk-between-Master-Bradford-and-two-Spanish-Friers.

Targoff, Ramie. "Mortal Love: Shakespeare's *Romeo and Juliet* and the Practice of Joint Burial." *Representations*, vol. 120, no. 1, fall 2012, pp. 17–38.

Taylor, Anthony B. "Ovid's Myths and the Unsmooth Course of Love in *A Midsummer Night's Dream*." *Shakespeare and the Classics*, edited by Charles Martindale and Anthony B. Taylor, Cambridge UP, 2004, pp. 49–65.

Taylor, John. *A Juniper Lecture, With the Description of All Sorts of Women, Good, and Bad: From the Modest to the Maddest, from the Most Civil, to the Scold Rampant, their Praise and Dispraise Compendiously Related*. W. Ley, 1639. *Early English Books Online*, Wing (2nd ed.), J1192.

Terry, Ellen, performer. *The Sourcebooks Shakespeare: Romeo and Juliet*. Edited by David Bevington et al., Sourcebooks MediaFusion, 2005. Book and CD.

Thomas, Angie. *Concrete Rose*. HarperCollins, 2021.

Thomas, Phillip V. *Vagrancy in Elizabethan England and the Response of the Privy Council, with Particular Reference to Five Towns*. 1994. U of Adelaide, MA thesis. digital.library.adelaide.edu.au/dspace/handle/2440/115954.

Thomas, Vivian, and Nicki Faircloth. *Shakespeare's Plants and Gardens: A Dictionary*. Bloomsbury Arden, 2016.

Thomason, George, editor. "The Picture of an English Antick, with a List of His Ridiculous Habits, and Apish Gestures. Maids, Where Are Your Hearts Become? Look You What Here Is!" Thomason Tracts, 1646. *Early English Books Online*, Wing (2nd ed.), P2155, name.umdl.umich.edu/A90675.0001.001.

Thompson, John L. *An English-Language Finding Guide to John Calvin Opera Quae Supersunt Omnia, Edited by Guilielmus Baum, Eduardus Cunitz, and Eduardus Reuss; Calvin Opera 1–59, Corpus Reformatorum 29–88, Brunswick and Berlin, 1863–1900*. 2nd ed., John L. Thompson, 1995.

Tiffany, Grace. "About Grace Tiffany." *Grace Tiffany: Riveting Fiction and Shakespeare Chat for Lovers of the English Renaissance*, 2013–, shakespearefiction.blogspot.com.

———. "Behind the Story: Interview with Grace Tiffany." Conducted by Jim McKeown. *KWBU*, 9 Dec. 2016, www.kwbu.org/local-news/2016-12-09/behind-the-story-interview-with-grace-tiffany.

Tislar, Kay. *Investigating the Importance of Detail Interest Level and Learning Objectives on the Seductive Detail Effect*. 2017. Michigan Technology U, MS thesis. digitalcommons.mtu.edu/etdr/386.

Trask, Emily, performer. *Romeo and Juliet*, by William Shakespeare. Directed by Robert Richmond, Simon and Schuster, 2014. Folger Shakespeare Library Presents. Audiobook.

Turchi, Laura, and Ayanna Thompson. "Shakespeare and the Common Core: An Opportunity to Reboot." *Phi Delta Kappan*, vol. 95, no. 1, 2013, pp. 32–40, kappanonline.org/shakespeare-common-core-turchi-thompson.

Turner, J. M. W. *Slave Ship* [originally titled *Slavers Throwing Overboard the Dead and Dying—Typhoon Coming On*]. 1840. *Museum of Fine Arts*, collections.mfa.org/objects/31102.

Tyukanov, Sergey. *Town of Time*. 2006. *Visionary Art Gallery*, www.visionaryartexhibition.com/featured-artwork/time-the-dance-of-death-by-sergey-tyukanov.

V for Vendetta. Directed by James McTeigue, performances by Hugo Weaving and Natalie Portman, Warner Bros. Entertainment, 2006. *YouTube*, uploaded by YouTube Movies & Shows, 6 Apr. 2011, www.youtube.com/watch?v=Et6M2r3yTAw.

Van Eyck, Jan. *The Arnolfini Portrait*. 1434. *National Gallery*, www.nationalgallery.org.uk/paintings/jan-van-eyck-the-arnolfini-portrait.

Vaughan, Edward. *A Divine Discoverie of Death Directing All People to a Triumphant Resurrection, and Euer-Lasting Saluation*. William Iones and Richard Boyle, 1612. *Early English Books Online*, STC, 24596, name.umdl.umich.edu/A14280.0001.001.

Vendler, Helen. *The Art of Shakespeare's Sonnets*. Harvard UP, 1997.

Westover, Tara. *Educated*. Random House, 2018.

Whately, William. *A Bride-Bush, or A Vvedding Sermon Compendiously Describing the Duties of Married Persons: By Performing Whereof, Marriage Shall Be to Them a Great Helpe, Which Now Finde It a Little Hell*. 2nd ed. Nicholas Bourne, 1619. *Early English Books Online*, STC (2nd ed.), 25298, name.umdl.umich.edu/A14989.0001.001.

White Linen Handkerchief Decorated with Cutwork, Needle Lace, and Embroidery, Italian. Circa 1600. *Victoria and Albert Museum*, collections.vam.ac.uk/item/O85005/handkerchief-unknown.

Whittemore, Hank. *The Monument*, new.shakespearesmonument.com. Accessed 12 July 2022.

"William Shakespeare – Playwright | Mini Bio." *YouTube*, uploaded by Biography, 12 Dec. 2012, www.youtube.com/watch?v=geev441vbMI.

Young, Bruce W. "Haste, Consent, and Age at Marriage: Some Implications of Social History for *Romeo and Juliet*." Iowa State Journal of Research, vol. 62, no. 3, Feb. 1988, pp. 459–474.

Index

Note: A 't' following a page number indicates a table; an 'f' indicates a figure.

Author

Sheridan Steelman received her PhD in English from Western Michigan University and recently enjoyed her golden and final year of teaching high school English at Northview High School in Grand Rapids, Michigan, in 2021–22. She served as English Department leader and Curriculum Teacher leader, and is the author of several articles—most recently, "Whose Ghost Is It, Anyway? Teaching Shakespeare Using Primary Documents" in *English Journal*. Steelman was awarded two School Bell Awards, an Outstanding Thesis Award, an Outstanding Teacher Award, and several Oldenburg Writing competition awards for her prose and poetry. Dr. Steelman is an AP Literature reader and has presented at the Annual AP Conference, the American Literature Association, the Midwest Conference for British Studies, the Calvin College AP Best Practices Conference, the Louisville Conference on Literature and Culture, and the College Board MRO Regional Forum. She continues to facilitate the West Michigan AP Literature and AP Language Networking Group on Facebook and has orchestrated AP classroom learning labs in West Michigan. You can follow Sheridan on Twitter (@steelmsl) and Instagram (@dr.steelman.reads and @sheridansteelman).

This book was typeset in TheMix and Palatino by Barbara Frazier.

Typefaces used on the cover include ILShakeFest and DIN Condensed.

The book was printed on 50-lb. White Offset paper by Seaway Printing Company, Inc.